W9-BRJ-510

# NATURAL WONDERS OF NORTH AMERICA

# NATURAL WONDERS OF NORTH AMERICA

## Exploring our great scenic heritage

AAA

ISBN: 1–55001–141–3

Designed and edited by Marshall Editions

Publisher: Bruce Marshall
Editorial Director: Ruth Binney
Editor: Marilyn Inglis
Copy Editor: Lindsay McTeague
Contributing Editors: Barbara Newman, Maggi McCormick, Beverly LeBlanc
Contributing Writers: Cindy Low, Duncan Brewer, David Adamson, Ed Zahnizer, Michael Leech
Art Director: John Bigg
Art Editors: Eddie Poulton, Mike Rose
Design Assistants: Penny Smith, Paul Tilby, Emma Hutton
Computer Maps: Jonathan Bigg
Picture Editor: Veneta Bullen
Production: Barry Baker, Janice Storr
American Automobile Association: Alex Gamble, Michelle Brady
Avenues, Inc.: Stuart Campbell, Donna Hayes, Bryan Weaver, Mark Mailman, Thomas Burnside, Candy Lee
Avenues, Inc. Production: Angela Meredith

Typeset by Servis Filmsetting Ltd, Manchester

Originated by CLG, Verona

Printed in America

# Contents

## THE AMERICAN WEST AND THE ROCKIES

Redwood National Park 10
Point Lobos 14
Yosemite Valley and the Sierra Wilderness 18
Rivers of Ice 26
San Andreas Fault 28
Point Reyes 30
Death Valley 32
Crater Lake 34
Olympic National Park 36
Mount Rainier National Park 38
Grand Tetons 42
Yellowstone National Park 46
Devils Tower 52

## THE SOUTHWEST AND MEXICO

Great Salt Lake 56
Bryce Canyon 60
Rainbow Bridge 64
Cowboy Country 66
Monument Valley 68
Grand Canyon 70
Meteor Crater 78
Painted Desert and Petrified Forest 80
Carlsbad Caverns 84
White Sands 88
Big Bend National Park 90
Padre Island National Seashore 96
Mexico 98

Illustration captions

*Page 1:* *Blue Ridge Parkway, Linville Gorge, North Carolina*
*Page 2:* *Bison, Yellowstone National Park, Wyoming*
*Page 4:* *Deer, Olympic National Park, Washington*
*Page 5:* tl, *Killer whale, British Columbia, Canada;* tr, *Yellow-bellied sapsucker, Colorado;* b, *Maple and birch forest, Isle Royale National Park, Michigan*
*Page 6:* *Live oak motte, Padre Island National Seashore, Texas*

## THE CENTRAL STATES


Badlands 108
The Black Hills 112
Oglala National Grassland 116
Tornado Territory 118
The Ozarks 120
Isle Royale 124
The Mississippi River 126

## THE EAST AND SOUTHEAST


The Everglades 134
Hurricane Power 140
Mammoth Caves 142
Okefenokee Swamp 146
Great Smoky Mountains 150
Stone Mountain 156
Blue Ridge Mountains 158
Cape Hatteras 162
Assateague 164
Delaware Water Gap 166
Cape Cod 168
The Adirondacks 170
Mount Desert and Acadia 174


## ALASKA AND HAWAII


Mount McKinley 180
Glacier Bay 184
Earth Fire 188
The Volcanoes of Hawaii 190
Kauai 196


## CANADA


Niagara Falls 204
Bay of Fundy 208
Dinosaur Provincial Park 210
Glacier National Park 212
Northern Lights 216
Columbia Icefields 218
Wood Buffalo National Park 220

Gazetteer 224

Index 238

Acknowledgments 240

# Foreword

North America boasts an abundance of hidden natural wonders that surprise and delight even the most seasoned explorer. Through NATURAL WONDERS OF NORTH AMERICA, expert environmentalists, geographers, photographers, and writers have joined together to capture and share these amazing adventures.

With breathtaking photography and informative text, NATURAL WONDERS OF NORTH AMERICA tours, from coast to coast, our continent's most fascinating and unusual oddities of nature. For avid travelers, nature enthusiasts, and those with a desire to experience our continent's exciting natural wonders, this book is an essential component for your hands-on reference library.

Turn the page and begin an adventure that will excite your whole family. Or escape to your favorite reading nook and let NATURAL WONDERS OF NORTH AMERICA guide you on your own unforgettable journey through unique natural phenomena, scenic world record breakers, and rare wildlife.

Director, Consumer Publications
AMERICAN AUTOMOBILE ASSOCIATION

# The West and the Rockies

## In the West of our imagining

For a visual record of life in the West before any Europeans altered it, we are indebted to the painter George Catlin. Enthralled by the landscape and by the intimacy of the native cultures with their environment, Catlin proposed a preserve to protect them both. Catlin's idea was decades before its time. Years later, when Henry David Thoreau proposed an eastern preserve, he already knew how imagination had shaped the West.

Yosemite became a state preserve during the Civil War. Eight years later, in 1872, Yellowstone was proclaimed the world's first national park. The motivation for its creation was not Catlin's proposal or Thoreau's, but a young nation's cultural insecurity. The United States was seeking peerless natural wonders of its own to rival Europe's spectacular antiquities. The idea of preserving natural wonders has grown toward Catlin's and Thoreau's notions and become an American contribution to world culture. Wildlife that Yellowstone's first proponents took for granted attracts international visitors today as a natural wonder in its own right.

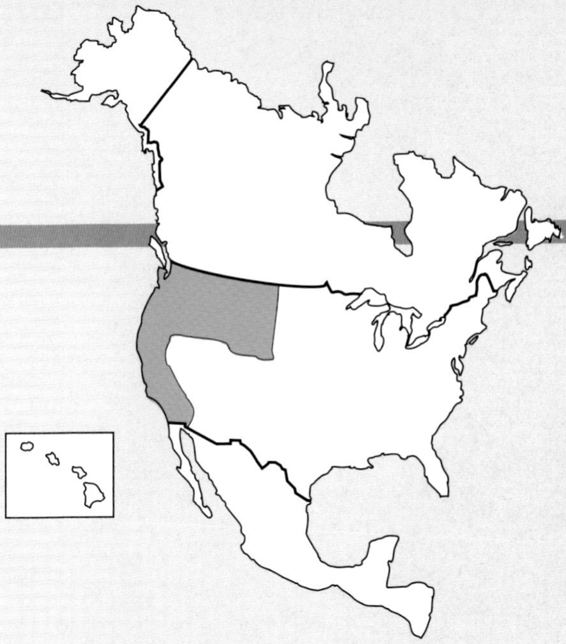

A wealth of nature's extremes occur in the West: the nation's tallest mountain outside Alaska; the continent's hottest and lowest points; its first ecological preserve; the world's largest and tallest living things; and its greatest geyser collection. America's romance with its rich stock of natural wonders has endured for more than a century and now attracts admirers from Tokyo, Berlin, Paris, London, and Nairobi as well as New York and Chicago. Many return home newly committed to protecting their own natural treasures. No contagion could be more beneficial to the planet we share.

CALIFORNIA

# REDWOOD NATIONAL PARK

REDWOOD TREES DOMINATED northern hemisphere forests 25 million years ago with a dozen or more redwood species sharing that landscape with saber-toothed tigers, mammoths, and mastodons. Today, only three species survive: the world's tallest living thing, the coast redwood; the world's largest living thing, the giant sequoia; and their diminutive cousin, the dawn redwood, which inhabits an isolated mountain range in China.

As global climates grew cooler and drier, the redwood species declined, edging into then-tropical California 20 million years ago. With the coming of the Ice Age, North America's two redwood species came to rest in their present isolation in California, giant sequoias on the western slopes of the Sierra Nevada and coast redwoods in a narrow strip of fogbound California coast continuing just into southern Oregon.

In 1850, redwood forests spanned 500 miles of Pacific Coast and covered two million acres. By 1965, they were reduced to 300,000 scattered acres, and commercial pressures to log those were intense. Many of the grand Victorian homes in San Francisco were built of straight-grained, weather- and rot-resistant redwood.

In 1968, three state parks and a connecting corridor of land were designated as Redwood National Park. Ten years later, Congress expanded the park significantly to encompass the world's tallest living things—the first, second, third, and sixth tallest trees—in the groves along Redwood Creek. The expansion also brought into the park logged-over lands that needed reforestation in order to protect the tall trees growing along Redwood Creek. Erosion on the denuded lands was causing siltation and flooding downstream that threatened to destroy the shallow-rooted trees in their streamside stands.

For all their colossal height, redwood trees have no tap root. Their root systems reach only 10 to 13 feet deep, spreading over a distance of just 60 to 80 feet. For

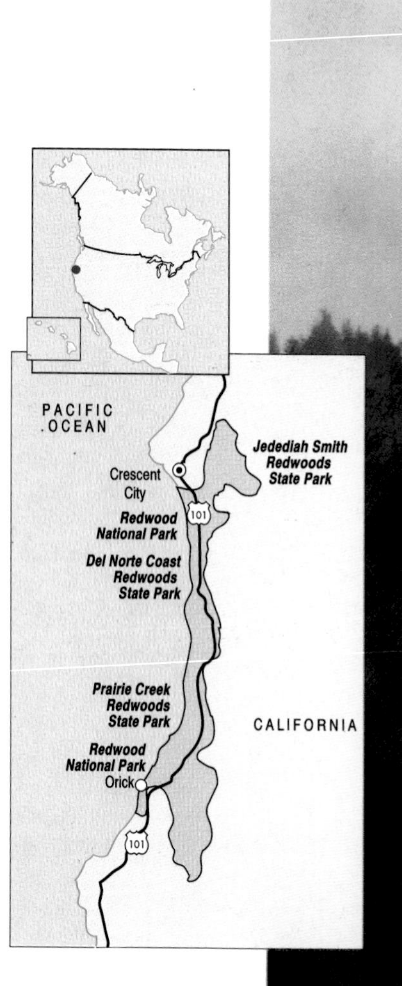


***Redwoods shrouded in mist*** *(right). These links to the age of dinosaurs live 2,000 years, weigh up to 500 tons, and grow taller than the Statue of Liberty. Ironically, their seeds are no larger than those of tomatoes, and their cones are about the size of a large olive.*

trees reaching over 300 feet in height, this provides minimal support. In fact, isolated trees readily topple in wind storms, lacking the safety in numbers provided by the awesome groves with their shoulder-high ferns and palpable stillness.

The protected coastline of redwoods, on the west slopes of the Coast Ranges, would justify national park status all by itself. Park rangers lead walks in summer to one of the world's most compactly diverse life zones, the tide pool. In the tidal zone where sea and land meet on more or less equal terms, life is stacked in layers according to the organisms' ability to withstand either drying sunlight or soaking salt water—or twice daily alternations of the two.

Intertidal aquatic plants have tenacious anchoring devices called holdfasts that keep the pounding surf from washing them away. Animal inhabitants of tide pools may cling to rocks much as barnacles do to ships. Few ecological niches on Earth are so demanding—or so fascinating, beautiful, and colorful—as this edge of sea and land.

Miles and miles of the bluff-headed coastline boast mostly rocky beaches but also sandy ones, and occasional offshore rocks or sea stacks attract myriad seabirds. More than half of the park's birds are marine species, many of them migratory or seasonal denizens, and include brown pelicans, cormorants, auklets, murres, gulls, and pigeon guillemots. The park's high sea bluffs afford many vantage points for watching the offshore spring and fall migrations of California gray whales or orca (killer) whales, seals, dolphins, sea lions, and porpoises.

The Smith River at the park's north end is named for the intrepid fur trapper, trader, and mountain man, Jedediah Strong Smith, who led the first overland trek to California. During this four year expedition, several of his men died in encounters with Indians in and near today's park. Smith trekked here in 1828, 20 years before the 1848 gold rush altered California's destiny forever.

A famous salmon stream, the Klamath River on the park's south, drains its namesake mountain range. When the sea-running cousins of the rainbow trout come back to their native stream gravels to spawn, their dramatic runs all but clog small tributary streams. Sea-run rainbow trout, called steelheads, are known as tackle busters here.

The availability of sea-grown protein in inland streams causes a temporary truce in these wilds. Otherwise solitary bears may fish side by side, ignoring or tolerating the presence of smaller mammals, to harvest the salmon made vulnerable by their reproductive single-mindedness and sheer numbers.

Once the domain of grizzly bears, today's park boasts several hundred black bears, although these are not often seen by visitors. Bears depend heavily on acorns for their yearly protein requirements, so they favor habitats like recently logged and reforested areas, where the vegetation they browse in produces abundant food.

Roosevelt elk, a Pacific Northwest subspecies slightly smaller than the elk of Yellowstone, are seen more often. Huge racks of antlers identify elk as opposed to blacktail deer. Elk favor open grassy areas called balds, which may have been cleared in the past by Indians who would burn them off to encourage the growth of food plants, which in turn would attract wildlife. Elk can often be spotted along the beach at Gold Bluffs Beach and at Prairie Creek campground. The bluffs were named for the gold found here in 1850 and extracted off and on until after World War II.

Nearby lies Fort Ross, whose apparently common name masks the fact that it is the only Russian fort in the Lower 48 states. Harbor seals, sea lions, and other pinnipeds (fin-footed furbearers) brought Alexander Baranov, a Russian nobleman and fur trader, ashore here.

Heavy plundering of sea mammals brought many close to extinction. Several species have now recovered their numbers, further benefactors of Redwood National Park's protection of the big trees' remnant coastal homelands.

***Naturally adapted for survival,*** *the massive redwoods' 12-inch-thick and highly acidic bark protects the trees from both insect and fire damage. As a tree grows older, its lower branches drop away, leaving a clean trunk. Since only a small proportion of their seeds germinate, most redwoods reproduce by stump sprouting. This reproductive process has the distinct advantage of providing the young shoots with the parent tree's root system. Tight stands of several trees, called family groups, often sprout from the same parent trunk.*

### Life on the shore

The highly vocal California sea lion (below) is perfectly described by its generic name, *Zalophus*, which combines the Greek words for surging sea and fabulous animal. Adult males 8 feet long weight in at 600 pounds. They range from Mexico's Baja California coast to the Channel Islands.

Brown pelicans (above) have returned from the brink of extinction through the protection of coastal lands and resources. An unusual seabird, this pelican is equipped with air sacs on the front of its body, which cushion the impact of its plunge into the water when it dives for fish, often from a height of 50 feet. Its catch is usually consumed on the surface.

***A member of the vast group*** *that includes an estimated 9,000 to 15,000 species, the sword fern (left) is properly named* Nephrolepsis exalta. *It is a pantropical species, whose dark fronds reach 3 feet in length. Its life cycle, which depends on the dispersal of spores that germinate in warm, moist, and shady sites, predates the seed-plant life cycle by many millions of years.*

*Ferns were the dominant land plants during the Carboniferous period, which began 260 million years ago, and the remains of what were once gigantic fern forests assisted in the formation of the Earth's coal supply.*

CALIFORNIA

# POINT LOBOS

POINT LOBOS MARKS THE STUNNING CLIMAX of the Monterey Peninsula's engaging natural beauty, culminating in a high and rugged headland where 35-foot storm waves assault the sea cliffs like artillery fire. "On no other coast I know," Robert Louis Stevenson wrote of this area in 1879, "shall you enjoy, in calm, sunny weather, such a spectacle of ocean's greatness, such beauty of changing color or such degrees of thunder in the sound." And this high Pacific headland harbors a wealth of marine mammals and birds that alone would justify its preservation.

The sea otter, a small marine mammal at Point Lobos, has had a disproportionately large influence on California's political destiny. Not quite 5 feet long and weighing up to 80 pounds, this largest member of the weasel family has thick, rich fur. Before any Europeans pushed north of Mexico, the Russian explorer Vitus Bering entered the Gulf of Alaska and bumped eastward along the Aleutian chain of islands to the North American mainland. Scurvy killed Bering and many of his men, but news of the copious fur-bearing animals they had found lining the coast of North America launched a rash of new expeditions.

Sea otter pelts became the rage of Empress Anna's Russian court, and Europeans also marveled at their quality and thickness. As the British, French, and Americans joined the trading frenzy, a fur rush ensued. The Russians put down roots in the land that stretched south from Alaska to northern California, all then unclaimed by European powers. The stockade and onion-domed church at Fort Ross (for Russia), once an outpost of Tsarist hegemony, are reminders of how surely the sea otter once shaped California's history.

Unlike most other sea mammals, sea otters do not depend on thick layers of fat to insulate them from the cold of deep ocean waters. They rely instead on air trapped in their fur and incredibly dense underfur, which can have more than 100,000 hairs per square inch. Such rich pelts brought them nearly to extinction at the hands of

***Sandstone strata*** *(right) reveal the geological complexity of the Coast Ranges of mountains, which formed about 64 million years ago, and emerge here as a shelf 15 to 30 miles wide. In the inlet called the Slot, 6-million-year-old sediment is thick with marine pebbles.*

aggressive fur hunters. Indeed, sea otters were considered extinct before 1925, but World War II submarine watchers noticed an isolated group of survivors just north of Point Lobos. That group was immediately protected and stern laws now protect the slow revival of the species. They add immeasurably to the allure of Point Lobos, since no national parks contain permanent colonies of sea otters.

Many people consider Point Lobos the treasure of California's state parks, and trees are numbered among its many jewels. With its lopsided, pear-shaped cones, the Monterey pine grows naturally in only three areas along the coast, sustained by the dripping fog which compensates for the rain-free summers. Like the bishop pines of Point Reyes, Monterey pines are linked inextricably to their ancient granitic soil which, in the case of Point Lobos's North Shore, solidified 110 million years ago. Sedimentary conglomerates such as those at Sea Lion Point often erode in complex and ruggedly beautiful patterns of cliffs, coves, and deep inlets.

Even more celebrated is the Monterey cypress that survives on the outermost granite cliffs. Away from sea breezes it succumbs to a fungus disease, so it cannot be cultivated elsewhere. But here, as the region's eminent poet Robinson Jeffers wrote, "the stiff plates of the cypress-boughs divide the sea's breath, /hard green cutting soft gray . . ."

About 750 of Point Lobos Reserve's 1,325 acres lie underwater and provide the richest marine habitat in California. Upwelling, mineral-rich waters feed the ecosystem and nourish its 100-foot-tall kelp forests, which are as productive per acre as fertilized agricultural land. Carmel Bay drops off steeply, and a mile north of the reserve lies a submarine canyon deeper than the Grand Canyon. Six miles offshore, it plunges to a depth of 7,000 feet.

Closer to shore, gray whales weighing up to 40 tons pass Point Lobos. Once hunted nearly to extinction, Pacific gray whales now number from around 15,000 to 21,000—estimates vary widely. More of them probably exist today than before commercial whaling began in the 19th century. Even the hidden features of stunningly beautiful Point Lobos embellish its status as a world-class natural wonder.

**Marine mammals**

Gray whales (far right) pass Point Lobos in December and May as they migrate between their Arctic feeding waters and their summer breeding waters in Baja California. They log up to 10,000 miles annually completing the round trip. One of the family of baleen whales, they feed by gulping ocean water and filtering the small marine organisms in it through plates called baleen, the same whalebone used for corsets.

Sea otters (right) feed and sleep floating on their backs, anchoring themselves at night with strands of the seaweed called kelp. Adept tool users, they crack open their staple food, sea urchins, on a stone balanced on their belly.

***Monterey cypress*** *(left), a gnarled and battered rarity, grows naturally at Cypress Point and Pinnacle Rock, at the northern end of the Point Lobos State Reserve, and nowhere else on Earth. It has battled the elements on these granite cliffs for more than 300 years, sending limbs and roots between and through the rocks to maintain its grip on the land, and twisting its trunk and branches to accommodate the strong gales.*

*Despite its strength, it suffers from root rot and has no resistance to severe frost. The region's fog, salt, and sea winds help sustain it, and its seedlings, which can only thrive after successive wet seasons, depend entirely on the local weather for their continued survival.*

*Though not often used for timber, cypress is light, quite hard, and extremely durable when set directly in soil.*

***Flowers of the Monterey pine*** *(above) are only seldom seen, since the tree itself is one of the rarest in the world. To protect the species* Pinus radiata *from extinction and assist with local reforestation, it has been planted in both New Zealand and Chile.*

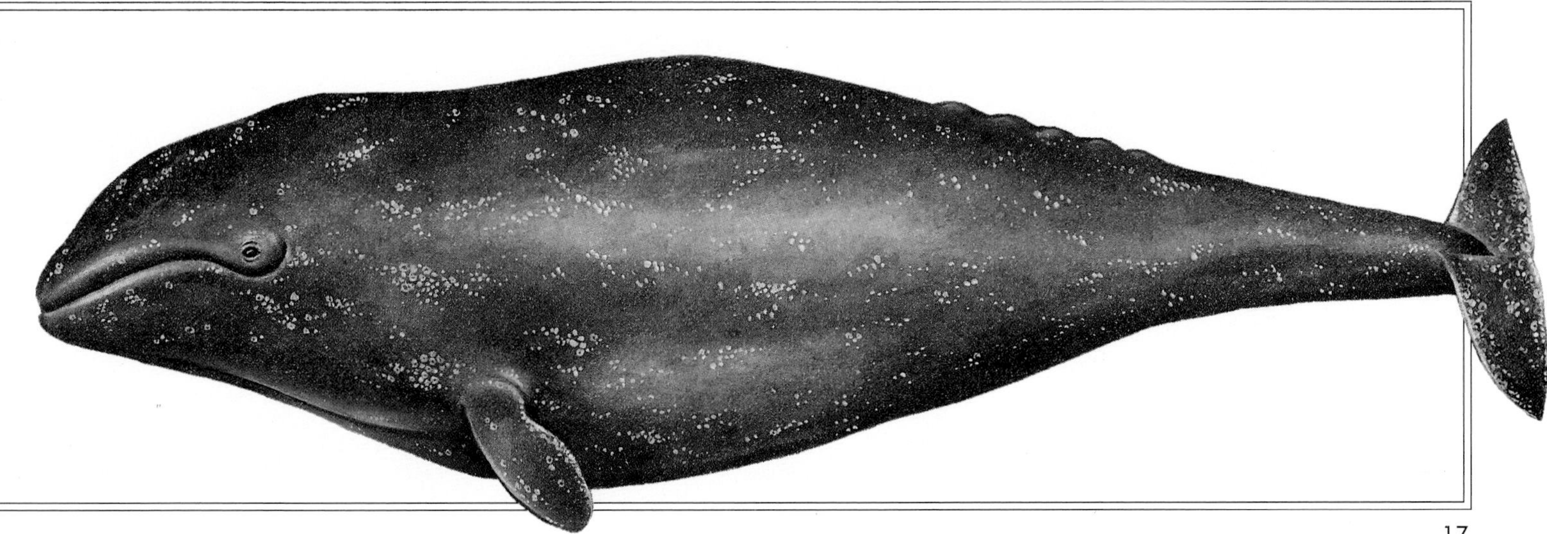

CALIFORNIA

# YOSEMITE VALLEY

## AND THE

# SIERRA WILDERNESS

JOSEPH WALKER'S PARTY OF TRAPPERS crossed the Sierra Nevada from east to west via Tioga Pass in 1833 and became the first non-Indians to see Yosemite Valley. They saw it from above as you can today from Olmsted Point and other scenic overlooks along the Tioga Road. Walker and his men were also the first non-Indians to see the giant sequoia trees of Tuolumne Grove.

Today's Yosemite National Park protects three major groves: the Tuolumne, Merced, and Mariposa. Yosemite Valley and the Mariposa Big Tree Grove were entrusted to California by the federal government in 1864 for protection as parklands, although Yosemite National Park was not created until 1890.

Parks chronicler Freeman Tilden notes how quickly Yosemite achieved popularity: "At a time when Yellowstone could record but a scant five hundred visitors, Yosemite Valley was already a thriving tourist resort." Discovery of the Mariposa Grove of giant sequoias two years later, in 1857, only increased the area's appeal.

Like the boldly sculpted granite megaforms of the valley, the giant sequoias inspire an awe that physical proximity only amplifies. Mid-19th-century Americans were in love with the big, the bold, and the vertical. Philosopher Ralph Waldo Emerson, visiting Yosemite in 1871, confided to his journal: "This valley is the only place that comes up to the brag about it, and exceeds it."

The most audible response at Glacier Point's scenic vantage point is silence, again an expression of awe. No visit to Yosemite should exclude the drive—or arduous hike up from the valley—to Glacier Point. Spread out through perhaps 270 degrees are El Capitan, Yosemite Falls, Half Dome, Vernal Falls, Nevada Falls, the

***Yosemite Falls*** *(right) is nearly half a mile from crest to valley floor and is actually two waterfalls. The Upper Falls drops 1,430 feet, nine times the height of Niagara Falls, while the Lower, which it joins without a break, tumbles another 320 feet.*

valleys of Tenaya Creek and the Merced River, and seemingly millions of peaks of the northern High Sierra, including its Clark and Cathedral ranges.

About 500 million years ago, what is now the Sierra Nevada lay below an ancient sea whose seabed sediments were eventually thrust above the surface while molten rock from deep in the Earth welled up beneath the sedimentary rock and cooled as granite. A fault-block range, the Sierra Nevada is a single block of the Earth's crustal plate that has been lifted on its east edge and tilted to the west.

The lift accounts for its long west slope and steep, short east slope. Years of erosion wore away the capping sediments—several thousand feet of superimposed rock—and exposed the granite to weathering, erosion, and repeated glacial episodes a million to 250,000 years ago. One and perhaps more glacial advances filled the valley to its brim.

Following valley paths cut by stream erosion, the glaciers' gouging left a spectacular series of hanging waterfalls. Yosemite Falls totals 2,425 feet, making it North America's highest waterfall and the second highest in the world. Half of the nation's highest waterfalls are here in the park. Windblown to a mistlike film, Bridal Veil Falls drops 620 feet into a lovely alcove, and mighty Nevada Falls on the Merced River plunges 594 feet with a contrasting thunderous pounding.

Retreat of the last major valley glacier 10,000 years ago left behind a shallow Lake Yosemite, the last of many in the valley. The glacier lacked sufficient power to gouge the valley floor deeply once again, so its deposits and sediments of the former lake account for the present lake's flat floor.

The first humans in the region probably witnessed the immediate aftermath of the last major valley glaciation. Evidence of human visitation to the region dates back 8,000 to 10,000 years, and the valley was settled 3,500 years ago when the predecessors of today's Miwok residents established themselves here by about 1000 or 1200 B.C. Miwoks called their homeland Ahwahnee, "valley that looks like a gaping mouth." Known as the Ahwahneechee, "people of Ahwahnee," they lived in the valley in summer and in the foothills in winter. They acted as go-betweens in trade for coastal Indians and the Mono Lake Indians over the Sierra Crest.

Ahwahneechee culture is well documented in the park by a museum, seasonal craft demonstrations, and the reconstructed Indian village behind the Valley Visitor Center. The traditional Indian dwelling, the u-mu-cha, was replaced with simple cabins by the 1890s. The park boasts a rich collection of tightly woven Miwok and Paiute basketry, which is

**Prophet of the wilderness**

"John Muir, Earth-planet, Universe" is the first entry in Muir's journal, *A Thousand Mile Walk to the Gulf.* Born in Dunbar, Scotland, in 1838, Muir emigrated to America in 1849 with his family.

Bound for South America via Cuba, Muir was diverted by illness to California, first seeing Yosemite Valley, at the age of 30, in 1868. It was love at first sight. "I only went out for a walk," Muir said, defending his zeal for nature, "and finally concluded to stay out till sundown, for going out, I found, was really going in."

In the Sierra Nevada, Muir

***Yosemite Valley*** *from the top of Half Dome (right). A corridor of rock 7 miles long and as much as a mile wide, Yosemite Valley lies between clifflike walls that rise more than 3,200 feet. The valley was carved by the relentless force of the Merced River and the steady advance of alpine glaciers. While the ice enlarged the river's canyon, it left some of the harder, more massive rocks in place; it created Half Dome's distinctive shape by shearing away layers of unjointed granite.*

studied glaciers and giant sequoias, becoming a regional expert on both. "Patient observation and constant brooding above the rocks," he wrote, "lying upon them for years as the ice did, is the way to arrive at the truths which are graven so lavishly upon them." In 1892, he founded the Sierra Club. Grasped firsthand in floods, blizzards, and earthquakes, Muir's cosmic vision articulated the importance of humans enjoying a living relationship with Nature.

John Muir was photographed in front of his beloved Yosemite Falls (left); and the same view of the falls is not much changed today (far left).

displayed at the museum. Baskets were used for sifting acorn flour as well as for cooking and eating the acorn mush. As you explore the valley floor, you may discover the heirs of the Indians' acorn economy. Some trees are riddled with closely spaced holes which acorn woodpeckers have jammed with acorns.

The National Park Service philosophy of natural management aims to restore the landscape to its condition in 1851, the year of the valley's discovery by non-Indians, and to preserve it in that state. Ecological processes were largely intact then, although the Ahwahneechee probably burned the valley floor periodically to encourage wildlife to forage and browse and to hasten the growth of the black oaks.

In accordance with the park's conservation policy, trout are no longer stocked, since only rainbow trout were native here. Grizzly bears were extirpated by the 1920s and black bears kept carefully separate from humans and their food by strictly enforced regulations. In recent years, one of the world's fastest living creatures, the peregrine falcon, and the California bighorn sheep have been restored to their native habitats here. Wild bighorn were decimated by the range encroachment of domestic sheep whose diseases killed most of the wild sheep. The domestic animals are still grazed in some High Sierra locations today, and their presence continues to plague bighorn restoration efforts.

The John Muir Trail links Yosemite Valley in the north with Sequoia and Kings Canyon national parks in the south, terminating on Mount Whitney whose steep east face Muir was the first to climb. The trail follows the crest of the Sierra, with parts of it tracing Muir's progress southward down the Sierra with his pack mule, Brownie. Muir was headed from Yosemite to the groves of giant trees in today's Sequoia National Park. He was also looking for glaciated valleys to rival Yosemite, and he found one in Kings Canyon. The trail threads through the John Muir Wilderness in today's Kings Canyon National Park,

***The Spanish explorers** called this waterway The River of our Lady of Mercy or the Merced River (left). It begins as a creek, falls casually over the Giant's Staircase—glacially carved steps in a sloping mountainside—in two successive leaps of 320 and 594 feet, and then crashes over Nevada Falls and Vernal Falls. In slightly more than half a mile, the Merced drops 1,200 feet before subsiding to a slow, gentle pace as it wanders along the valley floor.*

***The peregrine falcon** (above) is a robust predator that kills on the wing, often swooping hundreds of feet at speeds that reach 175 miles an hour to attack its prey.*

*Bighorn elk (left) stand 4 to 6 feet high. The male alone carries spiral horns, up to 3 feet 9 inches long, with which he fights his rivals during the rutting season in fierce, sometimes lethal, battles that can last for hours.*

one of the wildest portions of Muir's entire "Range of Light."

Mammalogists will explain the appeal of subalpine and alpine meadows by saying that our species evolved in grasslands and still responds to the familiar openness that meadows offer. Whatever its basis, their appeal needs no apology. Many of these high-mountain grassy fields blaze with wildflowers from late spring through the short summer season, and many are sliced with dancing rivulets.

The presence of water and grasses amid rocky crags makes meadows ideal for watching wildlife. Marmots graze in the open, all the while keeping watchful eyes on the sky for hawks and other birds of prey that cruise mountain heights. Spotting one, the groundhoglike marmot emits its piercing warning whistle and heads for rock cover. Smaller pikas harvest meadow grasses but are less often seen in the open. Sometimes called coneys, or rock rabbits, these big-eared, gerbil-sized rodents make hay piles to carry them through the winter. Unlike marmots, pikas do not hibernate so they must store overwintering calories in their hay piles rather than in body fat as marmots do.

Yosemite National Park boasts one of the largest and most famous of Sierran mountain meadows. Tuolumne Meadows sits at 8,592 feet in elevation not far west of the park's eastern entrance at Tioga Pass. Until the Tioga Road was put through, Tuolumne Meadows was known to many but seen only by hearty backpackers, most of whom reached it by climbing out of Yosemite Valley. It is 12 miles long and, in many places, stretches a full half mile in width. Having combined its Lyell and Dana forks, the Tuolumne River cuts through its namesake meadows as a respectable mountain river that shortly dives downward through the spectacular intimacy of the Grand Canyon of the Tuolumne River. The river then dances all the way to Hetch Hetchy reservoir where its waters are stilled behind O'Shaughnessy Dam, whose construction inside the national park broke John Muir's heart.

Tuolumne Meadows can be regarded as both a destination and a launching point. As a destination, its massive displays of such wildflowers as paintbrush and elephanthead make the journey more than

***The eerie landscape** of calcium carbonate towers rises farther above Mono Lake (left) as its waters are tapped; the water level fell 44 feet between 1941 and 1981. The three-million-year-old basin has held a lake for about a million years. Although it contains no fish, it is thick with brine shrimp, which supply food for more than 100 bird species. Over 800,000 feeding birds have been counted here in a single day.*

worthwhile. As a launching point, at 8,592 feet in elevation, the meadows give visitors a jumpstart on the high country. They are a wilderness threshold of unparalleled scenic beauty, ringed by peaks.

East of Tuolumne Meadows near the Tioga Pass through the Sierra Crest, the landscape changes abruptly. The clouds that carry warm, moist Pacific air are forced ever upward by the mountains. They cool as they rise and lose their moisture as precipitation. The rich forests of the western slopes dwindle to sparse ponderosa pines on eastern slopes that rapidly give way to arid conditions below.

In the basin and range topography that begins at the base of the Sierra's steep eastern escarpment, Mono Lake illustrates a local fact of life: east slope waters never reach an ocean. Here they flow into Mono Lake, a desert lake with no outlet. Its highly saline waters build exotic tufa formations—mineral deposits from the evaporating lake waters—that look from a distance like petrified forests.

The lake is important for the resident and migratory wildfowl, some of which nest on its islands. Recent drawdown of the lake water by inlet-stream diversions by the Department of Water and Power of the City of Los Angeles threatens these birds and their breeding grounds. As lake levels fall, coyotes and other predators are able to gain access to the islands and decimate the young birds.

Nevertheless, expansive in its otherwise arid setting and made eerie by its exotic tufa islands and towers, Mono Lake makes a fitting counterpoint to the stunning Range of Light whose mountain waters feed it.

**General Sherman Tree**

One of the natural highlights of nearby Sequoia and Kings Canyon national parks, the General Sherman Tree (right) is the world's largest living thing. Weighing roughly $4\frac{1}{2}$ million pounds, it stands 275 feet high and continues to grow. Its lowest branch is 130 feet above the ground, and the trunk beneath it is 101 feet in circumference; the maximum diameter, at the base, is 32 feet.

This tree has already lived for 2,200 to 2,600 years. Its bark, which can be nearly 2 feet thick, and its wood are fire-resistant, so sequoias easily survive the effects of lightning and brush fires.

Sequoia reproduction is a slow and difficult process. Compared to the gigantic bulk of the tree, seed cones are tiny, only the size of hens' eggs, and take 2 years to mature and, sometimes, 20 years to release their seeds. Douglas squirrels, which harvest fallen cones, and wood-boring beetles, which cut them off from their sap supply on the branches, both help free the seeds.

Fire is a helper, too, since seeds will only germinate in the nearly bare earth that only fire exposes. The flames of forest fires also thin the overhanging foliage, which allows sun to reach the seedlings.

***Glacier National Park*** *(right) in Montana, which is part of Waterton-Glacier International Peace Park that straddles the United States-Canada border, is a living testament to the awesome power of ice. The park is studded with 50 glaciers, most of which can only be reached by foot or horseback trail.*

***Wrangell-St. Elias National Park and Preserve*** *(left), in the southeastern corner of Alaska, contains glaciers five times the size of Manhattan and 9 of the 16 highest peaks in North America. The enormous icefields that blanket the mountaintops function as a natural system of refrigeration which can affect the climate in Chicago.*

*Muldrow Glacier (right), which lies between Mount McKinley's twin peaks in Denali National Park, is the largest north-flowing glacier in Alaska.*

GLACIERS FORM WHEN THE ANNUAL SNOWFALL consistently exceeds the annual snowmelt. As snowflakes pile up, their collective weight compacts old snow beneath them until it forms pellets or crystals. Solid chunks of ice made of old, granular snow can be as small as sand grains or larger than a human head. Gravity pushes the ice mass downhill as it grows in weight, and the friction of its movement produces a thin film of water beneath the mass, on which it slides. Glacial ice is a monomineralic, or single-mineral, rock like marble.

Valley head
Lateral moraine
New valley floor
Crevasse
Terminal moraine

Arctic
Alps
Interglacial stage
Glacial stage
Mediterranean

***The phases of an ice age*** *(below) may include both glacial periods of intense cold, when ice caps increase in size and glaciers dominate many areas, and warmer interglacial periods, when more temperate climates prevail. Geologists believe that subtle changes in the Earth's orbit around the Sun cause this short-term cycle.*

CALIFORNIA

# SAN ANDREAS FAULT

THE FACTS OF THE SITUATION are almost incredible. Slowly but inexorably, Bakersfield, California, moves toward Alaska. The two halves of Pinnacles Volcano lie 195 miles apart. Salt Lake City, Utah, and Reno, Nevada, have parted by 60 miles in the last five million years or so. Rocks in Point Reyes, California, match rocks that are found in the Tehachapi Mountains more than 310 miles south.

These phenomena result in part from the San Andreas Fault because, as historian Will Durant wrote, "Civilization exists by geological consent and is subject to change without notice." The San Andreas Fault, California's biggest and one of America's longest, exceeds 1,000 miles. At least 650 miles of the fault run through western California under areas with large urban populations, making abrupt slippage potentially devastating.

From the Gulf of California, the San Andreas Fault comes up to Los Angeles, bears left, heads north to San Francisco and through Point Reyes, and then tails off below the Pacific Ocean. It marks the zone of interaction between two of the Earth's crustal, or tectonic, plates which are egg-shell-thin compared to the Earth's mass.

The crust is not a single covering, but a series of plates that float on the liquid beneath them and bump into, pull away from, or move alongside each other. In the San Andreas Fault, the North American Plate is sliding westward while the Pacific Plate edges northwest by an inch a year, assuming enormous significance over the vast span of geological time.

In 1891, it was apparent that western California topography exhibited faulting. Three of California's mountain ranges are actually one system. The middle range trends east and west and links the Coast and Peninsular ranges which lie north-south. The east-west Transverse Ranges follow a bend in the San Andreas Fault, whose pressure pushes the Transverse Mountains up and shatters their rock.

Geologists have recently demonstrated that both the rise of California's coastal

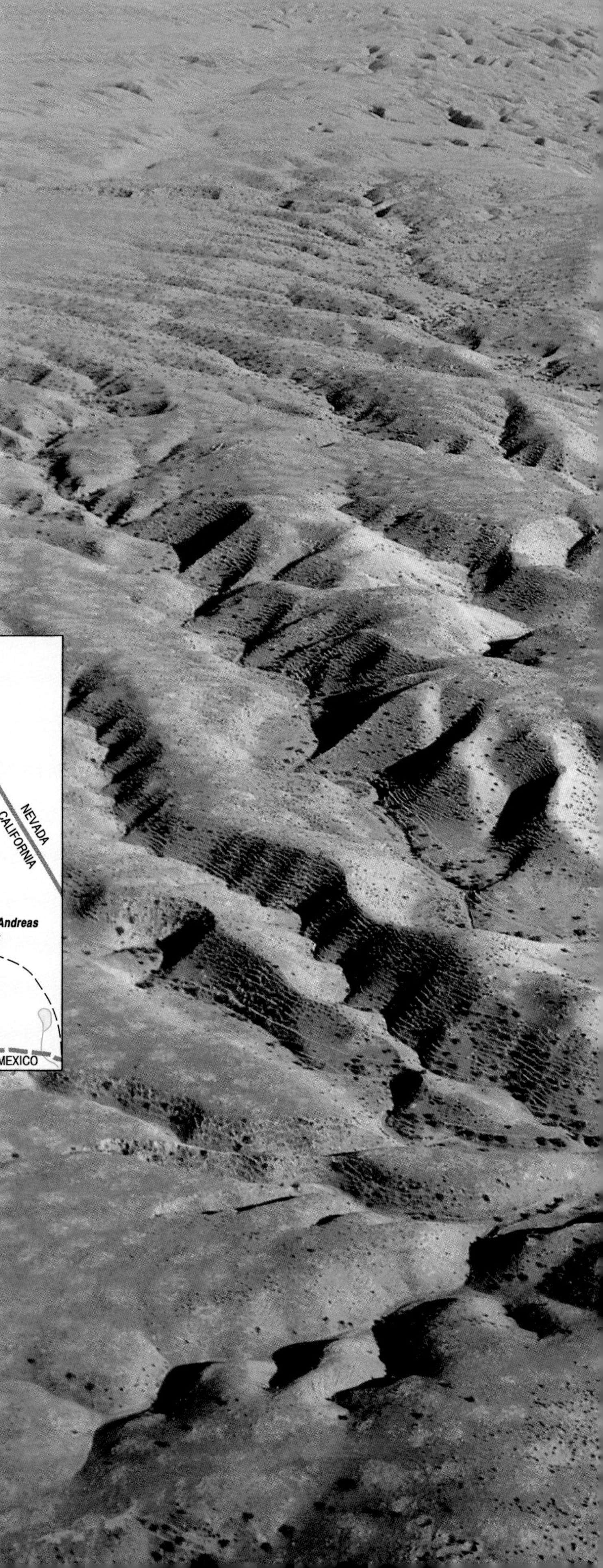


***Cracks in the California desert*** *(right) begin as tremors about 5 miles down in the bedrock. The fault's length was only recognized after the San Francisco earthquake of 1906, when buildings collapsed, fires raged, and almost 700 people died.*

***Buckled streets*** *(above) result as the pressures of parallel fractures in the fault compress the San Gabriel Mountains outside Los Angeles. The mountains' shattered western front sheds 7 tons of debris per acre every year, which slides dangerously toward the city.*

ranges and the spread of the Great Basin that stretches east from California to Utah result in part from San Andreas Fault pressures. The Great Basin's slow stretch explains why Reno now lies west of Los Angeles. Not always slow, however, the San Andreas Fault can propel California toward Alaska in 21-foot jumps. Civilization *is* subject to change without notice.

CALIFORNIA

# POINT REYES

SIR FRANCIS DRAKE, the first captain to sail his own ship around the world, dropped anchor at today's Point Reyes to repair the *Golden Hind*. An English adventurer serving Queen Elizabeth I, Drake could not have known that the high cliffs were not really North America. In the global scheme of crustal, or tectonic, plates that form the Earth's surface, Point Reyes marks the easternmost edge of the Pacific Plate, which grinds here against the North American Plate.

Point Reyes once adjoined the Tehachapi Mountains 300 miles to the south. Bodegas and Tomales bays at its northern end inundate parts of the San Andreas Fault, which, according to geologists, is prying Point Reyes toward Alaska at a rate of 2 inches per year. Like sutures through the fault line, Point Reyes's Inverness Ridge mountains are the crumpled result of crustal plate interaction.

In the great 1906 San Francisco earthquake, Tomales Point slid northward a distance of nearly 20 feet. The National Park Service's Bear Valley Visitor Center lies in the San Andreas fault zone. Nearby Earthquake Trail provides a short walk through the landscape resulting from the geological tumult underfoot, and two other trails explore Point Reyes's natural history and its horseranching days.

On the coast, Drakes Bay and Drakes Estero commemorate the adventurous Englishman who first reached their shores. The mile-wide estero, in which fresh and salt waters mix, is so protected by spits that it has four bays and has nearly become a lake. Lacking information to prove otherwise, we assume that Drake navigated the *Golden Hind* into the estero for repairs.

Waters of its estuary and of the adjacent Estero de Limantour are an important habitat for birds and serve as nurseries for marine organisms. It is possible to drive to Limantour Beach and walk its beachfront trail to Limantour Spit. Nearby trails give access to the estuaries for prime bird watching. The Limantour Beach trail penetrates a narrow strip of the park's substantial reserve of federally protected wilderness (74,000 acres) and its natural areas set aside for research.

When Drake arrived on these rocky shores, Miwok Indians had already been inhabiting the area for centuries. A peaceful tribe of hunters and gatherers, they lived comfortably on the natural riches surrounding them, harvesting and hunting according to the season.

Drake called the region Nueva Albion, New England. In 1603, the Spanish explorer Don Sebastian Vizcaíno dubbed it with its present name. After his stormy one-day anchorage in Drakes Bay on January 6, he named the land *La Punta de Los Reyes* for the Feast of the Three Kings that marks the 12th day of Christmas. England never pressed its claim here, and Spanish control lasted until Mexican independence in 1821.

When the U.S. took control of California, much of Point Reyes was converted into large beef and dairy cattle ranches. Examples of this lifestyle endure as mandated by the legislation creating Point Reyes National Seashore in 1962. A meeting place for sea, land, and tectonic plates, Point Reyes offers such unusual vistas as deer feeding near rocks where sea lions lie basking in the sun.

Point Reyes Lighthouse and a foghorn on the farthest point of this hammerhead peninsula both warn ships off this notorious rocky headland, where storm waves beach like artillery barrages. Adjacent waters are a graveyard of more than 100 ships that succumbed to the waves, often in choking fogs, before the lighthouse was built in 1870. Offshore, a gray whale may be making its less hazardous annual migration between Baja California to the south and the Bering Sea. Seals frequent the protected bays, and the estuaries are thronged with migratory shorebirds feasting in their brackish productivity.

Tomales Point harbors Tule Elk Range; Tule elk from an Owens Valley herd have been returned to their former habitat here. They are the smallest of North America's three elk subspecies, yet bulls weigh up to 550 pounds. In the mating season, in late summer, they rush at each other from 30-foot dueling distances to butt massive racks of antlers that span up to 60 inches and are shed and grown anew each year.

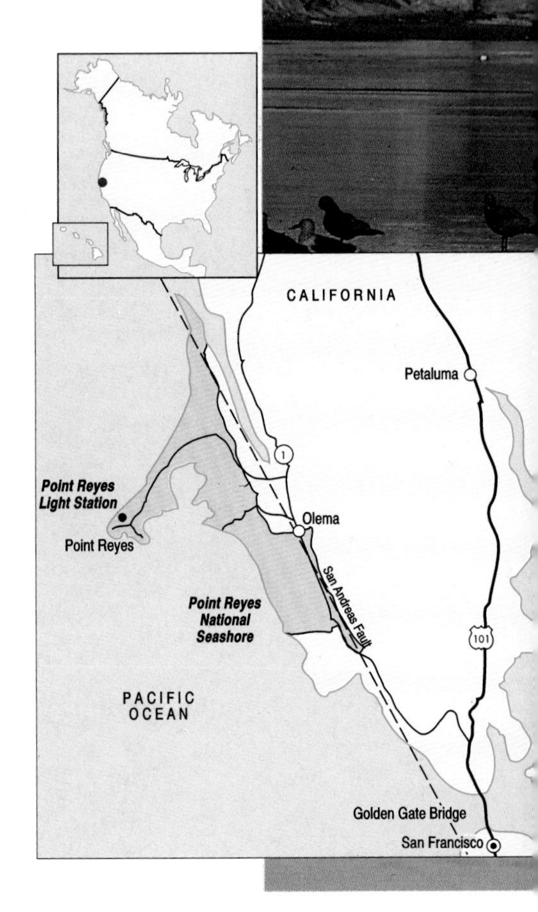


***Drakes Beach** (right) lies in a wide protected cove, ideal for swimming and so safe that a lifeguard is not considered necessary. Just beyond it, in the sheer cliffs and rocky shelves beneath the peninsula's lighthouse, thousands of common murre nest in the crevices. Each pair of seabirds lays a single egg.*

**Wildlife watching**

The male double-crested cormorant (right) can be seen dancing in the water while presenting the female with nesting materials as part of his courtship display. This medium-sized fish eater breeds close to dependable supplies of food in colonies of up to 3,000 pairs.

Seals can also be seen as they laze on the rocks or slip through the water. The body of a seal is typically torpedo-shaped, with thick layers of fatty blubber accounting for much of its weight. The flippers, as well as the body, are furred, and the seals undergo an annual molt.

Northern elephant seals (right) feed on fish and squid, and make long deep dives. In late November, at the start of the breeding season, males compete for a female partner. With the help of a greatly enlarged nasal chamber, which creates the elephantine snout, the males utter loud vocal threats against rivals.

CALIFORNIA

# DEATH VALLEY

ONE OF THE STRANGEST CORNERS of North America, Death Valley is packed with extremes and contradictions. Telescope Peak reaches 11,049 feet in elevation; nearby, the western hemisphere's lowest point rests 282 feet below sea level near Badwater. The bizarre beauty of this immense, unearthly landscape lures travelers back again and again.

Death Valley is so hot that July average high temperatures are 116.2°F—the record high is 134°F. Rainfall in July averages only one-tenth of an inch. This is the hottest spot in North America, but some of its mountains are snow-capped well into the summer and support bighorn sheep and bristlecone pines. These pines are the world's longest living things, although the age of the specimens in the park has not been determined.

The geologic faulting that created Death Valley's topographic extremes is relatively recent. It has left a record in rock that tells most of the Earth's history, albeit in a jumbled sequence. From Badwater to the top of Telescope Peak, the elevation rises more sharply and steeply than almost anywhere in the United States. The uplifted mountains keep moisture-laden clouds from reaching Death Valley itself, but more than 900 plants grow in the park.

Names such as Furnace Creek, Ground Afire, Chloride Cliff, and Devils Golf Course express the desert's nature, yet National Park Service maps carefully warn visitors to "Watch for flooding." More than one mining town has been obliterated by flash floods.

When it rains, boulders weighing up to 400 pounds scoot across the mud, propelled by the strong winds. Although it looks as arid as the moon, the landscape is torn at times by walls of water that are more like avalanches than floods.

A deceptive map and rumors of gold brought the first whites into this Shoshone Indian homeland in 1849. Their map of lies charted the course of Death Valley's illusionary history. Eventually, some gold was found in the land that came to represent hell on Earth in American folklore.

Later, paying silver was discovered in the area, and ultimately borax, which was eagerly consumed by the growing chemical industry—the brand name Twenty Mule Team Borax originated in Death Valley. A park canyon contains some lasting evidence; borax crystals lay like cotton bolls across Ground Afire, whose parched heat gave crazed men the illusion of drowning.

One of the park's biggest and most attractive sights is Scotty's Castle, which rises near a volcanic crater only 1,000 years old. It was begun in 1922 as a vacation retreat for Albert M. Johnson, a wealthy Midwesterner, but Johnson's friend Walter Scott lived there for six years after Johnson's death, spinning entertaining yarns about it that transformed it from Johnson's Death Valley Ranch into Scotty's Castle. Death Valley National Monument was created in 1933, and in 1970, the federal government bought Scotty's Castle and added it to the park.

Sunlight heightens illusion here. Burned to moonlike desolation at noon, Golden Canyon and nearby Zabriskie Point glow as golden as mother lodes in the rich early morning and evening sunlight. Death Valley's beauty is stark and fearsome.

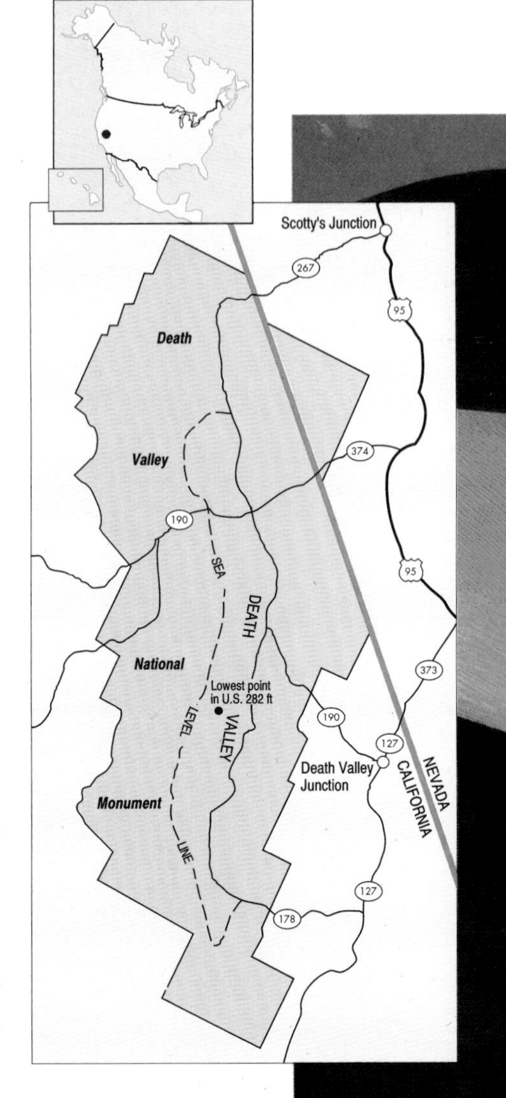

***Dunes at Mesquite Flats*** *(far right) rise to heights of 200 feet and shift in the wind. In this bleached landscape—one of the hottest, lowest, and driest places on Earth—the temperature often remains above 100°F during the night. The Indians called the valley* Tomesha, *Ground Afire.*

*Beavertail cactus (right) is named for the shape of its flattened stems; although spineless, it is dotted with barbed bristles. Some plants here only flower every ten years, and 21 species are found nowhere else on Earth.*

OREGON

# CRATER LAKE

How blue is it? It's like blue ink. Shamans forbade most Indians even to look at the lake because it marks the battleground of the earth-shattering conflict between the god of the world above and the god of the world below. Indians said nothing of it to the white men who began to roam these reaches of Oregon soon after the Gold Rush of 1848 led them to California. Not until 1853 was Crater Lake discovered—by a group of prospectors including John Wesley Hillman. They had found the nation's deepest lake. It is also the western hemisphere's second and the world's seventh, deepest.

The lake's water is not actually blue. It is so pure, however, that light penetrates very deep—apparently to a world record 725 feet. As the light probes deeper and deeper, one by one its colors are absorbed. The last color absorbed is blue, and only the deepest blues are then scattered back to the lake's surface. Similar phenomena make the sky look blue and sunsets red.

Crater Lake National Park enjoys some of the cleanest air in the United States. From Hillman Peak, at 8,156 feet above the lake surface the highest point on the caldera rim, you can see for about 100 miles.

The lake sits in the bowl-shaped caldera of collapsed Mount Mazama. Once 12,000 feet in elevation, Mount Mazama experienced cataclysmic volcanism about 6,850 years ago. It ejected so much ash and pumice that it collapsed into the emptied magma chamber. Rain and snowmelt began to fill the caldera once it had cooled.

Today's lake is 1,932 feet deep, and it has an average depth of 1,500 feet and a width of 6 miles. The lake has no inlet or outlet, but its replenishment is assured by ample precipitation including 50 feet of snowfall. As the amount of water it receives in precipitation roughly equals the amount lost through evaporation and seepage, the volume of the lake stays relatively constant.

Research conducted with an unmanned submarine device in the late 1980s suggests that some warm water may be vented into the lake from its bottom. Light-dependent blue-green algae exist at 725-foot depths,

***Wizard Island*** *(right), the most prominent feature of Crater Lake, was formed by a relatively minor volcanic eruption, which threw up this small cinder cone. The lake, one of the deepest in the world, maintains its depth with precipitation.*

***Clark's nutcracker** (above) remains near the lake year-round despite the harshness of the winter, which banishes most other birds. Officially a member of the crow family, it pecks at trees for the grubs in their bark, exactly like a woodpecker. It also eats evergreen seeds, prying them out of the trees with its bill.*

*Like other crows, Clark's nutcracker is a thief and frequently steals the eggs and young of smaller birds for its own meals. The explorer William Clark discovered the bird, which is named for him.*

but the clean, clear, and cold lake water supported no fish until freshwater shrimp were added to feed the rainbow trout and kokanee salmon introduced by anglers in the 19th century.

Crater Lake was discovered 20 years before Yellowstone became the world's first national park in 1872, but similar status eluded it until 1902, when it was proclaimed a national park through the efforts of William Gladstone Steel. As a Kansas schoolboy, Steel first learned of Crater Lake from a newspaper wrapped around his school lunch. He became obsessed with the lake, lobbying tirelessly on its behalf and finally appealing to the President in person. After 17 years of Steel's advocacy, Crater Lake became the nation's sixth national park.

WASHINGTON

# OLYMPIC NATIONAL PARK

JUTTING OUT OF WASHINGTON'S OLYMPIC PENINSULA, Cape Alva is the westernmost point of land in the contiguous United States, and it symbolizes the peninsula's intimate ties with the Pacific Ocean. Pacific air masses forced high by the Olympic Mountains dump moisture from 200 inches of annual precipitation on 7,965-foot Mount Olympus and drop 500 inches of snow on its Blue Glacier, which is 900 feet thick and one of 60 ice masses in the park.

Moderate temperatures, abundant rainfall, and protective fog have created Olympic's temperate rain forests. Rain drums into them, but scant light reaches the forest floor, which is so lushly carpeted with a 2-foot thickness of duff, moss, lichen, and ferns that its silence can be eerie.

Olympic's peninsular position also reflects its oceanic influences. Ice Age glaciers gouged out Puget Sound, Hood Canal, and the Strait of Juan de Fuca. They isolated the peninsula from the mainland ecosystems and left behind the deep soils that nurture the rain forest.

Because of its isolation, Olympic lacks 11 species of plants and animals you would normally expect to find here and has evolved 16 endemic organisms, including the magenta painted cup, Flett's violet, Piper's bellflower, Mazama pocket gopher, Olympic marmot, and Beardslee and Crescenti trout. The National Park was created in 1938, partly to protect the large herd of Roosevelt elk, which now numbers 5,000.

Fed by rain and snowmelt, 13 rivers radiate from the mountains. Some sustain annual runs of spawning salmon, bent on returning from the sea to their native streams. Mouths of several rivers open onto Olympic's 57 miles of wild ocean beach. Waters of the Hoh River run like milk in the spring, white with glacial flour, suspended rock powder ground fine by the glaciers' headwaters. The proximity of glaciated mountain to ocean beach lends the Olympic environments a startling, compressed diversity.

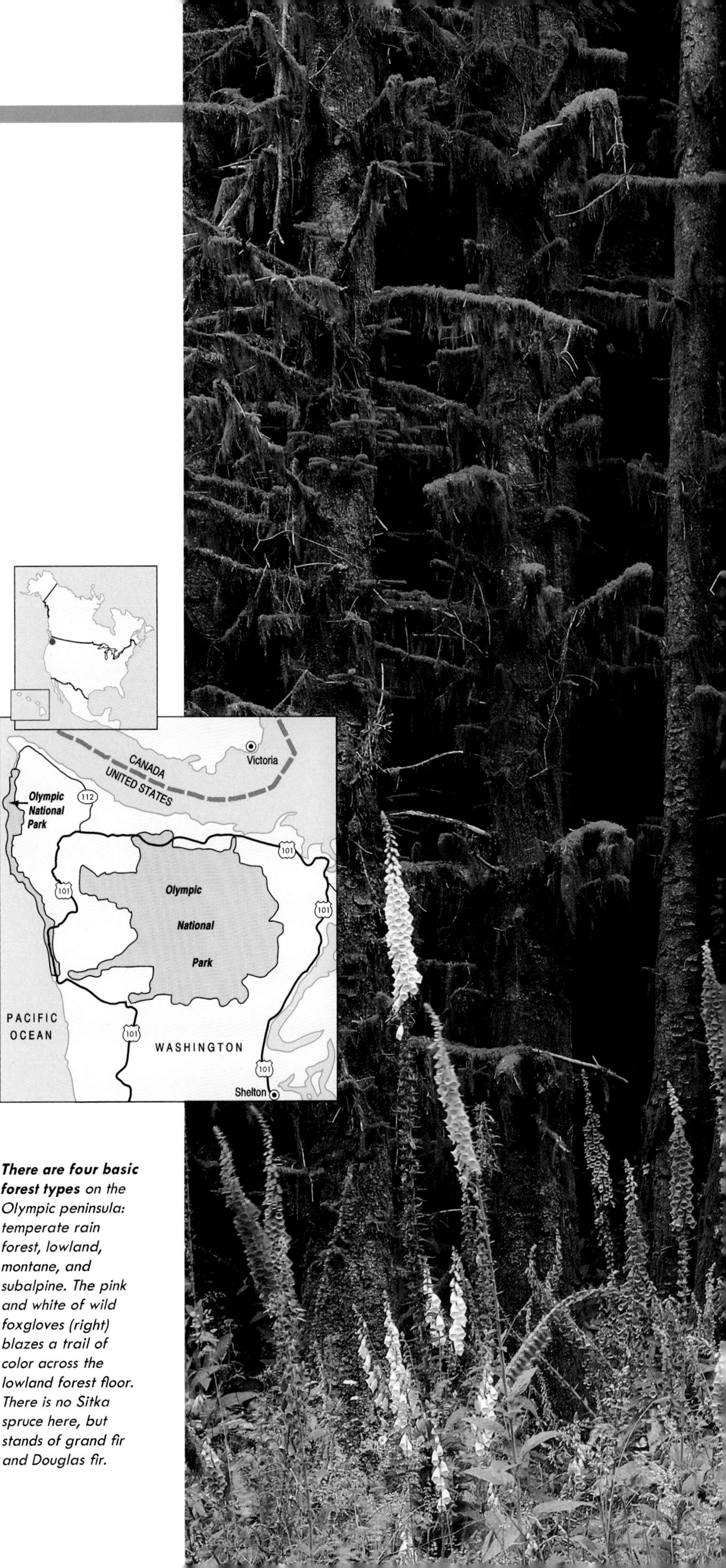


***There are four basic forest types*** *on the Olympic peninsula: temperate rain forest, lowland, montane, and subalpine. The pink and white of wild foxgloves (right) blazes a trail of color across the lowland forest floor. There is no Sitka spruce here, but stands of grand fir and Douglas fir.*

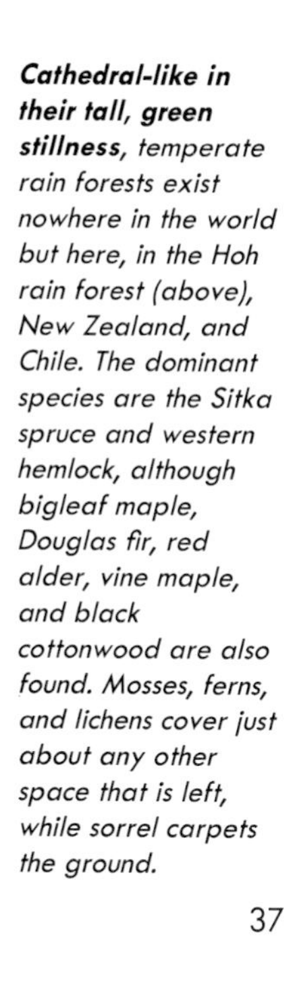

***Cathedral-like in their tall, green stillness,*** *temperate rain forests exist nowhere in the world but here, in the Hoh rain forest (above), New Zealand, and Chile. The dominant species are the Sitka spruce and western hemlock, although bigleaf maple, Douglas fir, red alder, vine maple, and black cottonwood are also found. Mosses, ferns, and lichens cover just about any other space that is left, while sorrel carpets the ground.*

WASHINGTON

# MOUNT RAINIER NATIONAL PARK

IN MORNING HAZE, Mount Rainier's peak looks like a phantom perched on layers of cloud. Forty-one glaciers make its conical shape dazzle and glisten. On some days, this volcanic mountain can be seen from 100 miles away; on others, not at all.

Although apparently solitary, Mount Rainier is actually one of many volcanoes in the Cascade Range, which runs from the Fraser River in southern British Columbia to California's Lassen Peak in the south. Now dormant, Mount Rainier last experienced minor eruptive activity approximately 100 years ago.

Once reaching 16,000 feet in elevation, the peak deteriorated over millennia. Then, about 2,000 years ago, new eruptions rebuilt Mount Rainier to its present height of 14,410 feet. It rivals the highest peak in the United States outside Alaska, 14,494-foot Mount Whitney in the southern Sierra's Sequoia National Park, California.

If fire built Mount Rainier, ice has sculpted it. Today's mountain glaciers are mere remnants of the huge Ice Age glaciers that once covered the present Seattle area to a depth of 4,000 feet. Mount Rainier's coastal setting on the Pacific provides it with masses of moist air, and its height guarantees it a fair share of the moisture. The peak forces the air masses to high elevations where cold temperatures then squeeze the moisture out of them as precipitation before they pass by.

North America's greatest snowfall in one season—a crushing 1,122 inches, more than 93 feet—was recorded at Mount Rainier in 1972. A single snowfall in 1956 dropped more than 30 feet—the greatest snowstorm recorded in the United States.

The mountain's lower slopes record an average 60 inches of precipitation each year; below the summit, that figure approaches 100 inches. The popular Paradise area of the surrounding national park averages 50 feet of snow per year, and

***Avalanche lilies*** *carpet the mountain meadows of Paradise Park (right). The plants bloom after the snow has melted, and the white trumpet-shaped blossoms can last until September. Dark green firs and balsams fringe the base of towering Mount Rainier.*

***Mount Rainier's snow-covered slopes** are mirrored in the flower-fringed Reflection Lakes (far right), which are glacier-carved lakes set in bowls scooped out by ice masses.*

*Wildflowers abound in the alpine meadows, including lupine (right), polygonum, Alaska spiraea, and carpeting moss campion.*

25-foot snowpack is common. As a result, roads can be closed into July, and high-country trails are often impassable until the end of the month.

Fabulous precipitation feeds Mount Rainier's glaciers, which represent the largest amassing of year-round ice on any peak in the contiguous United States. Nisqually Glacier is 4 miles long and flows downhill 12 inches on a summer's day. Emmons Glacier, the largest of all the glaciers on Mount Rainier, can be seen easily from Sunrise—elevation 6,400 feet—the highest point that can be reached by a park road.

As a glacier grinds along, it dislodges bits of rock that add to its earth-shaping potential. Embedded in its base or sides, these act as etching tools or as huge gritty abrasives like landscape sandpaper. Striae, straight lines etched into rock that record the passage of glaciers, are created by the embedded rocks.

Glaciation created many popular park features when global climates averaged a few degrees cooler than they do today. Having quarried vast heaps of rock debris, the glaciers deposited them at their margins or their terminus as at the mouth of rivers that were not frozen.

The Longmire to Paradise highway passes over the Nisqually River where the Nisqually Glacier deposited its terminal moraine in 1840. (Shortly after 1840, the glacier began retreating uphill 70 feet a year.) At Nisqually Icefall, the glacier still spills over a cliff in massive blocks of ice.

The park's many U-shaped valleys are also the work of glaciers. Stream-cut valleys begin as V-shapes, but glaciers gouge them to the distinctive U-shape. Such a canyon profile is visible at Stevens Canyon on the road leading from Paradise to Sunrise.

Mount Rainier's uppermost 6,000 feet are mainly bare rock and glacier ice. At about 7,500 feet, alpine plants begin to appear. Most grow close to the ground in protective, matted configurations. Many have hairy or waxy leaves and stems to help reduce moisture loss in the high winds they must endure. Describing these plant communities as alpine tundra acknowledges their great similarity to landscapes at lower elevations hundreds of miles to the north in Alaska.

Elk and other introduced species have created management dilemmas for the National Park Service, which pursues a philosophy of natural management. Its policy attempts to restore or perpetuate conditions and natural processes as they were in the mid-19th century before the arrival of Europeans.

In 1988, nearly 97 percent of the park was designated as wilderness for stringent protection under the National Wilderness Preservation System that was created in 1964. The idea of a national park is constantly changing, just like the dynamic landscape of dormant fire and retreating ice that created Mount Rainier.

WYOMING

# GRAND TETONS

"MAYBE THOSE ARE THE TETONS," people say as mountains appear to the west, but if they speak without gasping, chances are the Teton Range has not yet revealed itself. Long a landmark for trappers and traders who named them with the French word for breasts, the Tetons' naked geology lends them a stunning visual appeal.

A key to it lies atop Mount Moran: the sandstone capping its granite matches a sandstone formation that now lies 24,000 feet beneath the valley called Jackson Hole. Two massive blocks of the Earth's crust faulted here, slipping a total of 30,000 vertical feet over nine million years.

Today, the 40-mile-long mountain range juts abruptly skyward without foothills from Jackson Hole's comparatively flat floor, which is 6,000 feet above sea level. From the valley floor, it is more than 7,000 feet to the range's ultimate summit, the 13,747-foot peak of Grand Teton.

Contrasting with its steep eastern escarpment, the range's western face slopes toward Idaho's agricultural plains. In counterpoint to the mountains' starkly imposing granite reach, the string of lakes along its base possesses intimate grandeur. These lakes also illuminate the mountains' formations, since most rest in depressions gouged out by mountain glaciers and dammed by their morainal rubble piles.

Jackson Lake has been enlarged by a dam to benefit agricultural interests downstream on the Snake River, which carves its valley bed through the relatively loose rubble left by successions of valley and mountain glaciers. The Snake also provides one of the best avenues for seeing the park's astonishing array of wildlife. For some reason, many otherwise wary wild animals do not react to humans traveling on the river. Raft trips offered by concessioners—particularly morning and evening trips—make for wildlife-watching safaris that are unmatched in the Lower 48 wildlands.

Moose, beavers weighing as much as 40 pounds, various owls, ospreys, herons, ducks—the number of species that can be seen from a raft during an evening's float

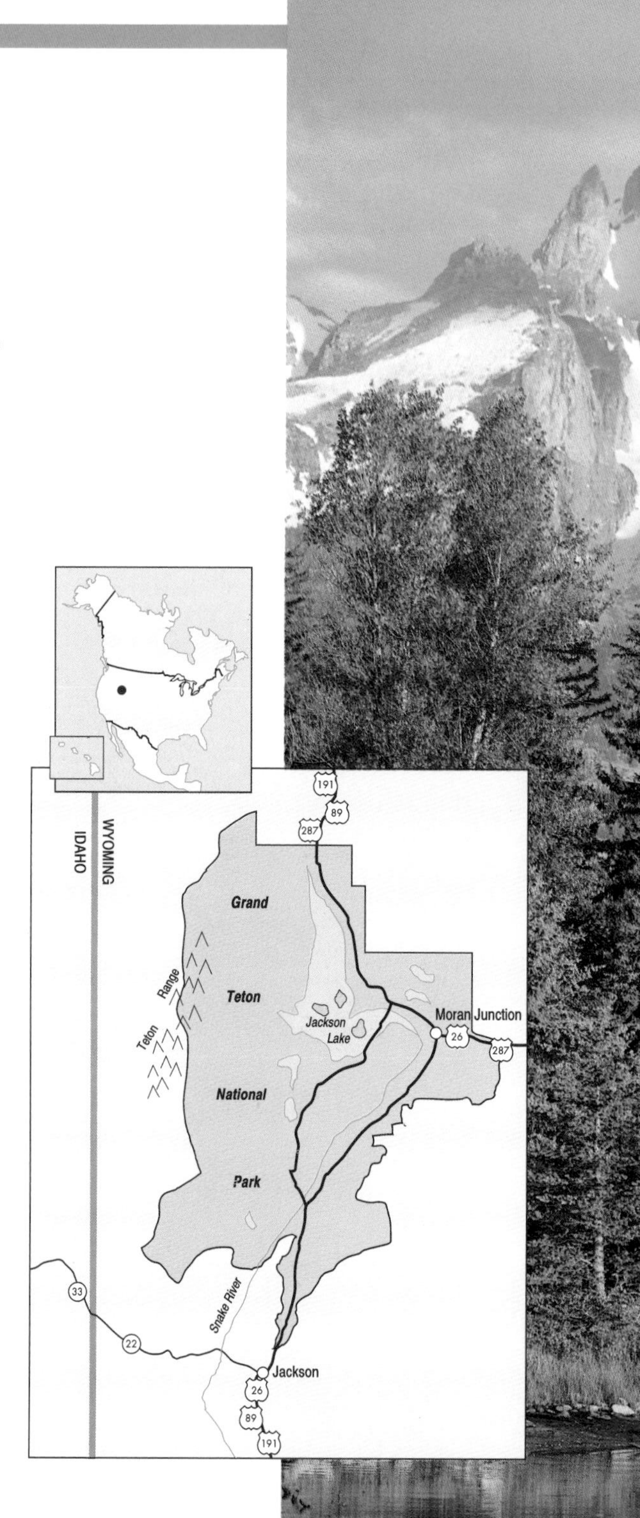


***The Teton Range*** *is the youngest in the Rocky Mountain chain, and the jagged peaks show no sign of the aging process that may one day wear them smooth. The river bottomlands and pond areas (right) provide a suitable environment for moose and beaver.*

***The moose*** *is the world's largest animal with antlers. It can be identified easily by its broad, overhanging muzzle and by the fleshy dewlap, known as the bell, hanging from its throat. The massive antlers of the male are palm-shaped and flattened. Bellowing males (above) engage in fierce contests with rivals for the attention of females.*

*Like most members of the deer family, the moose sheds and regrows its antlers in an annual cycle. They are shed in late winter or early spring, and grow again in summer before the fall rutting contests. To feed, moose eat bark and grasses, or wade into the water in search of aquatic plants.*

staggers the imagination. Ecologically, float travel is more benign than hiking, and elk (wapiti), moose, mule deer, black bears, buffalo (bison), and coyotes roam the bottomlands and valley pond areas. In fact, river bottomlands are prime spots to see all the park's larger mammals except bighorn sheep and pronghorn, or antelope.

It is possible to get a distant view of elk (about 3,000 summer in the park) and a panoramic view of Jackson Hole's flat valley with its abrupt Teton backdrop from on top of Signal Mountain. Here, at the top of the 7,500-foot peak, wary grouse slink through the shrubbery. Much of the range was taken over by ranching and other development, so the National Elk Refuge was created along the park's southern boundary, and masses of elk winter here.

Only black bears now inhabit the park. Grizzlies rarely, if ever, range down this far from their core habitat in the Greater Yellowstone area. Black bears are not the fierce predators that grizzlies are, but, along with occasional mountain lions here, they top the food chain with the help of opportunistic coyotes.

With elk, the park's chief wildlife spectacles are its herd of bison, or buffalo, and the seemingly ungainly moose with its incredible rack of palm-shaped antlers. No

**Mountain men—trappers, traders and mappers**

Why Kansas cowboys should personify popular Western myth stumps many historians. Far better candidates are the mountain men who rode their horses ahead of advancing European culture, not behind a bunch of cows. Jim Bridger (above) should be more popular than Roy Rogers.

Bridger roamed the Rockies beginning in the 1820s and overstated the western wonders he saw, but usually with a kernel of truth. Old Gabe, as trappers called him, said Yellowstone boasted a glass mountain, petrified birdsong, and a six-hour echo he used as an alarm clock. Yellowstone's obsidian cliffs are indeed glassy, but its petrified forests attract living birds. (The echo remains mysterious.)

Although illiterate, Bridger was keenly intelligent. He learned French and Spanish from fellow trappers and mastered several Indian languages. His peers considered him the best trapper, hunter, and Indian fighter of all. As for veracity, the map drawn from Bridger's memory in 1851 remained this region's most accurate one until the 1871 Hayden Survey. Surveyors with theodolites and transits could not compete with his canyon-by-canyon picture of the Rocky Mountain West. He guided the first military survey expedition into Jackson Hole in 1860.

creature can be judged ungainly, however, that negotiates the wilds at speeds of 35 miles an hour or more while carrying such a heavy rack of antlers. Moose feed on willows growing along streams and on pond-bottom plants. As they lift their heads from under the water, they create a memorable vision when the trapped water pours from their antlers like tiny, ephemeral waterfalls.

Its so-called Cathedral Group includes the three Tetons—Middle, South, and Grand—Mount Owen, Teewinot ("Many Pinnacles") Mountain, Nez Perce, Cloudveil Dome, and several spires. Mount Moran to the north, with its skillet-shaped glacier, adorns many postcards. Good views of this sandstone-capped peak can be seen from Jackson Lake Lodge, Oxbow Bend, and the Willow Flats pull-out on the park road.

A dozen glaciers have re-established themselves on the Teton peaks. One exhibits characteristics so classically common to mountain glaciers that it has been named Schoolroom Glacier. Today's small ice masses merely suggest the massive glaciers that worked major Teton canyons; they are ice cubes compared to the Ice Age valley glaciers which covered this area. The ancient ones quarried the range's eastern escarpment, gouged out Jackson Hole, and then filled it with glacial rubble.

The shatter lines on many Teton peaks show that the range's uplift was not a smooth event. Although they are composed of ancient rock, the Tetons themselves are very young mountains, only 9 million years old compared to the Rockies' 60 million years or the Great Smoky Mountains' 200 million years.

However, the Tetons' crystalline rock is the same as the three-billion-year-old core of eastern North America's Allegheny Mountains. Hard and stable, the rock draws climbers, who are also attracted by the lack of foothills. Alpinists can begin to climb immediately at the mountains' base; few major peaks in the Lower 48 states can be assaulted so directly.

The Tetons are still rising—although climbers will not notice it, since the rate of uplift is about 12 inches every 300 or 400 years—and this most compact of major ranges stands to maintain its awe-inspiring scenic beauty for eons to come.

*__Much of Jackson Hole's landscape__ is the result of glaciation, and this wintry scene (right) shows how relentless the weather can still be. A herd of cattle have come here for water and grazing, away from the deep and crusted snow. Winter can be a tough time for all the animals, and although coyotes may not attack healthy specimens, they will feed off the carcasses of dead animals.*

*In the spring, this valley floor will be a carpet of brilliant color. Sagebrush buttercups arrive after the snow, closely followed by spring beauties and yellowbells, and then scarlet gilia, lupines, larkspur, and wild buckwheat bloom.*

**Getting ready for winter**

Buffalo (left) roam the sagebrush flats and frequent watering holes in the park. Primarily grazers, these huge creatures, sometimes measuring 9 feet long, are covered in shaggy, brownish-black fur that grows thickly on the head, neck, and forelegs. Winter dominates this area for more than half the year, so protection against the elements is essential. Large numbers of elk spend summers in the park, putting on weight to help them through the harsh winter.

Black bears, and the occasional grizzly, forage in the canyons and woodlands to build up body fat. The American beaver (right) has dense fur to provide waterproofing and insulation, and special muscles close its ears and nostrils when it is underwater. Fall is the time when beavers are busiest, making repairs to their lodges and dams, and stockpiling food for the winter.

WYOMING

# YELLOWSTONE NATIONAL PARK

HERE IN YELLOWSTONE, WITH ITS GUSHING GEYSERS, bubbling mud pots, piping hot thermal pools, and dramatic waterfalls, America launched its love affair with wild nature's superlatives. It has been a protracted romance, and the lovers have worked themselves so far into each other's psyches that Yellowstone National Park symbolizes the American experience just as much as the Gilbert Stuart portrait of George Washington does.

Yellowstone is a high plateau built up by the lava flows of ancient volcanoes. Its thermal features result from the thinness of the Earth's crust here; throughout the world the crust varies from 5 to 25 miles thick, but at Yellowstone, it is as thin as 1 mile. Surface water percolating downward as much as 2 miles is superheated and pressurized, and explodes back to the surface as the multiple steamy and sulfurous wonders for which Yellowstone was set aside four years before the nation's centennial.

It is the largest and only major undisturbed geyser field in the world, with an estimated 10,000 thermal features. Twenty times more heat flows out of Yellowstone than the average for the rest of the continent's surface. In one geyser basin, that figure rises to more than 800 times the continental average. There is as much thermal activity here as in the volcanoes of Iceland and Hawaii.

Earthquake activity is common: a 1960s earthquake created Quake Lake; a 1983 quake altered the intervals between Old Faithful's eruptions. Many of Yellowstone's awe-inspiring waterfalls occur at eroded edges of its vast lava plateau. Even its trout bask in the park's thermal legacy. Yellowstone National Park boasts a vast underwater wilderness; by the late 1970s, the number of fish-watchers in the park had topped that of anglers. Three subspecies of cutthroat trout—named for the red marks behind their gills—inhabit park waters. Their June or July spawning runs up streams out of Yellowstone Lake are as

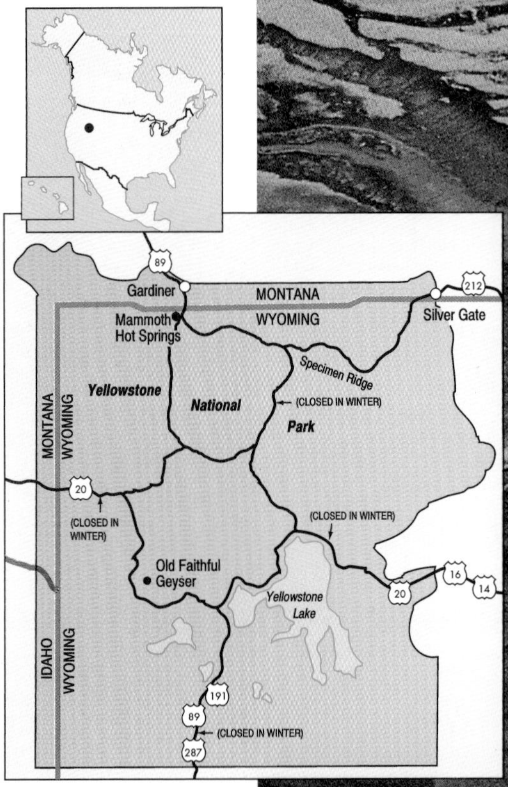

89
Gardiner
MONTANA
WYOMING
212
Mammoth Hot Springs
Silver Gate
Specimen Ridge
Yellowstone
National
Park
(CLOSED IN WINTER)
MONTANA
WYOMING
20
(CLOSED IN WINTER)
(CLOSED IN WINTER)
Old Faithful Geyser
Yellowstone Lake
16
14
20
IDAHO
WYOMING
191
89
(CLOSED IN WINTER)
287

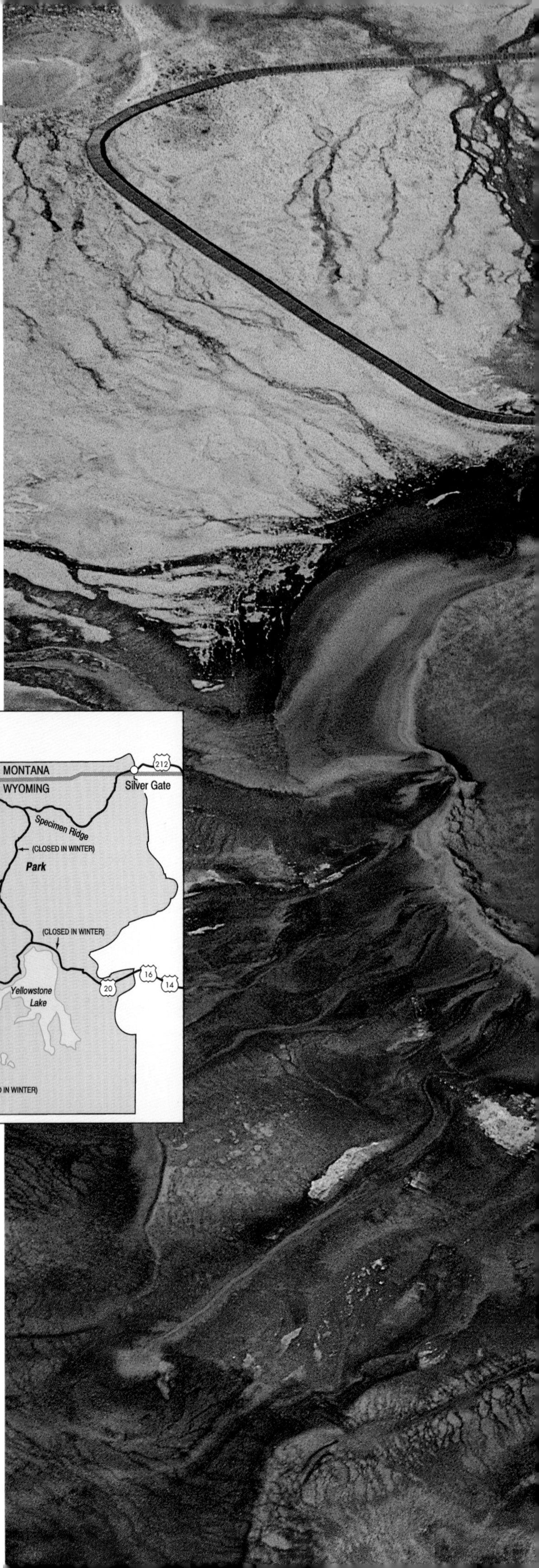

***Bands of color*** *(right), tinted by various algae that thrive at different temperatures in the hot springs, reveal the heat of the water that has bubbled up from the Earth's interior. The green band is coolest. Life near the boiling center is colorless and invisible.*

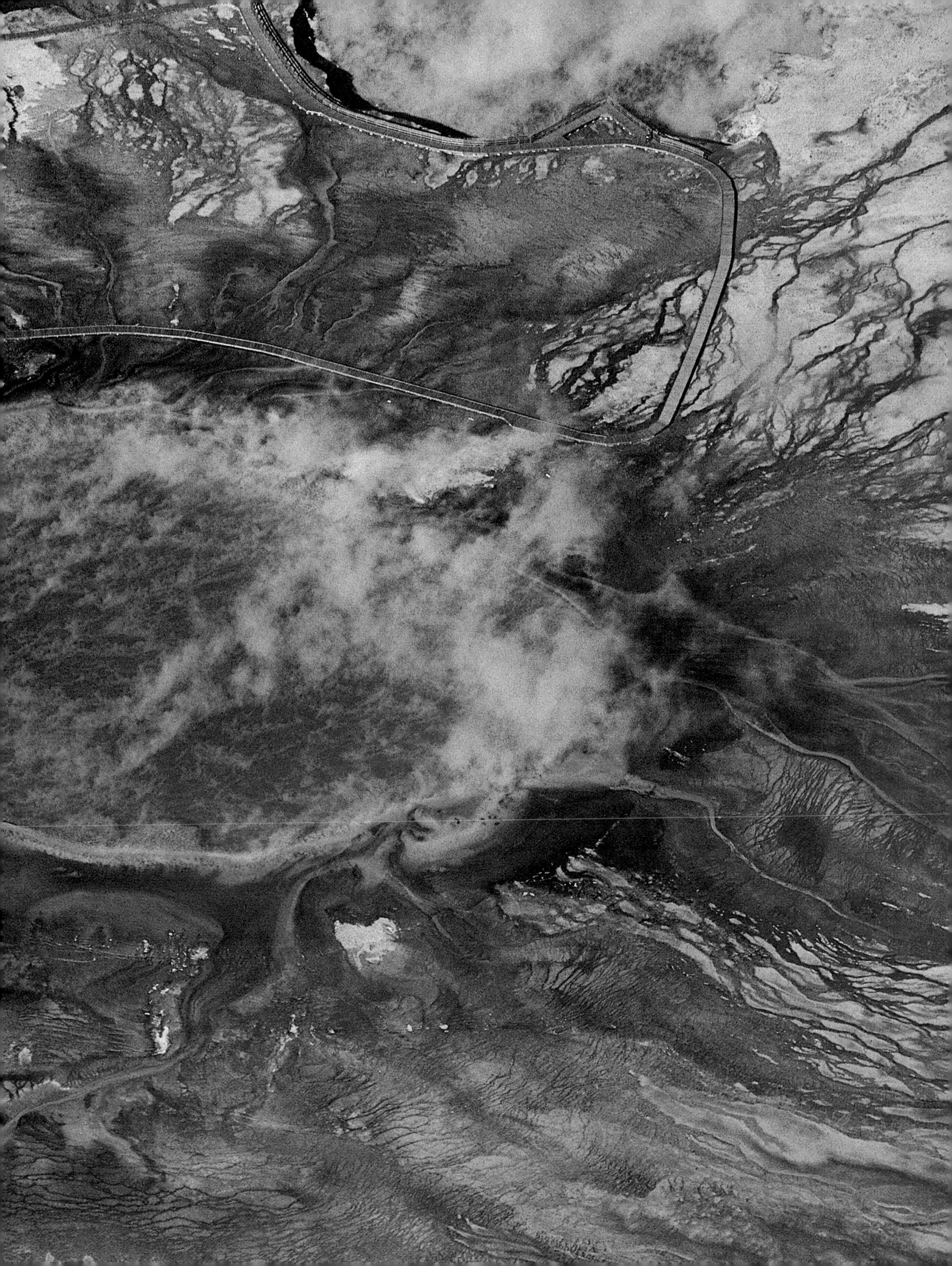

thrilling as the sighting of grizzly bears, bald eagles, or trumpeter swans.

Yellowstone Lake is easily one of the world's largest natural lakes at its elevation, and its 139 square miles make it the largest of its kind in North America and the last large lake formally discovered on this continent. At various times in its past, the lake has flowed into the Pacific Ocean, the Atlantic Ocean, and Hudson Bay. Today it averages a depth of 139 feet and contains 12 million acre-feet of water that completely replaces itself only every 10 or 11 years.

Stately trumpeter swans, which weigh 20 pounds and support wings spanning 10 feet, are linked to the park waters for survival. By the 1930s there were fewer than 100 of these birds in the U.S., two-thirds of them in southern Montana and the rest in Yellowstone. With protection afforded by the park and adjacent wildlands and the 1935 creation of a refuge in Montana, trumpeter swans began to multiply and now they number about 10,000.

Given today's keen interest in wildlife watching, it is difficult to appreciate that the park's large animals were of no particular interest to early park advocates. Public concern only came to the defense of wildlife well after the park was established and the nation's hordes of buffalo were reduced to the very brink of extinction. In fact, the only wildlife species the park has lost is the wolf, which was killed off by the 1930s, largely by park rangers and government hunters, as an unwanted predator of livestock and big game species.

Grizzlies dominated their homelands for so long that they evolved an extremely low reproductive rate that now threatens to undo them. Remnant populations today exist only in the Yellowstone area and in Idaho and Montana, in high-mountain wilderness. Of the roughly 250 grizzlies in Yellowstone, only around 30 are breeding females. Some bear researchers feel that this low number may result in the species' demise in the park as wildlands outside park boundaries continue to shrink because of logging, mining, and second-home development. These females can produce only ten cubs per year at best. Once numbering in the hundreds of thousands, grizzlies now total 600 to 700 in the Lower 48 states.

Grizzlies challenge Park Service management because the agency has been

***Magnificent debris*** *(right) remains in the stunning landscapes of rock and forest that characterize the park, the result of a volcanic outburst that took place 600,000 years ago and threw ejecta over more than 1,000 miles.*

*When the twin magma chambers responsible for the blast were empty, they collapsed inward, leaving a bowl-shaped depression, or caldera, so large—almost a mile deep and up to 50 miles wide—that it can only be seen in its entirety from the air. Most of the park's major thermal features ring the fracture zones that surround the rim of the caldera.*

***The grizzly bear*** *(below), scientifically called* Ursus arctos horribilis, *possesses extremely hard muscles, a large heart, astonishing speed, and great agility. Nearly 18 feet tall when standing and weighing up to 900 pounds, it can run downhill at 30 miles an hour.*

*Most visitors no longer see grizzly bears because the Park Service makes a concerted effort to separate this beast of myth and legend from humans and their food sources.*

*Elk (above) graze in bands in winter for the quantities of grasses and leaves they need for food. The animals are drawn to the warmth given off by the hot springs during the cold winter months. The thermal heat and steam help to melt some of the snow covering the ground, making it easier for the elk to break through the icy covering to reach the fodder below.*

charged with keeping Yellowstone as it was before the encroachment of humans. The grizzly's plight first focused attention on the need to coordinate federal management of the Greater Yellowstone Area. Known early on as the Greater Yellowstone Ecosystem, the designation includes parts of two national parks, six national forests, national wildlife refuges, unreserved public domain, and state lands totaling 11.7 million acres in 12 counties of three states.

Despite discrete official designations, the lands and their plants and animals are interdependent ecologically. Grizzly bears can roam over distances of up to 100 miles in 24 hours, often passing out of park boundaries onto lands in which they can run foul of poachers, trigger-happy hunters, or livestock operators.

The Greater Yellowstone lesson could have been learned as well from the earlier plight of trumpeter swans. Today, a nonprofit coalition of federal and state interagency grizzly bear management teams negotiate cooperation and compatible regulations. The bureaucratic altruism harks back to Yellowstone's creation as a park more than 100 years ago.

Contemporary East Coast centers of power were slow to accept the truth of Yellowstone's manifold scenic and geologic wonders. Beginning in the 1850s a succession of expeditions sought to verify the Yellowstone stories. These culminated in the 1871 Hayden Survey, part of the U.S. Geological Survey.

Artwork by painter Thomas Moran and photographer William Henry Jackson lent tangible reality to the scientific assessments and prodded Congress to create the world's first national park. Today, Yellowstone is also a World Heritage Site and an International Biosphere Reserve, designations only underscoring its global role as a natural wonder.

The massive forest fires that swept through the area in 1988 likewise provoked international stewardship of Yellowstone. World news coverage brought spontaneous outpourings of money and offers to help recovery efforts. Today's traveler can see ample evidence of the fires, but equally evident are the park's natural recovery mechanisms. In the end most people realized that the 1988 fires also gave us a glimpse of the natural processes of Earth.

***The widespread underground heat** in the park has attacked these lodgepole pines (right) at their roots; all that remains are the dead trunks. About 80 percent of Yellowstone is forest, and in 80 percent of the forests, the lodgepole pine dominates. Rhyolite rock that was once lava breaks down to form sandy, coarse soil, poor in mineral nutrients, but it is all the lodgepole needs to survive.*

*Volcanic episodes 50 million years ago repeatedly buried the trees here. The petrified forests created by these eruptions are unusual because they contain layers of many different forests and entire trees buried upright. Vandals have taken many pieces of fossilized rock over the years, but one fossil stump still stands near Tower Junction.*

### Old Faithful

Rudyard Kipling found Yellowstone "a howling wilderness . . . full of all imaginable freaks of a fiery nature." Members of the 1870 Washburn Expedition named Old Faithful for its frequent and predictable eruptions—18 to 22 every day. A 1983 earthquake nearby lengthened the average interval between eruptions from 69 to 78 minutes. The interval now averages 76 minutes and ranges from 33 to 93 minutes. Old Faithful plays to a height ranging from 106 to 184 feet and averaging 130 feet.

Between eruptions, Old Faithful (right) must refill its reservoir with groundwater and build a superheated head of steam under pressure in order to play again. Eruptions spew from

3,700 to 8,400 gallons at a temperature of 203°F—here, at 7,366 feet above sea level, water boils at 199°F.

Dissolved silica from deep in the ground evaporates out of geyser water as sinter or geyserite, which has built a mound around Old Faithful. Riverside Geyser on the Firehole River features an angled cone like a mortar launcher and plays at a 70-degree angle over the river. Riverside and Old Faithful are in the Upper Geyser Basin, whose 2 square miles boast the world's largest concentration of geysers. Another of the park's wonders, Minerva Terrace (left) at Mammoth Hot Springs, consists of spectacular calcium carbonate formations.

WYOMING

# DEVILS TOWER

"There are things in nature that engender an awful quiet in the heart of man," author N. Scott Momaday writes. "Devils Tower is one of them." Momaday's grandmother, a Kiowa Indian, told him the flutings in the tower walls were made by a great bear's claw as it climbed a huge tree stump after seven terrified children.

As the bear climbed, according to the Indian legend, the stump rose in the air to protect the seven sisters. The bear "rose against the tree and scored the bark all around with its claws," Momaday's grandmother said. "The seven sisters were borne into the sky, and they became the stars of the Big Dipper." Indians called Devils Tower Mateo Tepee, or Bear Lodge.

Roughly 60 million years ago, volcanic activity forced molten magma up into the sedimentary rock then capping this landscape. The cooling magma formed a volcanic neck like a huge inverted plug or cork. Over millions of years, the softer sedimentary rock eroded away, leaving this tower of magma isolated 867 feet above its base and 1,267 feet above the nearby Belle Fourche (Beautiful Branch) River. Its summit stands 5,117 feet above sea level. This geological wonder resulted from the different erosion states of sedimentary rock and volcanic lava. Accentuating its strangeness, columns formed as the cooling magma contracted and fractured.

Devils Tower was named in 1875 by a scientific survey team; it made a superb landmark for pioneers traveling west. Troops led by Colonel Richard I. Dodge escorted the survey, which violated a treaty reserving this region for exclusive Indian entry and use.

Above the stark rock walls, the top of Devils Tower supports grasses, sagebrush, currant bushes, and prickly pear cactuses which provide food for chipmunks and woodrats which in turn feed snakes. Birds, including hawks and rock doves, come and go. Rock climbers report having seen snakes and rodents working their way up the rock fissures.

***The stony outlook** of Devils Tower (right) is reflected in Belle Fourche River. The top of this remarkable formation provides climbers with a panoramic view of the meeting point between the dense forests of the Black Hills and the grasslands of the plains.*

**Blacktail town**

As engaging as the tower is imposing, the park's prairie dog colony occupies its southeast corner, near the Belle Fourche River alongside the main park road. Observing these blacktail prairie dogs' town doings brings out the child in visitors of all ages.

Their multi-chambered burrows have mounded entrances that serve as dikes against flooding in downpours. Home-building for these energetic rodents includes scraping, bulldozing, and tamping. Burrows have a main plunge hole and a connecting safety hatch, usually about 30 feet apart. The burrow bottoms out about 15 feet below ground, slightly below the level of the main nesting chamber. Nest chambers are lined with soft plant fibers for comfort, insulation, and protection against damp.

Prairie dogs are preyed upon by now extremely rare black-footed ferrets—large members of the weasel family—as well as coyotes, badgers, bullsnakes, golden eagles, and prairie falcons. Burrowing owls nest in old prairie dog burrows, hence their name. They sometimes prey on pups, but the prairie dogs may also eat the owls' young and eggs. Badgers, being formidable diggers, specialize in preying on new burrows that have only one entrance.

Prairie dogs stand erect to scout for danger, sound alarms, and eat. Pups learning the eating posture are comical as they try, unsteadily, to balance before toppling over. Much of the grass cutting that these animals do around their burrows is defensive, to reduce predator hiding places. Prairie dogs' grooming behavior and constant colonial bickering makes for delightful natural drama against the lordly backdrop of Devils Tower.

# The Southwest and Mexico

**Bones and heart of the planet**

In the southwest of North America and the borderlands that sprawl into Mexico, the raw power of geological processes can be felt more strongly than in any other region of the continent. Prettiness exists in the birdsong, the spider webs, and the first snowfalls of winter, but it seems peripheral to deeper, infinitely slower, more powerful rhythms in these stupendous landscapes.

The salt crystals of the Great Salt Lake are both a nuisance and a source of wealth; the process that created them also left a tidemark 1,000 feet over the shining city beneath. The ravishing painted pinnacles of Bryce Canyon perch on the edge of a plateau that was raised by the same force that helped cut the Grand Canyon a mile deep in the ancient schists that spawn mountain ranges. Those gleaming, dark rocks, which are older than all life on Earth, put human efforts—rafts, dams, expeditionary forces—into a new perspective. Humankind impinges on that world at its peril. It is thrilling, beautiful, and inspiring, but it does not care about us.

Gentler landscapes than these are reassuring. It is possible to relate to the seasons and the life cycles of animals and plants, even to the oldest of all living things, the bristlecone pine. But the landscapes of the Southwest, with their science-fiction suns, grumbling volcanoes, crystallized tree trunks, and soaring fragments of primeval seabeds challenge us to understand processes on which we can make no impression and in which people play no part.

Not everything here is that daunting. Approachable activities like exploring the wildlife habitats of Big Bend National Park, beachcombing for shells on Padre Island National Seashore, and watching for the great sperm whales in the Sea of Cortés are all things that enable us to reassess our own humanity. But the most lasting impression is of having glimpsed something both beautiful and terrifying: the bones and heart and rhythms of the planet.

UTAH

# GREAT SALT LAKE

GREAT SALT LAKE STANDS IN ITS OWN DESERT; now a drainage basin, the desert was once a huge primeval inland sea. Three rivers—the Jordan, the Weber, and the Bear—feed the basin and the lake, and in the spring their waters often swell with melted snow.

Yet no water flows out of Great Salt Lake. Any water leaving it does so by evaporation, a process which produces an ever-increasing concentration of mineral salts. Three-fourths of this mineral load is in the form of common salt, sodium chloride; the balance includes potash, magnesium, and potassium.

Over 70 miles long and 30 miles wide, the Great Salt Lake is so heavily saturated with mineral salts that it is almost too buoyant to swim in. But the intrepid can float with ease, with feet, arms, and head well clear of the water. As the sun dries swimmers off, they become coated with a powder of tiny salt crystals that prickle the skin and can sting the eyes. Swallowing or inhaling the brine can cause painful choking.

The sun gleams off dazzling salt deposits everywhere. Salty crusts thicken the outline of the sparse plants at the water's edge, and birds and small animals that fall into the lake surface in a mummifying jacket of crystals.

The original inland sea, Lake Bonneville, was ten times the size of the present lake and occupied parts of Utah, Nevada, and Idaho. Its almost 20,000 square miles were formed from the meltwater of glaciers at the end of the Ice Age when meltwater and rains filled the mountain-rimmed basin to overflowing. The excess water surged through the Red Rock Pass and flowed down into Idaho, swelling the waters of the Snake River and eventually joining the Columbia River to reach the Pacific Ocean.

As the climate warmed up in the wake of the glaciers, evaporation overtook the inflow from streams and rivers. The long, slow lowering of the lake's surface began,

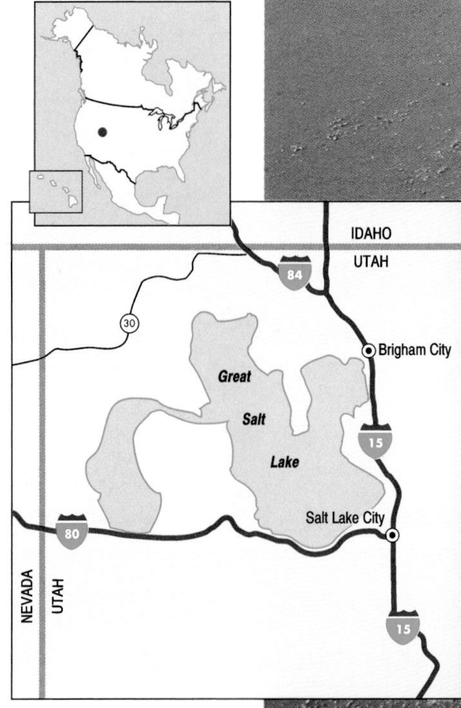

***The salty shoreline*** *of Great Salt Lake (right) has shrunk over the ages, concentrating the salt levels as moisture evaporates. With no rivers running out of the lake, water is lost almost entirely through evaporation.*

**Mormon leader**

Brigham Young was born in Whitingham, Vermont, on June 1, 1801. His father was a farmer, and in 1804 the family moved to a farm in western New York, where Brigham spent most of his early years. By 1829, he had settled in Mendon, New York, where he worked as a carpenter, joiner, and painter.

*The Book of Mormon*, published by Joseph Smith, theological founder of the Church of Jesus Christ of Latter-day Saints, or Mormons, came to Young's attention, and on April 14, 1832, he was baptized into the Mormon Church. After the murder of Joseph Smith in 1844, the Mormons left the city they had built at Nauvoo, Illinois, and moved west, led by the forthright Young, now head of the Church. Young was a strong-willed worker who had a vision of finding a place where the Mormons could develop their own community without fear of persecution.

In 1848, with the first 148 settlers, Young got his first glimpse of the Great Salt Lake and declared "This is the right place." Salt Lake City was founded the same year, and Young marked off an area for Temple Square, the future spiritual center for the Kingdom of God on Earth. He worked hard to build the Mormon community, but trouble arose between the government and the Mormons because of their practice of polygamy and a general fear of Mormon power. This led to the Utah War (1857–58), a bloodless conflict, but it ended with Young's removal as governer.

and with it came the increasing concentration of minerals. Terraced steps on the surrounding mountains mark the lake's earlier levels; the highest is 1,000 feet above the current level of the Great Salt Lake.

The first white man to see the Great Salt Lake was the trapper and mountain man, Jim Bridger, who reached it by traveling down the Bear River in 1824. The U.S. Army then surveyed and mapped it during the 1840s and 1850s. Traveling westward through the passes of the Wasatch Mountains to escape religious persecution in the Midwest, the Mormons looked down over the valleys, salt flats, and marshes toward the Great Salt Lake for the first time on July 21, 1847.

The lake reached its present level about 8,000 years ago, having achieved a balance between the volumes of water entering it as inflow and leaving it as water vapor. Within those 8,000 years, the surface level has twice risen more than 4,230 feet above sea level, but for most of the time since the settling of the community, the water level has been falling gradually.

Some plants have developed a salt resistance that enables them to live in briny conditions that would quickly kill most vegetation. Goosefoot plants (Chenopodiaceae) grow on the shoreline, along with salt grass (*Distichlis spicata*), shadscale (*Atriplex confertifolia*), greasewood (*Sarcobatus vericulatus*), pickleweed (*Allenrolfea*), and creosote bush (*Larrea*). Undisturbed by occasional flooding, these plants all flourish in compacted, salt-heavy soils.

In the waters of the lake, the largest living organisms are the brine shrimp (*Artemia salina*) and the brine fly (*Ephydra*), which the locals call the buffalo gnat. Hatchings of the brine fly can coat large areas of the shallows and shore in the summer. The gulls that abound on and around the lake feed on the flies, and the flies themselves feed on algae and bacteria.

Two forms of the minute, one-celled *Dunaliella* plant thrive in the lake. *D. salina* is pinkish in color and turns the waters pink where it grows. *D. viridia* is green, turns the water green, and has the same effect on the brine shrimp that feed on it. Other single-celled plants living here are *Chlamydomonas* and *Aplanotheca*, both of them green. The smallest of all the salt-surviving life-forms that inhabit the lake are the microscopic bacteria.

The brine shrimp's egg is marvelously adept at surviving. It can be dried out, sunbaked, frozen in ice, and deprived of water for years at a time. Yet, despite all this, it will happily revive and hatch when exposed to saline water.

The largest of the eight islands in the lake is Antelope Island, named by the explorers Kit Carson and John Fremont in 1843 for the pronghorn antelope they found here. Antelope Island is a state park, 15 miles long and 5 miles wide, with a mountain at its center—the 6,956-foot Frary Peak—and buffalo and deer have the run of it. At low water, it can be reached by means of a causeway.

Despite the great expansion of Salt Lake City and the mineral industries busily leaching valuable chemicals from the "liquid mine," the Great Salt Lake and its desert surroundings have not been entirely tamed by human presence. The floods of the late 1980s reminded the inhabitants that nothing, particularly nature, can be taken for granted. They turned off the pumps that were transferring lake water to West Pond in 1989, when the danger of flooding had past, but now everyone watches the snow and rain levels with great attention. High on the Wasatch Mountain ridges, 1,000 feet above the city, Lake Bonneville's highest bench mark is a constant reminder of the true power of nature.

**Salt Lake bird haven**

The unexpectedly high water levels that inundated the salt flats and marshes around the Great Salt Lake between 1982 and 1987 threatened regions that provide one of the largest havens in the United States for migratory birds. As many as two million birds a year use the freshwater marshes and islands in the lake itself as short-term refuges during their great spring and fall migrations. More than 250 species have been identified.

North America is traversed by broad flyways, the major routes taken by migrating birds, mainly along a north-south axis, but with some lying east-west as well. The Great Salt Lake and its environs lie close to the merging point of two of these routes, the Pacific and Mountain flyways, that follow the parallel lines of the Pacific Coast and the Rocky Mountains.

Predominant among these migrants are water birds, including snow geese, Canada geese (right), western grebes, eared grebes, whistling swans, great blue herons, white-faced ibis, American white pelicans, and a large variety of ducks and gulls. Gunnison Island, in the northwest of the lake, is less than 170 acres in area, rocky, and the largest single breeding site of American white pelicans in the country. Nesting on the island to keep clear of marauding jackals and other predators, the pelicans commute daily, 25 miles each way, to the Bear River Migratory Refuge with its freshwater streams and marsh pools. Some go as far as Utah Lake, which is 80 miles away, to hunt its rich depths for fish.

The high water levels of 1986 and 1987 flooded the marshes that serve as refuges, destroying the nesting sites, shelter, and food supplies vital to the migrants. The birds began stopping elsewhere on their annual migrations. By the spring of 1991, however, birds were beginning to return to major sites, although vegetation was sparse compared to previous years.

***Spread out in shattered patterns,*** *the cracked mud of the salt flats (left) provides a home for a variety of plants, like greasewood and salt grass, that can both tolerate their salinity and resist long periods of drought. In other parts of the flats, salt lies in meandering crystallized ridges on the smooth, firm surface.*

*So much rain evaporates every year over Great Salt Lake Desert (below) that the annual rainfall totals only 4 inches. However, during the 1980s, the lake's level rose dramatically. Record rainfalls and heavy snow and thaws brought unprecedented runoff into streams and rivers. The lake began to reclaim farmland, wash out bird sanctuaries, and threaten buildings and roads. Emergency legislation authorized a pumping project to move lake water to West Pond in the Great Salt Desert.*

UTAH

# BRYCE CANYON

BRYCE CANYON IS NOT A CANYON AT ALL, but an amphitheater of eroded cliffs facing east over the valley of the Paria River. Along with Zion Canyon to its west, Bryce forms part of the great complex of plateaus and canyons that sits astride the Utah-Arizona border. The Grand Canyon, south of the border, is the third part of the jigsaw, and all three are awesome monuments to the erosive powers of water and weather.

Bryce Canyon is capped with layers of geologically young rock, the limestone, sandstone, siltstone, and shale of the Wasatch formation. Bryce has been carved out of an escarpment known as the Pink Cliffs, although the word pink scarcely does justice to the kaleidoscope of vivid colors, from pale lavender to deep terra-cotta, that reveal the metallic traces in the rock and change constantly according to the time of day, the season, and the weather.

The layers of the Bryce region come virtually up to the geological present; they were formed over the last 65 million years, during the period known as the Cenozoic. The rim region of the Grand Canyon, by contrast, consists mainly of Kaibab limestone from the Mesozoic period, 570 million to 225 million years ago.

The Pink Cliffs from which Bryce Canyon was shaped mark the eastern brink of the Paunsaugunt Plateau, a huge block of the Earth's crust forced upward from sea level to its present elevation. Rain, floodwater, and cycles of freeze and thaw began to eat away at the exposed rock. The hard limestone, once the bed of an ancient sea, resisted, while the sandstone and shale broke down quickly. Walls and columns of rock took shape, divided by deep fissures, and their surfaces glowed with color as the oxygen in the air changed the metallic content of the rock chemically.

The entire plateau was scored with a network of vertical cracks and stress faults, which were subject to rain seepage and winter freezing. Expanding ice enlarged the fissures. Nature still gnaws at the ranks of fantastic pinnacles in all these ways, and flash floods in summer still scour the deep

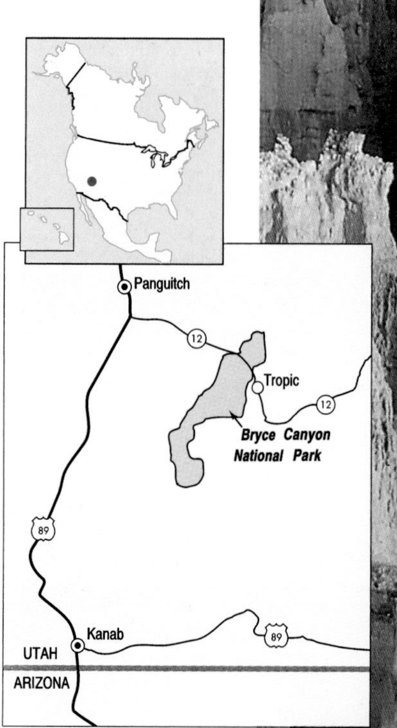

***In Silent City** in Bryce Canyon (right) the towering pinnacles glow with added color during late summer rains. The region was named after rancher Ebenezer Bryce, who called it "a hell of a place to lose a cow."*

***The elegantly named*** *Wall of Windows (above) is just one of the works of art that have been sculpted by nature in this breathtaking landscape.*

*Other rocky features resemble exotic architecture and bear evocative names such as the Cathedral, Temple of Osiris, and Hindu Temples. The aptly named Wall Street is a canyon full of shadows and "skyscraper" cliffs.*

***A variety of trees*** *adorns the upper and lower limits of the park. On the low, woodland slopes, oaks, Utah junipers, and pinyon pines abound. Farther up (right), shrubs such as the greenleaf manzanita are dwarfed by great ponderosa pines.*

*At elevations of more than 8,500 feet, white fir and Douglas fir thrive alongside blue spruce, limber pine, and the ancient bristlecone pine.*

## Animals: the permanent residents

Bryce Canyon National Park harbors a rich cross-section of southwestern wildlife, from ground squirrels, chipmunks, and yellow-bellied marmots to bobcats, coyotes, black bears, and mountain lions. Mule deer, skunks, gray foxes, porcupines, badgers, and prairie dogs roam the region, too.

The porcupine (left) is slow and clumsy, but climbs trees readily to feed on buds, twigs, and bark. In summer, it also feeds on roots and the stems of flowering plants. Badgers are solitary creatures and generally become active at night. They are excellent diggers and will burrow rapidly after rodents—their main food. The badger sleeps for much of the winter, but, unlike true hibernators, it is active during mild spells.

The coyote (right), is a highly adaptable animal which manages to thrive in diverse habitats. Its diet is varied as well—rodents, rabbits, snakes, insects, carrion, fruit, berries, and grasses are eaten along with fish, frogs, and crustaceans.

Many of these creatures keep to the high altitudes during the summer months to take advantage of the cool air and then wander down to the river valleys, woods, and meadows when winter comes.

ravines with pebbles, rocks, and silt.

At the same time as the pinnacles are being constantly remolded, pared down, and eventually felled by their own weight, the rim of the escarpment is in retreat. Abraded by the weather, the lip of Bryce Canyon backs westward at the rate of about 2 feet each century.

One of a dozen small amphitheaters chewed out of the Pink Cliffs by the elements, Bryce Canyon is 8,000 feet above sea level at its rim. The Paiute Indians explained the eerily human shape of some rocks with a story about the Legend People, who were turned to stone by the god Coyote as punishment for their bad behavior. The lengthy but accurate Indian name for the Bryce formation is "Bowl-shaped Canyon Filled with Red Rocks Standing up like Men."

This is high country which lends itself to walking, strolling along the gentle rim, or trekking more energetically through the zigzagging loop trails. The upper and lower limits of the park span over 2,000 vertical feet, and the wildlife and vegetation vary according to altitude. The terrain below the 7,000-foot line can be markedly warmer and drier than at the higher levels. The environment on the low, woodland slopes suits trees like oaks, Utah junipers, and pinyon pines. In the vegetation zone at 7,000 to 8,500 feet, shrubs such as the greenleaf manzanita are dwarfed by the great ponderosa pines. At the highest level, over 8,500 feet, white fir and Douglas fir thrive alongside blue spruce, limber pine, and bristlecone pine.

Linking Rainbow Point and Yovimpa Point in the south of the park, Bristlecone Loop Trail lets hikers take a close look at the ancient bristlecone pines along the rim of the escarpment, some of them more than 1,500 years old. The bristlecone pine is the oldest living thing on the planet—specimens in other parts of the country are close to 5,000 years old. Almost indestructible, the bristlecone survives in terrains where nothing else can get a roothold.

In the spring and summer, the colors of the rocks are challenged by the wildflowers, which include primroses, irises, blue flax, paintbrush, and Mariposa lilies. The scale and prettiness of Bryce, together with the variety of its environments, flora, and fauna, make it strangely approachable.

UTAH

# RAINBOW BRIDGE

RAINBOW BRIDGE, THE LARGEST NATURAL ARCH in the world, is a soaring span wide enough to contain the Capitol building in Washington, D.C. Yet despite its awesome size, it remained unseen and unknown by white Americans until the early years of the 20th century.

Tucked away in a remote branch of the Colorado River near Glen Canyon, just north of the Arizona border, the breathtaking arch of warm, pink sandstone was known to local Paiute and Navajo Indians. The Navajos called it "The Rock That Goes Over" and the Paiutes called it "The Stone Rainbow."

Stretching 290 feet from the base to the top of the arch, Rainbow Bridge has a span of 275 feet. It is 42 feet thick at its apex and 33 feet wide across the top, wide enough for two-lane traffic. Jutting out from the cliff of which it was once a spur, it vaults high over Bridge Creek. Swollen by seasonal torrents and laden with abrasive silts, this modest trickle carved the arch in the sandstone buttress over the course of thousands of years, and the smooth lines of the bridge were rounded and polished by the wind.

Blackened stones found at the site indicate that Rainbow Bridge may have been sacred to the local tribes in past centuries. But access to it was so difficult that, when the first white men reached it, most local tribes had no idea where it was. It is hidden away in a narrow canyon in some of the wildest country in the whole United States.

Declared a national monument in 1910, it was for many years the most difficult site to reach in the entire national park system. Glen Canyon Dam, completed in 1963, and the resulting Lake Powell raised the water level in the Colorado River, turning fiendishly difficult trails into easily navigated water passages.

Visitors can now travel by boat to within a short stroll of Rainbow Bridge, or can take the 6-mile Forbidden Canyon hike that was unavoidable before Lake Powell was created. Reflected in the widened waters of its creek, the great and extremely beautiful arch is now as accessible as it is impressive.

*The arch of* ***Rainbow Bridge*** *soars skyward, lending credence to the Navajo belief that this is a sacred place. The base of the bridge is Kayenta sandstone laid down hundreds of millions of years ago; the arch itself is Navajo sandstone.*

***The clean, white flowers*** *of the datura, with their long, cream-colored stamens, make a striking contrast with the sandstone wall. These sweet-smelling flowers appear in July and August, and are also known as angels' trumpets, or moonflowers.*

*One variety, known as thornapple or Jimson weed, is known to be an hallucinogen and was given to Algonquin boys as part of their ceremonial rites of passage to adulthood. The flowers are pollinated by evening-flying moths, and seeds may remain dormant for many years.*

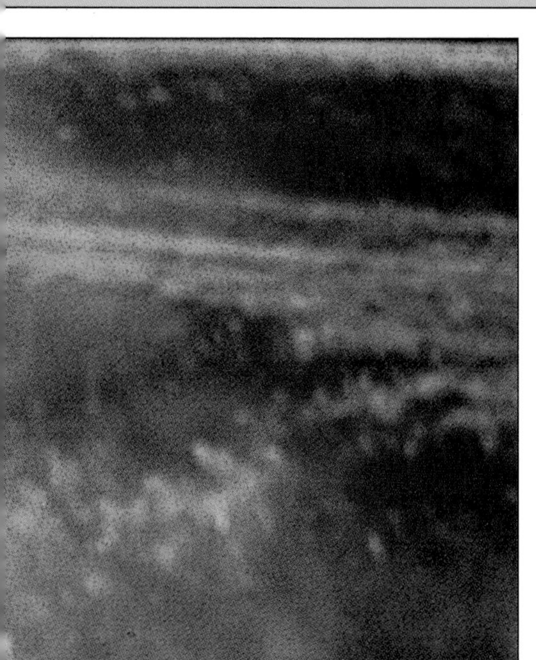

***Saguaro at sunset*** *(above), framing the jeweled lights of Tucson, create a scene combining old and new Arizona. Just east of Tucson, in the Saguaro National Monument, forests of saguaro tower 50 feet tall. Also in the park, the Tucson Mountain Unit protects rock formations with Indian pictographs and designs (left) showing early drawings of the horse.*

AS MUCH A PART OF THE SCENERY as the open country that was his home, the cowboy still holds his place as a legendary figure of the old West. Pioneers first acquired their cowboy skills from the Spanish *vaqueros* in Texas around 1820; they quickly learned to ride with a saddle and spurs, to handle a lariat, and to use a branding iron.

After the Civil War, the market for beef developed rapidly, and soon cattle herds spread west across the plains from Texas to the Rocky Mountains. The cowboy was king then, and the man in a broad-brimmed hat, high-heeled boots, and denim jeans dominated the landscape.

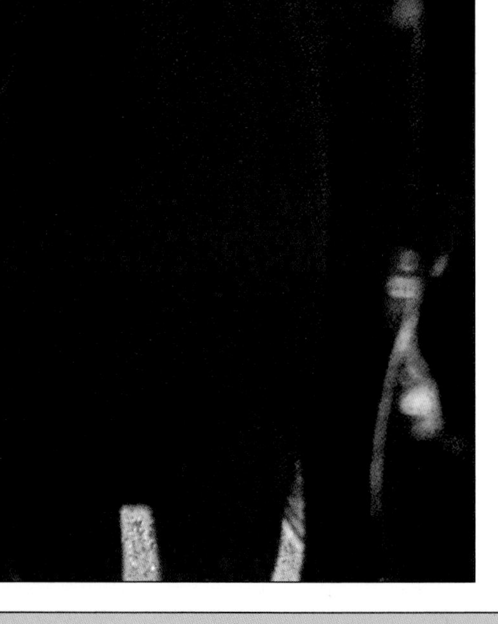

***The thundering of hooves*** *and clouds of dust conjure up the atmosphere of the old days. Much like his ancestors, this modern cowboy (left) rounds up a herd of horses in Colorado.*

*Texas Longhorns were the first cattle in the Americas. The open plains and sandstone canyons, like Bryce in Utah (right), were home to Longhorns which could travel without water for 100 miles.*

UTAH, ARIZONA

# MONUMENT VALLEY

REARING LIKE ANCIENT TEETH from sloping shale bases on the valley floor, the majestic buttes of Monument Valley are among the most evocative emblems of the Southwest. For many people they bring back memories of a hundred western movies shot here—John Wayne's *Stagecoach* is probably the most famous of them.

Monument Valley straddles the Utah-Arizona border and lies within the Navajo Indian Reservation. The plateau that forms the valley floor is over a mile above sea level, and some of the buttes rise a further 1,000 feet above that. Millions of years ago, when the area was covered with water, the land surface was at the same elevation as the tops of today's buttes. Upheaval of the Earth's surface drained the water into river systems that carried away quantities of soft shale and sand, leaving the harder material jutting above the valley floor.

The air here is dry and clear, with annual rainfall barely exceeding 8 inches. The clarity deceives the eye, making distances seem much less than they are. In fact, it is a giant's landscape. At sunrise and sunset, the shadows of the natural monuments stretch for miles across the scrubland, adding violet and purple to the smoldering red and terra-cotta of the sandstone.

Like much of the Southwest, Monument Valley is intensely beautiful, but hostile to human habitation. The arid dunes and scrubland sustain no game except rabbits, and the only creatures that really thrive are the reptiles, such as the collared lizard, the horned toad, and the prairie rattlesnake. The lack of water limits the vegetation to hardy species—scrub juniper, sagebrush, pinyon pines, and cacti—that can survive for months without rain. A rare rainstorm will startle brilliant wildflowers out of the earth, but the blossoms are short-lived.

The permanent beauty of Monument Valley resides in the rocks, the crystal air, the changing play of light and shadow, and the almost imperceptible alteration and erosion of the buttes, mesas, and pillars as they return, grain by grain, to the dunes they once were.

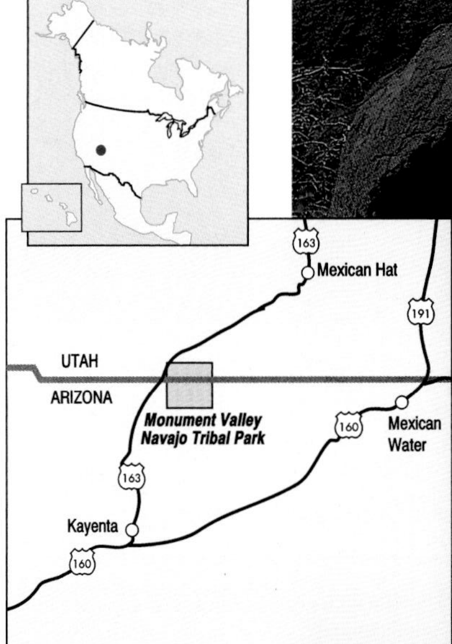

***Distant monuments*** *(right) and all the impacted sand dunes that surround them were once blanketed with a sheet of ice. Monument is a geological term attached to the remnants of erosion that are higher than they are wide. Many of these resemble living creatures or man-made edifices, which their names reflect.*

***Navajo herders*** *(below) now graze their sheep and goats on the sparse vegetation that once sustained Pre-Columbian tribes of cliff-dwelling Pueblo Indians. Cave villages of up to 200 rooms have been discovered here, as have various rock paintings. White handprints decorate an adobe ruin called the House of Many Hands. In the 1860s, some Navajos moved here to avoid being forcibly relocated to New Mexico.*

ARIZONA

# GRAND CANYON

NO PHOTOGRAPH OR DESCRIPTION can adequately prepare the visitor for his or her first glimpse of the Grand Canyon. Most people approach it, through shielding woods of stunted oaks and pines, from the South Rim, where the immense rift is suddenly revealed. That great wedge of space, impossibly deep and bounded by cliffs, headlands, and buttes of startling, glowing colors, stuns most first-timers into silence or incoherence.

A great cataclysm seems to have rent the Earth apart. Until the late 19th century, some scientists were still convinced that a massive earthquake must have split the red rock of northern Arizona into a chasm 277 miles long, a mile deep in places, and up to 18 miles wide, rim to rim.

However, in common with the stately structures of Monument Valley and the evocative shapes of Bryce Canyon, the event that created the Grand Canyon took millions of years. Water, wind, and temperature shaped it, not sudden shifts in the Earth's crust. Yet slower, more deliberate earth movements did play a vital role.

The great crustal warping that created the Rocky Mountains 60 million years ago also pushed upward into the elongated Kaibab Plateau. What is now the Colorado River, winding its way along the Canyon's foot, was then two components, separated by the plateau. East of the plateau, the Ancestral Colorado flowed south and east, eventually reaching the Atlantic Ocean at the Gulf of Mexico. To the west, a river system called the Hualapai flowed westward to the Gulf of California.

The upper tributaries of the Hualapai dug backward into the plateau toward the Ancestral Colorado by a sort of uphill nibbling known as headward erosion. About 12 million years ago, during a renewed period of doming throughout the west, the Ancestral Colorado was somehow blocked in its southeastern course and built up a huge lake, known now as Bidahochi, southeast of the plateau.

Roughly two million years later, the headward erosion of the upper Hualapai

***The Colorado River*** *(right) runs between mile-high walls of Vishnu schist, a hard rippling rock that is the only Canyon layer too old to bear any fossil traces. The formations of Vishnu schist are among the oldest exposed rocks in the world, dating back about 1.7 billion years.*

system cut through to join the Ancestral Colorado. The great lake emptied westward through the new channel, and the modern Colorado River was born.

The enormous cutting power of the new river system scored a V-shaped slot deep into its bedrock, removing millions of tons of material daily. In modern times, before the construction of the system of dams that now slows its seaward rush, the river in full flood carried an incredible load of over 25 million tons of suspended material past a given point every 24 hours. The daily average over a 12-month period was about 500,000 tons of silt and sand. These figures would have almost doubled if they had included material rolling along the river bottom. Today, with the dams regulating the river flow, the daily average is about 40,000 tons.

As the newborn Colorado tore at its bed, the rock beneath it was still doming upward. The rate of uplift was not dramatic—maybe a hundredth of an inch a year—but over the next five million years the plateau rose over 4,000 feet. At the same time, the abrasive particles in the rushing, rasping river dug deeper and deeper into the riverbed, carving a gorge inch by inch.

While the river cut downward, other erosive forces were working—and still work—on the rock face it exposed. Freezing and thawing widened the cracks; winter storms and spring snowmelts continually removed debris; wind wore at the softer formations. Soft stone layers were eaten away beneath harder ones, until gravity forced huge ledges to collapse. In the last ten million years, the Canyon has widened many times faster than it has deepened.

Visitors descending into the Canyon today, on foot or by mule, get a close view of the rocky bands that mark the sediments of the numerous seas that have repeatedly flooded the region and receded during the course of almost two billion years. Adventurous souls who ride the river rapids can almost touch the oldest layer of all at the bottom of Granite Gorge.

Man hunted in the Grand Canyon at least 4,000 years ago. The earliest evidence, found in a cave at the eastern end of the Canyon, consists of little models of deer and bighorn sheep, fashioned from willow twigs and pierced by tiny spears. Many more of these graphic hunting charms have now been found throughout the Canyon.

In about A.D. 1000, Pueblo Indians built their cliff houses and food stores in side canyons, out of sight of the main channel. In 1937, exploration of the 200-acre top of Shiva Temple, a large butte near the Canyon's North Rim, revealed that 1,000 years earlier they had climbed the butte to dig flint out of the butte's cap of Kaibab limestone to use for tools and weapons.

The Pueblo Indians left the Canyon in about A.D. 1150, but other tribes replaced them, including people of the Cerbat culture, some of whose descendants, the Havasupai, are the last indigenous inhabitants of the Canyon. They live in Havasu Canyon on a reservation of 518 acres, the smallest and most remote reservation in the country. The canyon, together with Havasu Creek, lies west of the river bend that skirts Great Thumb Mesa and can be reached by steep tracks from the South Rim. The Havasupai are hunters and farmers, and about 300 of them live in the lush valley with its 100-foot waterfalls.

Today, the National Park Service maintains two of the traditional trails into the Canyon. Bright Angel Trail and the Kaibab

***In September 1540,*** *an expedition of Spaniards became the first Europeans to see the Canyon, reaching the South Rim (above) while seeking the fabled "Seven Cities of Cibola." They failed to climb down to the river, since their Pueblo guides hid their knowledge of the existing trails.*

***Impressive falls*** *in Bright Angel Canyon (right). Despite the natural abundance of water, hikers to the inner canyons must carry their own supply. In dry heat, a person can lose up to 2 gallons of water every day in evaporation. As baggage, that amount will weigh 20 pounds.*

Trail both descend from the South Rim. The Bright Angel Trail winds 9 miles down to the Colorado River, 4,460 feet below the rim. The Kaibab Trail is a little shorter; at the bottom, you can cross the river on a suspension bridge and continue for another 13½ miles up Bright Angel Canyon to the North Rim.

A separate network of trails was originally cut by deer and bighorn sheep, then taken over by Indian hunters and, eventually, prospectors. However, these trails are unmaintained, and rockfalls and slides make them even more hazardous.

In 1776, a priest, Francisco Tomas Garces, visited the Havasupai Indians. U.S. military surveyors began to explore the area in the 1850s, and Lieutenant Joseph C. Ives sailed up the Colorado to within 75 miles of the western end of the Canyon before running aground in Black Canyon. Ives continued upstream by mule along the South Rim, making excursions down precipitous trails into side canyons. He reported that although the "Big Cañon of the Colorado" was beautiful, it was a "profitless locality."

In 1869, Major John Wesley Powell, one of the great American explorers, set off with nine handpicked companions to travel all the way down the Colorado River from its tributary, the Green River, in Wyoming. The one-armed Civil War veteran, a scientist and geologist, loaded his expedition into four wooden boats. They set off on May 24, gained the mouth of the Paria River just above the current entrance to the national park at Navajo Bridge, and emerged on August 29 at the other end of the Canyon.

By then, Powell had only two battered boats and five companions. One man had left the expedition after six weeks. Three others had left only a few days before the end of the journey and been killed by Indians. Powell kept a detailed journal during his three-month adventure and gave names, which still exist, to many of the distinctive sites he had seen, including Glen Canyon, Marble Canyon, and Bright Angel Creek.

In 1963, the gates were closed in the newly completed Glen Canyon Dam, upstream of the Grand Canyon, and the water accumulating behind it began to form Lake Powell, which was named for the intrepid major. Since the Colorado River is now controlled at both ends of the Grand Canyon, it can no longer clear itself of boulders and debris washed down from the side canyons with the same efficiency as before, and the flow of the river within the Canyon is regulated according to the electricity needs of the towns served by the powerful generators in the dams.

Upstream of Glen Canyon Dam, a large amount of silt and sand is also trapped now in Lake Powell, so the river within the Canyon runs much clearer than previously. The clearer waters attract trout, which avoided the river when it was muddy and uncontrolled. But trout are voracious eaters, and they are destroying the eggs and young of fish which once thrived in the Canyon waters.

The Grand Canyon may resemble a dead, unearthly landscape at first sight, but it is, in fact, alive with animals and plants, some of them unique to the locale. Because of the widely varying conditions between the canyon floor and the rim, a broad spectrum of plants and creatures is concentrated in a relatively small area (see box p. 77). Within the Canyon and its rim regions live typical inhabitants of geographical

***From Toroweap Overlook** (right) on the North Rim, 3,000 feet above the winding river, the thundering rapids of the Colorado look like gently tossing whitecaps. The river runs here through the Canyon's narrowest passageway, between nearly sheer walls that are only half a mile apart. The land across which the Canyon slices tilts steeply to the south, and the river runs closer to the South Rim than the North and collects water draining from the north.*

**Shooting the rapids**

After the mighty Colorado River enters Marble Gorge, at the Canyon's northern corner, it plunges south and downward over a series of 200 rapids that for many years were thought to be the wildest continuous stretch of white water in the world. Intrepid explorers set off from Lees Ferry in long, bulbous, inflatable rafts or, more hair-raisingly, in small wooden dories. By the time they reach Lake Mead above Hoover Dam, they have dropped 2,200 feet in roughly 240 miles of river passage, over some of the wildest rapids. At Lava Falls, where the river drops through 37 feet of boulders, massive standing waves, and swirling currents in the course of 30 seconds, a volcanic flow once blocked the Canyon with a lava dam 1,400 feet high. Eventually, the river wove around and over this obstacle and then destroyed it completely.

latitudes from the Mexican deserts to the Canadian forests.

The temperature at the bottom of the Canyon is, on average, 35°F warmer than at the North Rim. In summer, temperatures on the floor of the Canyon regularly reach 120°F in the shade. In spite of this, certain plants like mesquite, the catclaw shrub, and the barrel cactus thrive, giving shelter and sustenance to a number of small mammals, reptiles, and insects, including the pink Grand Canyon rattlesnake, which is shy and seldom seen.

Set on the flank of the Kaibab Plateau, the North Rim is a good 1,000 feet higher than the South Rim and receives more rainfall and snow. This abundant precipitation allows for more diversity of plant life and in turn supports a wider variety of animal species.

The lushly watered Havasu Canyon is rich in wildlife. Along the streams grow cottonwood, wild grape, willow, box elder, and hackberry. Bird watchers can spot cormorants, hummingbirds, mallards, swifts, swallows, warblers, goldfinches, buntings, grebe, teal, and the great blue heron, while visitors watching the ground might see bighorn sheep, deer, rock squirrels, and even beavers.

The impact of visitors on Grand Canyon National Park is tremendous, since it is the most popular of all national parks. Thousands raft down the river each year, hundreds of thousands hike down the trails, and millions cram the roads to the most popular lookout points. Yet it is still possible to find an isolated spot.

Only 15 percent of all visitors approach the Canyon from the north, and the great forested length of the North Rim is still largely unspoiled. On the popular South Rim, most visitors cluster at the most accessible viewing points, so a short hike should lead the more determined nature-lover to a quiet spot where he can watch the colors change.

Within the Canyon itself, hikers and rafters enter a mile-deep world of primeval rocks, rushing waters, and wild creatures. The banded sides of the immense chasm are like corridors through geological time. Outside the most popular vacation periods, visitors can pass through the layers of ancient history without too much jostling from the 20th century.

***Point Imperial** (left), the highest viewpoint on the North Rim of the Canyon, soars to 8,803 feet above sea level. The astounding walls contain at least 20 layers of rock, and each layer reflects millions of years of geological history. The chemical reactions of air and water on the minerals within the rocks give them their distinctive hues. Ancient schist is reddish-black, while granite shows pink, shale red, limestone yellowish-white, and sandstone anything from white to brown.*

## All creatures great and small

The dry heat of the canyon floor supports a variety of desert creatures that includes spotted skunks (above), yellow scorpions, tarantulas, and whiptail lizards. The Kaibab squirrel, one of the tassel-eared family, is unique to the North Rim and has evolved to suit the changing temperature patterns; its cousin, the Abert squirrel, lives on the South Rim.

The sides of the Canyon, which are cooler, provide homes for mammals such as the Arizona gray fox and cliff chipmunks. Mountain lions (below) also roam the Canyon, although they are increasingly rare. Most active in the early morning and evening, the cat may emerge at any time in search of prey.

ARIZONA

# METEOR CRATER

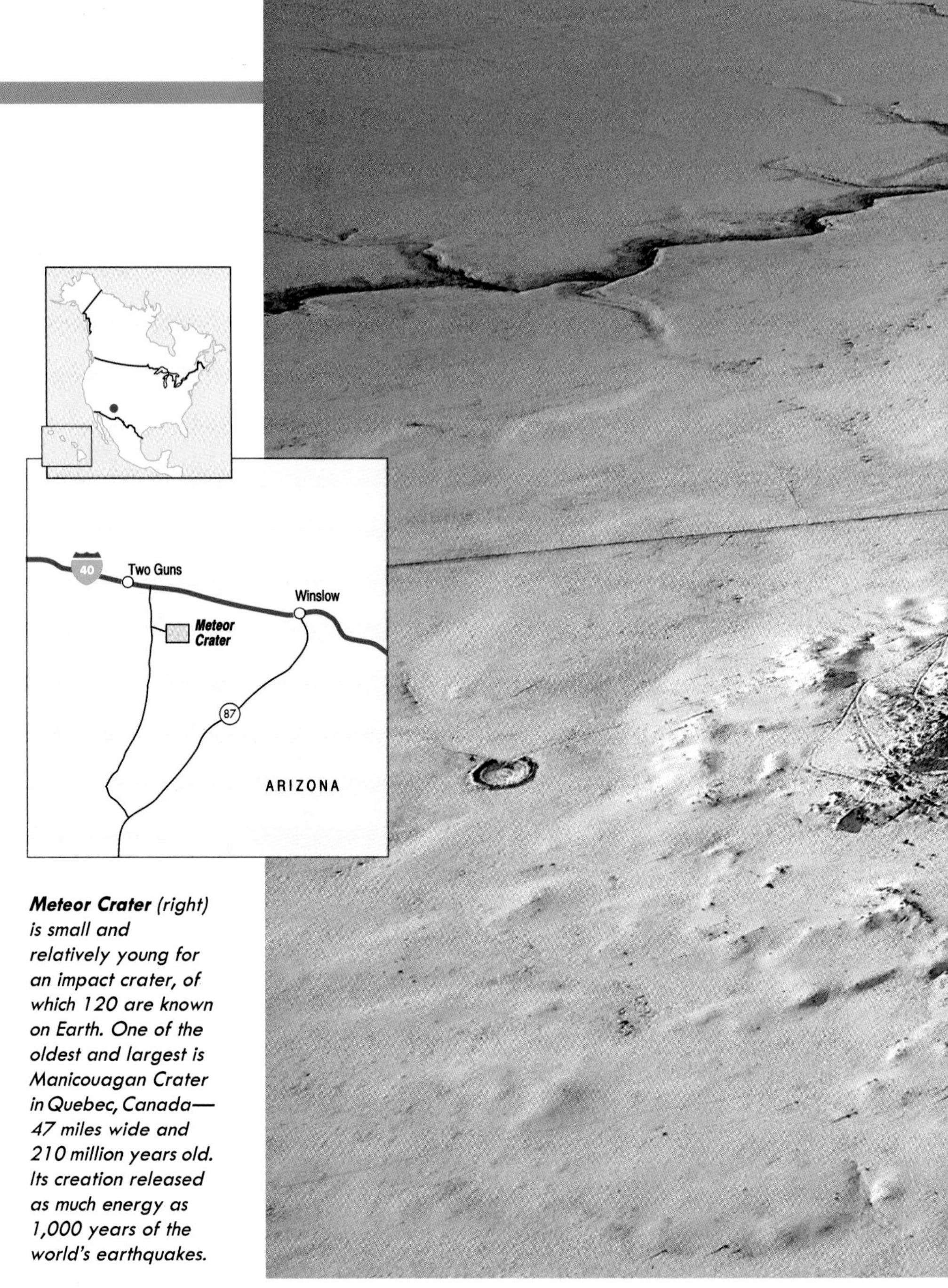


***Meteor Crater** (right) is small and relatively young for an impact crater, of which 120 are known on Earth. One of the oldest and largest is Manicouagan Crater in Quebec, Canada—47 miles wide and 210 million years old. Its creation released as much energy as 1,000 years of the world's earthquakes.*

FROM THE AIR, METEOR CRATER looks strangely familiar, like the astonishing but now familiar pictures of craters on the Moon. Like the lunar craters, Meteor Crater is an impact crater, formed by the disintegration of a solid body from beyond Earth's atmosphere.

No meteoritic crater on Earth is as well defined as this, for the simple reason that Meteor Crater is relatively young; the meteorite that created it roared through the Earth's atmosphere no more than 50,000 years ago. Most other meteoritic craters on Earth are much older, and erosion, along with the movement of the Earth's tectonic plates, has obscured or totally removed the evidence of their existence. Because the Moon lacks an erosive atmosphere and moving crustal plates, its craters—some of them many times larger than Meteor Crater—have remained sharply defined for millions of years.

Meteor Crater is over 4,000 feet across and almost 600 feet deep, and its rim is 200 feet higher than the surrounding desert. When the meteorite fell, it was a massive lump of nickel iron, perhaps 190 feet across and weighing around 70,000 tons, that plowed into the ground at a speed of almost 30,000 miles an hour. Abruptly blocked by the Earth's mass, it exploded with a force equivalent to half a million tons of TNT, more than 12 times greater than the force of the atomic bomb that destroyed Hiroshima. The explosion threw 100 million tons of pulverized rock high into the atmosphere and piled up the layer of material that now forms the crater's rim.

Metal droplets from the meteorite sprayed over a 100-square-mile area, and some of the rock fragments that were hurled up to 6 miles from the point of impact weighed as much as 1,400 pounds. The sandstone and limestone thrown outward were the remains of fossil-bearing lake deposits, and a thick, lens-shaped layer of this broken material, known as breccia, lies on the crater floor. The bottom of the breccia layer is about 1,200 feet beneath the crater's rim.

The lump of nickel iron that created the crater is known as the Cañon Diablo meteorite. Although no substantial remains lie within the crater, over the years roughly 20 tons of fragments have been recovered within a 6-mile radius of the crater, varying from solid droplets to chunks weighing 100 pounds. It is thought that most of the meteorite's bulk vaporized in the impact explosion and that the millions of tiny metallic grains that have been found in and around the crater condensed from the cloud of vaporized material.

The first reports of Meteor Crater appeared in 1891. For a long time, many scientists believed it was volcanic in origin, although others, after finding iron fragments, preferred the meteorite theory. In 1906, mining engineer Daniel Barringer, who had bought the site, began to drill, but failed to find a massive iron core.

Later, in the 1930s, large amounts of money were invested in further drilling, in the hope that iron deposits might be found somewhere beneath the breccia and profitably mined. However, the drill bits encountered undisturbed sandstone beneath the broken limestone of the breccia, and the prospecting was abandoned. The meteoritic origin of the crater was confirmed in 1960 with the discovery of rare silicas that could only have been formed by the immense pressure and heat generated by a meteorite impact.

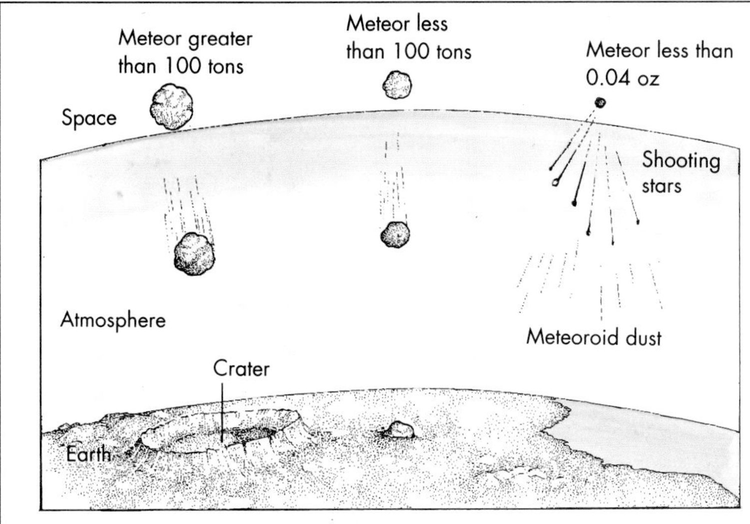


**Meteoritic impact**

Meteor Crater is a misnomer, since a meteor is a body which burns up in the Earth's atmosphere before it reaches the surface. Meteorites, however, survive the friction of the Earth's atmosphere and land on the planet.

Over 50 tons of meteoritic material reach Earth every 24 hours. Most of it consists of small grains, but up to ten meteorites a day are thought to weigh 2 pounds or more. About 65 percent of all meteorites are stony, and 35 percent are metallic, formed mainly of iron and nickel.

ARIZONA

# THE PAINTED DESERT AND PETRIFIED FOREST

SOUTHEAST OF THE GRAND CANYON, the region known as the Painted Desert stretches across the plateau of northern Arizona to the Petrified Forest National Park. To the south of the park runs the Little Colorado River, the last trace of the Ancestral Colorado which carved the Grand Canyon when it changed its course.

The Painted Desert, 150 miles long and up to 50 miles wide (7,500 square miles in total), lies between the Kaibab and Kaibito plateaus. Along with Grand, Bryce, and Zion canyons, it is one of the best places in the world to view the exposed layers of millions of years of sedimentation and erosion.

During the latter part of the Triassic period, 200 million years ago, much of Arizona was a swampy jungle, completely different from today's barren desert lands. Great cone-bearing trees 200 feet high and more grew in the lush, wet plain and in the hill country to the south. As trees died or were felled by storms and torrential floods, they were washed northward onto the plain, where they bogged down and were eventually totally submerged in mud and sand deposits.

Most of these trees were members of the *Araucarioxylon* genus, of which a modern descendant is the Norfolk Island pine. The tops and roots rotted away or were torn off, leaving the huge trunks behind. The muddy silts that buried the logs when they settled also contained volcanic dust and ash that were carried into the region by wind and water. This imported dust added silica to the mud and contained various minerals such as iron oxide, copper manganese, and chromium.

Water seeping down through the layered sediment collected strong concentrations of dissolved silica, which eventually permeated the buried logs, replacing each cell of organic material with a perfect replica in minerals. Gradually, the wooden trees

***The Painted Desert*** *(right) has millions of years of erosion on display. The brilliant colors of this geological history blaze from the desert's hillsides, and the rocky sediments glow through a spectrum of orange, pink, lilac, and blue, reflecting a remarkable fossil record.*

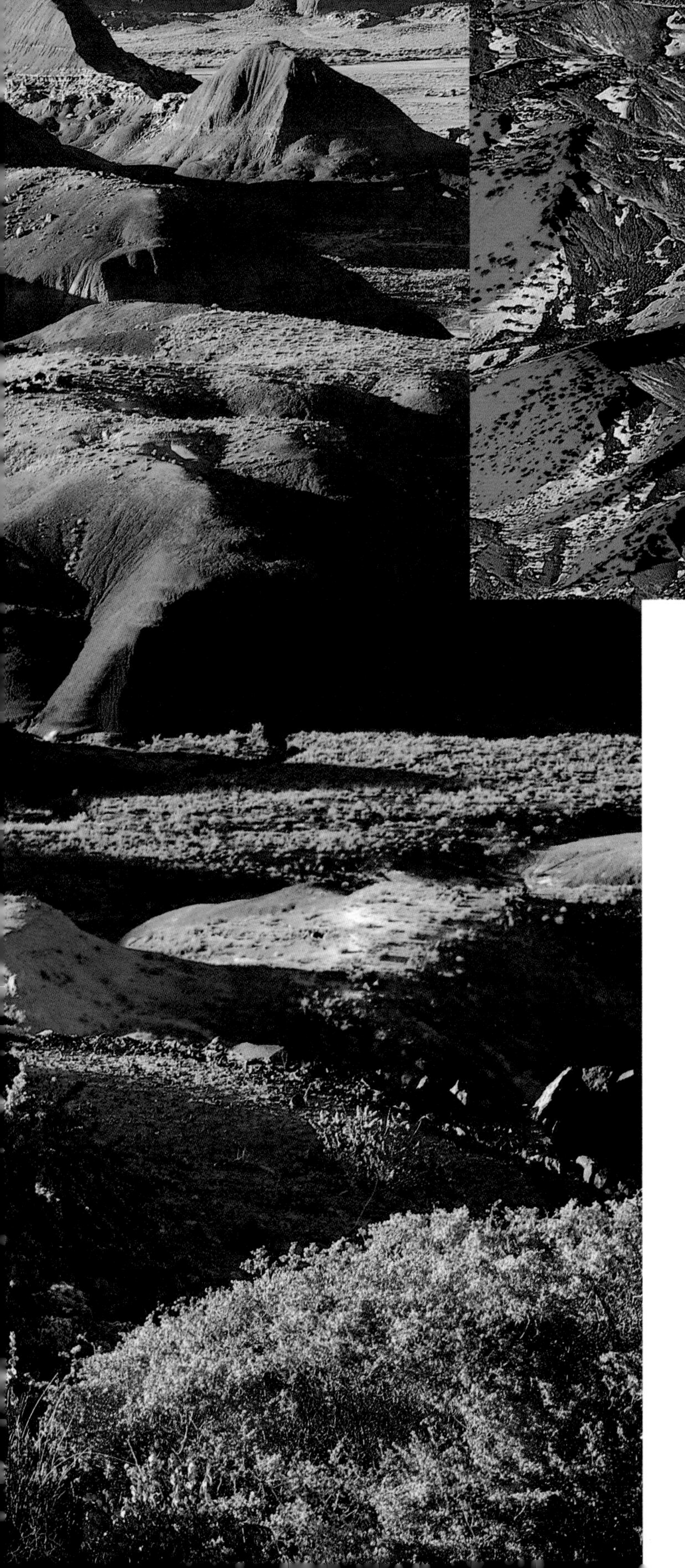

***The snow-softened contours*** *of the desert (above) paint a gentle picture. The Painted Desert lies at 5,000 feet in elevation, and every spring the waters of the Little Colorado River are swollen with run-off. Torrents of floodwater thunder over the 100-foot cliffs of the Grand Falls, where volcanic lava once blocked the entire river canyon. Over the centuries, the river found its way around the basaltic plug and re-entered the canyon over its eastern rim, where the Grand Falls now descends in terraces 400 feet wide. The wild power of the red, silt-laden waters provides a colorful exhibition of sediment on the move.*

became crystal trees, and the silica turned to quartz, in the form of pure crystals as well as combinations of brilliant semi-precious varieties such as jasper, onyx, amethyst, carnelian, and agate.

More sedimentary layers were added to the beds holding the trees as seas came and went across the region. Eventually, the original swamp levels were capped with thousands of feet of sedimentary rock. As the land began to warp upward 65 million years ago, the seas disappeared, and earth tremors fractured many of the now brittle logs into sections.

Over the intervening millions of years, the erosive powers of water, wind, and weather have stripped back the thick sedimentary cap. The process has cut through thousands of feet of sediment to lay bare the original shale and sandstone layers encasing the logs. These layers of shale and sandstone, in turn, are particularly vulnerable to erosion, and as the fine amalgam of shale, clay, and sandstone has washed away, the great logs—over 200 million years old—have surfaced.

The Petrified Forest was initially made into a national monument under the Antiquities Act in order to preserve it from

a commercial scheme to build a crushing mill on the site to turn the ancient trees into abrasive material for industrial use. Over the years, tons of petrified wood have been removed by souvenir hunters, but it is now strictly forbidden to remove any fragment, however small, from the national park.

The logs of the giant pines are by no means the only fossils to have surfaced in the Petrified Forest. The great swamplands where the logs were buried were once lush with plant and animal life. Dinosaurs wandered there when the trees were still growing. Huge crocodile-snouted phytosaurs hunted fish-eating metoposaurs that weighed half a ton. Large, armadillolike aetosaurs preyed on herds of 2-ton vegetarian *Placerias*, a type of three-eyed rhinoceros with large tusks. All these creatures have turned up as fossils in the soft Chinle Formation, a compressed amalgam of mud, silt, and bentonite, the clay formed from volcanic ash.

Each year, the region's 9 inches of rain falls in a few drastic downpours and pares away another inch or so of sediment. The rain washes away the soft sandstone and transforms the sunbaked clay of the desert

***Almost 90 percent of the wood*** *in Petrified Forest National Park is formed from an extinct relative of the Norfolk Island pine. These trees grew more than 100 feet tall with a diameter of 10 feet. Shown in cross-section, a petrified log (above) reveals its history in rings of quartz.*

***Scattered around*** *the tinted hills of Blue Mesa (right), the once great conifers are now a landscape of glittering minerals. Erosion of the earth has left some petrified logs stranded on columns of clay. Pedestal Log, in the left foreground, stands out against the colorful, banded mesas.*

***The Puerco Ruins,*** *the largest of the park's ancient sites, was built on the edge of a bluff. It was occupied until A.D. 1400, but the only remains are sandstone walls, a ceremonial kiva, and petroglyphs carved into the rock (above).*

*The Navajo Indians, whose reservation lies next to Petrified Forest National Park, created legends in which the crystalline logs were the bones of a giant called Yietso. The Paiute Indians believed the logs were massive arrows left behind by Shinauv, their thunder god. The Indians who lived there from A.D. 500 to 1400 used petrified wood to build their homes.*

into a temporary quagmire. As a result of the erosion, the remains of about 40 different vertebrate creatures and over 200 plant variations have so far been identified in the fossil beds.

The creatures that now inhabit the Petrified Desert are a great deal smaller than the dinosaurs, but a lot smarter in most cases. They include badgers, coyotes, bobcats, rabbits, mice, and deer antelope, as well as reptiles such as the poisonous Arizona coral snake. The mammals did not exist during the time of the dinosaurs and the fossil trees, but their prototypes may have been starting to evolve as the trees were being sealed into their preserving, metamorphizing sedimentary layers.

Petrified trees and fossils are found throughout the Painted Desert, but the 147 square miles forming the Petrified Forest National Park contain the largest concentration of petrified trees in the world. It is also much larger in area than the other notable petrified forest at Sigri on the Greek island of Lesbos. Below the trees now visible are almost certainly thousands more, waiting to be released from their ancient logjams by relentless erosion.

NEW MEXICO

# CARLSBAD CAVERNS

ON THE EASTERN FLANK OF THE GUADALUPE MOUNTAINS, Carlsbad Caverns National Park covers about 73 square miles. Above ground, canyons and rough country lead to the Guadalupe Ridge, which reaches an altitude of 6,350 feet. However, most visitors to the national park are far more interested in descending into the earth than climbing over it.

Carlsbad Caverns forms a huge, interconnected complex of underground passages, caves, and high-ceilinged chambers. More than 70 distinct caverns make up the network, which is remarkable for the diversity and beauty of its deposit formations, which have been sculpted by 3.5 million years of dripping water.

Carlsbad Caverns and the Guadalupe Mountains are part of the Capitan Reef, a layer of marine limestone 1,600 feet thick that was formed 200 million years ago on the floor of the ancient Permian Sea, which covered much of western Texas and southeastern New Mexico. When the continent began buckling upward 65 million years ago, in an upheaval that also created the Rocky Mountains, the Capitan Reef was pushed toward its present elevation.

Its movement caused great cracks to develop which allowed surface water and rain run-offs to permeate the Earth's surface. The water was slightly acidic, and over millions of years, it dissolved limestone and carved out the caverns and interconnecting channels. Eventually, the climate changed, the water table dropped, and air replaced the water in the tunnels and caves.

Carlsbad Caverns contains structures and shapes from an unfamiliar world. Some are on a gigantic scale, while others are as detailed and fragile as lace. Motionless waterfalls and cascades, curtains, chandeliers, and organ pipes have been sculpted from the deposits of countless billions of water drops, turning caverns and chambers into cathedrals, enchanted forests, and science fiction landscapes. Guides and visitors have struggled to give familiar names to the exotic shapes and assemblages

***After leaving the last shaft of warm sunlight*** *behind, visitors descend into the underground world where the temperature is a constant 56°F. At a depth of 829 feet, the scenic King's Palace and Queen's Chamber lead to the exquisite Papoose Room (right).*

that loom throughout the system, but the fanciful names fall far short of the magical architecture itself.

In 1901, a cowboy named James Larkin White became the first white man to explore the depths of Carlsbad Caverns, and he later became the site's first guide. White groped his way into the tunnels, lighting his path with a kerosene torch. Four thousand years earlier, Basket-maker Indians left their wall pictures at the entrance and one of their sandals, which gave a date to their presence.

Visitors who descend the Main Corridor come across forms called the American Eagle, the Three Little Monkeys, and the Baby Hippo. At the bottom of the Main Corridor, 830 feet below the surface, lie the "scenic rooms," such as the Green Lake Room, the Queen's Chambers, the Papoose Room, and the King's Palace. A series of floodlights dramatizes the shapes, casting evocative shadows.

A climb up Appetite Hill, which rises 100 to 200 feet, attains the level of such features as the Hall of the Giants, Fairyland, and the Temple of the Sun. The largest of all the caverns has defied every attempt to find a name that matches its majestic dimensions and is simply called the Big Room. Spreading over an area of almost 14 acres, it is large enough to house a dozen football fields, and the great vault of its roof is 255 feet high in places.

Because of the dangers inherent in a huge cave system, visitors to the park are only able to see a portion of the Carlsbad Caverns complex. But the two guided tours take in the most stunning formations and chambers and seem to satisfy everyone, especially since the problem of climbing back to the surface has been solved by the installation of an elevator.

In 1986, cavers discovered a major new cavern system within the national park, just 5 miles from the Carlsbad Caverns. Investigating an old 90-foot pit, where strong winds blowing up from the bottom indicated the possibility of extensive caverns below, they worked their way through to an amazing world now named Lechuguilla Cave. It has turned out to be the country's deepest cavern, 1,565 feet below the surface at its deepest point. Fifty miles of passages and chambers have been explored, and no one can even guess how much more remains to be discovered.

***Caves provide a summer home*** *for hundreds of thousands of bats (right), whose daily feeding sorties alerted ranchers to the existence of the caverns in the 1880s. Every day at dusk, from late spring to early summer, bats stream out of the caves ready for the night's insect hunt. They emerge in waves, at a rate of thousands a minute, and the air is filled with the beating of their wings.*

***The amazing dripstone formations*** *(left) take shape as stalactites, when water drips from the cavern's ceiling and leaves its deposit behind, or stalagmites, which form when rising columns develop from the accumulated calcite on the cave floor.*

Lechuguilla was formed quite differently from most cave systems. Hydrogen sulfide from oil deposits rose through fissures in the Earth's crust and mixed with oxygen and water to form sulfuric acid. This strong acid then scooped out the limestone and created the cavern system. Its dripstone features are among the most sumptuous and intricate ever seen, and its chambers gleam with magnificent crystalline displays of gypsum, aragonite, and other minerals.

Entry and passage require considerable caving and climbing skills, so Lechuguilla is likely to be off limits to the general public for some time. It is being fully explored and mapped by members of the Lechuguilla Cave Projects under the auspices of the National Park Service.

**Bat behavior**

One species of mammals in every four is a bat, yet remarkably little is known about them. They are the only mammals capable of sustained flight, which they achieve by means of their well-designed wings.

More than 95 percent of the half a million bats that roost in Bat Cave are Mexican free-tails, which migrate from Mexico each year to give birth in June and raise their young. For four to five weeks, the babies cling to the ceiling each night while the adults fly southeast toward the Pecos and Black River valleys to hunt for enough insects to sustain them until the following evening. In late October, adults and young return to the warmer climes of Mexico.

Other, more unusual bats found in the cave are the big brown bat and the western pipistrelle. All these bats make use of echolocation, a natural sonar system, for finding prey and plotting their flight course.

NEW MEXICO

# WHITE SANDS

TUCKED BETWEEN MOUNTAIN RANGES, the San Andres in the west and the Sacramento in the east, White Sands National Monument covers an area of 275 square miles. At first, the sands present a shocking sight, since they look like a slice of snow-covered tundra dropped into the arid desert of the Southwest.

Rolling dunes gleam brilliant white against the blue sky, but this is not powdery snow that stretches so invitingly under the hot New Mexico sun. White Sands is the world's largest surface deposit of gypsum, or calcium sulfate, which in crystal form is called selenite and is perhaps best known as the basic material of plaster of Paris.

Despite the heat of the day, the fine gypsum forming the dunes is relatively cool to the touch, due to surface evaporation and high reflectivity. It is also silky smooth and soft, without the abrasive texture of quartz sand. When they are rubbed between the fingers, the gypsum grains crumble to a powder as fine as talc. Unlike ordinary sand, gypsum is soluble in water, which explains how the white sands arrived at their present site between the mountains in the Tularosa Basin.

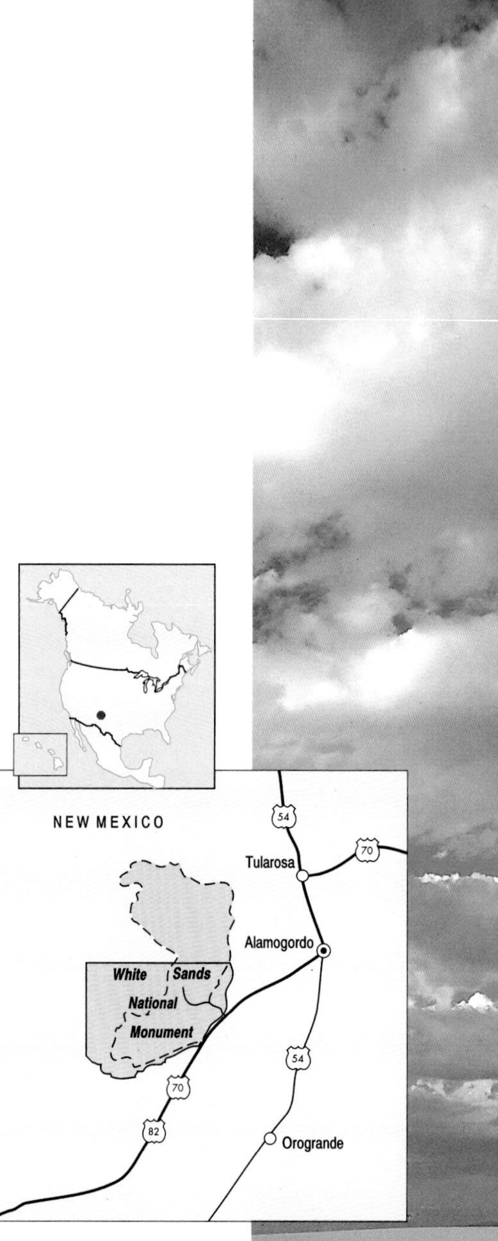


When the Permian Sea that once covered much of North America began its long retreat 100 million years ago, gypsum was one of the minerals that remained behind, lying in thick strata. More gypsum was shoved to the Earth's surface when the North American landmass began to hunch upward 65 million years ago. The San Andres and Sacramento mountains slowly took shape, with the Tularosa Basin between them.

Winter rains and spring meltwater began to leach away the gypsum in the sedimentary layers of the new ranges, running in almost saturated solutions down to Lake Lucero, at the foot of the San Andres Mountains. There is no exit for water from the lake except by evaporation, which leaves behind thin sheets of crystalized gypsum, or selenite, which the wind erodes into fine sandlike grains.

The prevailing winds from the southern end of the basin carry the crystals northeastward, piling them up in steep dunes;

***The ever-shifting nature*** *of the gleaming white dunes poses a problem for plant life. The yucca (right) tries to stay above the piling sand by stretching its stem farther and more swiftly than usual to keep its leafy head clear. Some yuccas have grown from 20 to 30 feet of slender stem.*

***The vivid colors*** *of the* Echinocereus triglochidiatus, *or hedgehog cactus (above), are found all over New Mexico; bushy specimens may be 50 years old.*

*Animals that live in the White Sands region have adapted their coloring to match the brilliance of the sands. The bleached earless lizard (below) has added a bright white skin to its stock of survival techniques.*

gypsum will form steeper dunes than quartz sand because of the sharper angles of its grains. The dunes are not a static feature; they move with the wind as much as 33 feet a year. More gypsum joins White Sands from deep beneath the basin as water seeping upward from 1,000 feet below brings it in solution and deposits it in a thin crust on the surface.

White Sands is one of the few national monuments where visitors are positively encouraged to walk and play. No number of dune-leaping tourists can possibly harm these mobile and rapidly regenerating gypsum mounds, and a slight night breeze is guaranteed to erase all signs of human disturbance before the dawn breaks.

TEXAS, MEXICO

# BIG BEND NATIONAL PARK

BIG BEND NATIONAL PARK, established in 1944, constitutes 801,163 acres of some of the wildest country in the National Park System. The great size of the park swallows up the relatively few visitors to make this one of the least crowded national park destinations in North America.

The Rio Grande interrupts its southeasterly journey with a 90-degree turn that loops it beneath the Big Bend region of Texas like a sagging hammock. The park that nestles snugly in the crook of that run is a continent in microcosm, with low-lying terrain, river systems, upland desert, and a mountain range merging with one another in a relatively confined area.

The Rio Grande defines the park's 118-mile border with Mexico, and in that distance it runs through three important canyons it has carved into the rock: Santa Elena in the west, Boquillas in the east, and Mariscal between them. From its source, 12,000 feet above sea level in Colorado's San Juan Mountains, the Rio Grande travels 1,885 miles to the Gulf of Mexico.

For much of that distance, it is controlled and depleted by irrigation. However, the section that stretches along the park forms a unique area of wild, unspoiled river and terrain. Thanks to Mexico's Rio Conchos, which enters it from the west, the Rio Grande has become a deep, swift flow with powerful currents by the time it reaches the park and funnels into the Santa Elena Canyon.

The absence of people encourages wildlife. Collared peccaries, or javelinas, mule deer, and coyotes come to the water's edge to drink at dusk. Mountain lions, bobcats, and the almost extinct Mexican wolves more wary of humans, are harder to spot.

There are 30 snake species at Big Bend. Where the canyons widen, the banks are home to two of the park's five poisonous snake species: the Trans-Pecos copperhead snake, which favors cane patches, and the western diamondback rattlesnake. The Rio Grande leopard frog, the spiny softshell

***This lonely stretch of river*** *(right) through the Mariscal Canyon has been designated the Rio Grande Wild and Scenic River. The chief indicator plant of the region, part of the Chihuahuan Desert, is lechuguilla, a clump of dagger blades that protrude from the desert floor.*

turtle, and large catfish thrive, and a unique minnow, the Big Bend gambusia, is found only in a pond in the park's southeastern corner.

The Chisos Mountains soar up from the desert, dominating the entire park. Although the Rio Grande flows around the park at an altitude of 1,800 feet above sea level, the Chisos peaks look down on it from a great height. Loftiest of all is Emory Peak, which stands 7,835 feet high.

The Chisos Basin is a natural amphitheater at an altitude of over 5,000 feet. Emory Park overlooks it, as do Casa Grande (7,300 feet) and Lost Mine Peak (7,550 feet). Visitors frequently camp in the basin which is an ideal base for mountain hiking in the summer, when the desert far below is uncomfortably hot.

The enormous range of altitude and terrain within Big Bend means that at certain times of the year snow and sleet showers fall among the high peaks early in the day and temperatures blaze at river level, 6,000 feet lower, at noon of the same day. The sudden contrasts of terrain create some unique environments where widely disparate species meet and intermingle, and cacti usually found in the desert often grow alongside mountain pines.

Although some of the Chisos peaks are bare rock, others are thickly forested. Ponderosa pines cloak the highest levels, and below them stand junipers, Mexican pinyons, and at least three varieties of oak. Douglas firs, Arizona cypresses, and quaking aspens are also found in the uplands.

The highland meadows are lush with grasses and flowers in the spring and summer. Laguna Meadows, a haunt of the rare colima warbler, extends from the basin area toward the escarpment known as the South Rim, passing through dense growths of aspen, oak, maple, and cypress. The South Rim itself, 2,000 feet above the sloping desert floor, is almost bare.

The meadows and woods of the Chisos Mountains provide a refuge for many

***The Chisos Mountains and the Grapevine Hills*** *(left) cut through Big Bend country, offering cool relief from the desert floor. Formed from volcanic outpourings that burst through the sedimentary layers of an ancient inland sea, the Chisos have been carved by time into ridges and canyons.*

***Prickly pear*** *(right) is just one of 70 species of cactus that flourish in the hot, dry conditions of Big Bend's desert regions. Hardiest of all desert cacti, the prickly pear owes its survival to the speed with which it establishes a root system in the poorest soil. Anchored by a long, depth-seeking taproot, it can take up water quickly and efficiently during rare rainstorms by means of a wide-ranging shallow root system.*

*The flowers range from pale and bright yellow to strong pinks and reds. The fruit is reddish-purple when ripe.*

animals rarely seen lower in the park. Mountain lions seldom make an appearance, since they hunt by night and sleep during the day. The Sierral del Carmen whitetail deer usually graze at elevations above 5,000 feet, where they share the terrain with the kit fox.

Lower down, the gray fox predominates; mule deer graze, and occasionally a black bear is seen in the woods. Reptiles tend to stay at the lower, hotter altitudes, but the black-tailed rattlesnake prefers the hills.

The desert regions of Big Bend are part of the great Chihuahuan Desert that lies between the two parallel mountain ranges of the Mexican Sierra Madre. Most of the

***One of the park's*** *most eccentric birds is the roadrunner (right). It uses its tail as a steering device and a brake, and has been clocked at almost 20 miles an hour on the run. It feeds on ground-living insects such as crickets, as well as lizards, snakes, and fruit such as the prickly pear. It gets much of its required moisture from the body juices of prey.*

## The Birds of Big Bend

Big Bend National Park contains more identified bird species—over 400—than any other national park. Positioned squarely beneath one of the great migratory flyways used annually by vast numbers of American birds, the region forms the northern extremity of the range of many birds from the south, and the southern edge of the range of many others from farther north.

The canyons that force the Rio Grande into a rushing torrent are the favorite nesting places of peregrine falcons, which build their eyries high above the river. Swallows nest low on the rock faces, snatching mud for building material from the banks and shallows. Predatory birds include golden eagles (left) and bald eagles, red-tailed hawks, and American kestrels. Screech owls and great horned owls hunt at night.

At the other end of the size scale are the wrens. The melodious canyon wren frequents the river; in the desert, the cactus wren lives among the spines of the cholla cactus. Flycatchers and woodpeckers (above left and right) occur throughout the park. Some Big Bend birds are found nowhere else in the country. The Lucifer hummingbird frequents the desert, drinking nectar from agave flowers, and the colima warbler has also been seen.

***Slowly snaking its way** across the park, the Rio Grande (above) provides a perfect place for creatures not happy with the dry areas of desert. Beavers live in bank burrows, and their teethmarks in the trees along the river's edge show where they have been busiest. Garfish and turtles also swim in the river and are living fossil reminders of the savanna and swamp that existed here almost 50 million years ago.*

Chihuahuan Desert lies south of the Rio Grande in Mexico, but its northern reaches embrace a large area of Texas.

The park's desert receives an annual rainfall of about 7 inches, only half the amount that falls in the mountains, but still enough to make the huge variety of cacti and other desert plants bloom as if by magic after the rain. Over 850 flower-bearing desert plants have been identified here.

Like the plants, the desert creatures are often superbly adapted to the arid environment. Many avoid the sun completely, coming out in the cool of the night to forage and hunt. The kangaroo rat does not drink water at all. It takes moisture from its food, mainly seeds, and from the humid air of its burrows. Its body recycles its own water, and its kidneys excrete uric acid in almost solid form. The pronghorn antelope, which is making making a comeback in the park, also has efficient moisture-processing equipment.

The black-tailed jackrabbit is common throughout the park and a favorite meal for a number of predators, including coyotes, bobcats, and eagles. The open desert country seldom provides a hiding place, so the jackrabbit relies on its speed and maneuverability to keep out of trouble. In short bursts, it can reach speeds of up to 45 miles an hour, take 20-foot leaps, and change direction with bewildering rapidity. The jackrabbit's enormous ears help it listen for danger and serve as heat exchangers, carrying heat away from the body in their blood vessels and dissipating it into the air.

Other mammals, including skunks, mice, and badgers, are outnumbered by the cold-blooded creatures. The park is home to 22 species of lizards and 30 kinds of snakes, as well as a dozen different species of scorpions, which are nearly always encountered at night. A scorpion's sting can be painful, but it is lethal only in exceptional circumstances. Big Bend is also home to some fearsome tarantula spiders. Despite their appearance and reputation, they only bite in self-defense and are rarely lethal to humans.

Since the park was established, most signs of human encroachment have begun to disappear, returning the region to a true wilderness where river, desert, and mountain coexist naturally as they once did across the continent.

TEXAS

# PADRE ISLAND NATIONAL SEASHORE

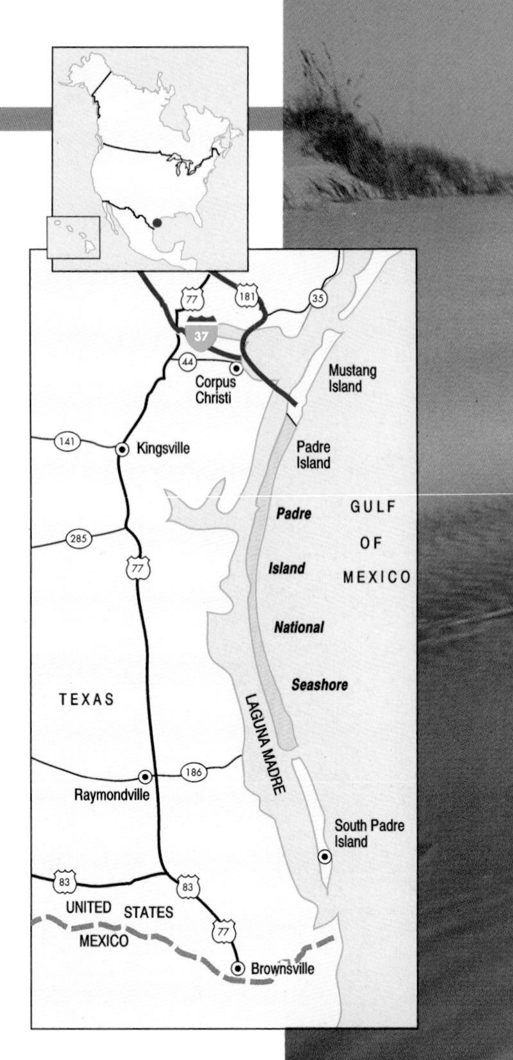


***Often battered by tropical storms,** this wild shore, with its ever-changing nature, is anchored by the roots of sea oats (seen in background right). This plant takes hold in the shifting sands of Padre Island and holds the dunes in place.*

PADRE ISLAND NATIONAL SEASHORE, established in 1962, is part of the long series of barrier islands that runs parallel to the Gulf coastline of south Texas. Padre Island stretches along 113 miles of this barrier, from Mansfield Channel in the south, which was dug in 1964 and divides it from South Padre Island, to the occasionally flooded Corpus Christi Pass in the north, which separates it from Mustang Island. It is the longest unbroken barrier island in the world, and 66 miles of it have been designated the Padre Island National Seashore.

Early in the 16th century, when Padre and South Padre islands were a single strip inhabited by Karankawa Indians, Spanish colonists called the island *Isla Blanca*. At the end of the 18th century, Padre Nicholas Balli bought land rights from the Spanish and after his death, the island was renamed in his memory.

Between the island and the mainland lies Laguna Madre, which is no more than 3 feet deep and varies in width from 10 miles at its southern end to about 2 miles near the northern end of Padre Island. The artificial channel of the Gulf Intracoastal Waterway slices through its center. Excavated in 1949, it is 14 feet deep and about 225 feet wide. Since little fresh water runs into it, the Laguna Madre is very salty. From Father Balli's time until the 20th century, the lagoon was an obstacle that kept the island relatively free of human incursions.

The Gulf side of Padre Island, an almost unbroken, sandy beach pounded by Atlantic surf for more than 100 miles, will never be developed as long as the National Park Service controls it. Surf fishermen cast here for tarpon, mackerel, sand trout, and pompano. Offshore, boat fishermen go for sailfish, marlin, bonito, and red snapper.

The beach gives way to a shingle of small shells, which in turn leads into the dunes. Winds and tides litter the sand with flotsam from as far away as the Azores, as well as from the Caribbean, Yucatan, and South America. The dunes form a ridge parallel to the beach which is anchored by salt-resistant plants. At some points, the dunes are breached by washover channels that flood at certain high tides. When the large washover channel that forms at the northern end of Padre Island is not flooded, Padre Island and Mustang Island form an unbroken, 130-mile strip.

The width of Padre Island varies between 1,400 feet and about 4 miles. Low-lying grasslands, sometimes covered in salt water, extend along the lagoon side of the central dunes, and marshy tidal mud flats form the final zone between the grasslands and Laguna Madre.

A causeway leads to the north end of the island, but it remains unspoiled and uncrowded, particularly in the National Seashore area. While it shelters extensive wildlife, birds are the most visible inhabitants; in fact, the region is a paradise for bird watchers. Many varieties of shellfish, crabs, and shrimp spawn and grow here, sometimes migrating to the Gulf side of the island when they reach maturity.

Padre Island's mammal population

includes white-tailed deer, jackrabbits, coyotes, and moles. Over 30 species of snakes have been identified, including the western diamondback rattler, although harmless varieties like the western coachwhip and the checkered garter snake are more common.

Padre Island National Seashore is an environment constantly on the move, where tides change channel depths and dunes slowly shift in the prevailing winds. It is also one of the rare corners of the country where the landscape is still as it must have been a thousand years ago.

***Gulls, herons, and ducks*** *live by the water's edge on Padre Island (right). Here, brown and white pelicans flap heavily along the surf line; waders spear fish and scoop up mollusks; and skimmers snatch tiny fish from the surface. Bitterns, spoonbills, cormorants, and oyster catchers also feast here.*

# MEXICO

MEXICO'S LANDSCAPE IS WILD AND DRAMATIC. Its cities, like cities all over the world, are growing fast, but much of the country's exciting terrain is still relatively undisturbed by human activity.

A giant wishbone of mountains contains Mexico's central plateau. The Pacific coast, in the west, is lined with steep foothills of the Sierra Madre Occidental. In the east, the long ridge of the Sierra Madre Oriental borders an increasingly narrow coastal plain while progressing south along the Gulf of Mexico. Between these two mighty ranges, the Mexican Plateau climbs steadily from the U.S. border in the north as it stretches toward the southern mountains of the Sierra Madre del Sur.

Separated from this plateau and its mountainous walls by the narrow Isthmus of Tehuantepec, the flat lowlands of the Yucatan peninsula curl northward, separating the Gulf of Mexico from the Caribbean Sea. In the northwest of Mexico, separated from the mass of the continent by the Gulf of California, the peninsula of Baja California seems to exist on its own.

The arid peninsula of Baja (Lower) California is 760 miles long and less than 100 miles wide for most of that length. Steep mountain ridges run parallel to its coasts all the way from Cabo San Lucas at its southernmost tip to its northern border with the state of California.

This is a land of dry, empty wildernesses, granite rock, and upland deserts. Flanking the Gulf of California, which is also known as the Sea of Cortés, the mountains rise so steeply that the sheer rock face often falls into the water.

Some parts of Baja California receive no rain at all for years on end, and most of the peninsula qualifies as desert, with less than 10 inches of rain per year.

Many of Baja's species have evolved in isolation and become unique to the peninsula, found in their particular forms nowhere else. Among the wildlife that have adapted to the arid conditions are the kangaroo rat, which stores moisture-absorbing seeds; the desert toad, which remains buried underground in a comatose state during dry spells, waking only when

***Mount Orizaba** (right), more commonly known as the volcano Citlaltépetl, is Mexico's highest peak, standing at 18,701 feet. Located 60 miles east of Puebla, it has lain dormant since 1687. Beneath it are high plateaus and rich farm and meadow lands.*

***Volcanic ash formations** at Isla Partida, Baja, (above) offer the region's arid face to the baking sun and brilliant blue sea. The western slopes of Baja's Las Tres Virgenes (right) are more gentle.*

rain falls; and the chuckwalla lizard, which can drink and desalinate sea water.

Of the 120 cactus species that have been identified in the peninsula and the Gulf islands, the most distinctive is the cardon. This towering plant has a short, robust trunk, up to 5 feet in diameter, from which a number of vertically pleated arms soar to a height of 50 feet or more. The cardon is only found here and in one region of the Sonora Desert on the opposite side of the Gulf, and 50 of Baja's cactus species grow nowhere else on Earth.

Baja California attracts half a million tourists a year; its Mexican population, concentrated in the few towns, is about $2\frac{1}{2}$ million, which makes it the most sparsely populated of all the Mexican states. The Mexican government has established two national parks in the north, Sierra de Juarez and Sierra de San Pedro Martir. It has also created refuges for gray whales in the Laguna Ojo de Liebre in the west and for marine mammals such as the California sea lion and the elephant seal on an island in the San Benito group off the Pacific coast. In the Gulf of California, almost 50 islands are official wildlife sanctuaries.

The Sea of Cortés is a vast underwater canyon with the San Andreas Fault at the bottom. The deep ravines and basins of the sea floor send cold, extremely nutritious water welling upward, contributing to the food chain in one of the richest marine ecosystems in the world.

The Gulf is an important haven for a great range of whales and dolphins. Gulf of California harbor porpoises, known locally as *vaquitas*, inhabit the northern waters and are found nowhere else. Gray whales, finbacks, blues, humpbacks, and sperm whales all flourish here as well and are most easily spotted in the channels between the peninsula and the islands of the Bahia de Los Angeles, where the Gulf is narrowest.

The most frequently seen are the finbacks, the second largest whales in the world after the blues. Finback whales remain in the Gulf year round, feeding on tiny creatures and plants strained out of the water with their specially adapted mouths.

Most of the Gulf's fish stay close to shore, and, since the inshore waters can drop steeply to depths of hundreds of fathoms, the variety of fish near the shore is very wide. Farther down, sierra mackerel surge in hungry schools, as do other school fish such as goatfish, mullet, and green jacks. Deeper still, grunts and groupers feed on the bottom and around the rocks.

The waters of the Gulf are renowned for their large sport fish, including marlin, swordfish, and the brilliantly colored dorado. Giant manta rays sail like spaceships through the depths, occasionally surfacing to leap clear of the water, and in the deep waters hammerheads, leopard sharks, and tiger sharks lurk.

The great western ridge of the Sierra Madre Occidental has an average altitude of 5,000 to 10,000 feet. It is mainly volcanic in origin, unlike the Sierra Madre Oriental on the eastern edge of the Mexican Plateau, which is composed chiefly of folded layers of sedimentary limestone and shale.

At the northern end of the Sierra Madre Occidental, southwest of the city of Chihuahua, lie half a dozen barrancas, or canyons, immense rifts which rival Arizona's Grand Canyon in depth and far exceed it in width. The rivers and streams that carved them, flowing west over millions of years, cut down through thousands of feet of volcanic rock, aided by the seasonal floods caused by thundery summer rain.

Largest of the barrancas is Barranca del Cobre, or Copper Canyon, which was named for the now disused mines in its sides. Copper Canyon is large enough to contain three or four Grand Canyons, but its floor, unlike the Grand Canyon's desert, is green with tropical jungle. At its deepest, Copper Canyon cuts 5,577 feet into the Sierra Madre Occidental.

The Urique River also carved the adjacent Barranca de Urique, on whose lower

slopes the Tarahumara Indians spend the winter growing oranges and bananas. In summer, when rain swells the river, they climb back to the canyon's higher levels and its rim. The Tarahumaras are superb mountain climbers and long-distance runners, and spend a large portion of their lives in ritual gatherings. They are among the most remote and isolated Indian tribes in Mexico. About 50,000 of them inhabit the Barranca region, living in caves and simple houses, growing their staple crops of fruit, beans, and corn.

The Sierra Madre Oriental is mainly composed of limestone. It is steep on the

***The brown pelicans*** *(left) that dive for their food in Magdalena Bay on the southwestern coast of Baja must compete with the local fishermen, whose fleets dot the 1,600 miles of Baja's coastline.*

*At Cabo San Lucas (right), on the southern tip of Baja, and throughout the Sea of Cortés, the variety of fish is enormous. More than 800 fish species have been identified in this sea, along with literally thousands of species of mollusks, shrimp, crab, and other invertebrates.*

*Enormous shoals of sardines stay close to the water's surface, while king angelfish (below left) prefer the rocky crevices and protective caves at lower depths in the Sea of Cortés.*

eastern side, facing the broad coastal plain of the Gulf of Mexico; the western side of the Oriental slopes gently into the arid vastness of the Chihuahua Desert.

Monterrey, Mexico's third largest city, is hemmed in to the west and south by the ridges of the Sierra Madre Oriental's spine. The bones of the mountain here are a particularly soluble form of limestone which is very susceptible to erosion and to the acidic action of water, and as a result the region is scored with impressive cave systems and gorges.

Huasteca Canyon, just southwest of Monterrey, is a narrow gorge 1,000 feet deep. The Garcia Caverns, about 20 miles east of the city, contain some of the largest caves in Mexico and must be reached by cable car. In this craggy, gaunt upland terrain, bare rock alternates with stretches of forest, and stream-fed valleys wander between the ridges. Close to the Garcia Caverns is the spectacular Cola de Caballo, or Horsetail Falls. The waterfall is about 115 feet high and its water cascades into a natural garden at its base.

South of Mexico City and Cuernavaca, underground streams and rivers have carved the limestone into Mexico's most famous cave network. Some of the streams no longer exist, but at least two of them, the San Geronimo and the Chantocoatlan, flow into the ground here and re-emerge as a single river, the Rio Amacuzac.

The Cacahuamilpa Caverns are surrounded by a landscape of mountains and valleys covered with lush tropical vegetation. After running water had scooped the caves and galleries out of the rock, seeping and dripping water began to build their renowned stalactite and stalagmite formations. The caverns form the most extensive system of stalactite caverns in Mexico, and only a few of their galleries have been fully explored.

One of the galleries is 4,528 feet long, as much as 325 feet wide at certain points, and 230 feet high. The stalagmites rising from the cavern floors reach heights of 130 feet, and their diameters measure up to 65 feet.

Mexico forms one arc in the Pacific Ring of Fire, the great string of volcanoes that encircles the section of the Earth's crust known as the Pacific Plate. Many of Mexico's southern peaks are volcanic, and the entire country is one of the world's most active volcanic and seismic regions.

Citlaltépetl's symmetrical, snow-laden peak, the third-highest in North America, was first scaled in 1848. Set in its own national park, the volcano overlooks the plain that falls to Veracruz and the Gulf of Mexico.

Farther west along the same range of volcanic peaks, Popocatépetl, the Smoking Mountain, 45 miles southeast of Mexico City, can easily be seen from the nation's capital. Mexico's second highest peak rivals Mount Fuji in Japan with the beauty of its balanced form. The volcano was violently active until 8,000 years ago, and Spanish historians recorded more recent eruptions in the 16th and 17th centuries. In 1921, it vented smoke and fumes for several months, and it still smokes sporadically from vents within the crater at its summit, which is 17,887 feet above sea level, 2,000 feet wide, and 500 feet deep.

Still farther west, Nevado de Toluca is 40 miles southwest of Mexico City. Once as high as Popocatépetl, it lost a large portion of its summit in a mighty explosion 25,000 years ago. A second series of blasts, 11,500 years ago, reduced the volcano to its present height of 14,977 feet.

Between Guadalajara and Tepic, the volcano Ceboruco marks the western end of the range of volcanoes that spans the entire country from the Pacific Ocean to the Gulf of Mexico. The valleys of the state of Nayarit sweep down toward the ocean here, and Ceboruco's highest point is about 7,100 feet above sea level, only as high as its cousins to the east.

***Urique Canyon*** *(left), named for the mighty Urique River which carved it out of the barren landscape, is only one of the several giant canyons contained in Barranca del Cobre, or Copper Canyon. The walls of the canyon are not precipitous, but descend in a series of massive, sloping steps through a maze of secondary and side canyons.*

*The extinct volcano Nevado de Toluca (right) is plugged with solidified lava. Its broad, eroded caldera now contains two sparkling blue lakes known as the Lake of the Sun and the Lake of the Moon. The peak looks down across the wide, fertile Toluca Valley to the Pacific Ocean in the far distance.*

Valleys lined with farms and oak woods lead to Ceboruco, but the luxuriant terrain gives way to a bleak, lifeless landscape closer to the dormant volcano. The slopes are composed of rough, gray basaltic spills, and nothing grows here. Ceboruco put its grim stamp on this land in a series of eruptions, the most recent of which ended in 1870.

Ceboruco and the other volcanoes in the chain could erupt again any time, as others have this century. The taming of Mexico's wilderness is a slow process which may never be completed, and the volcanoes are a constant reminder that some parts of the natural world will never be tamed.

# The Central States

## Heartland of the nation

East of the Rocky Mountains, the Great Plains sweep southward through the central states. Prairies and rich agricultural land intermingle through North and South Dakota, Nebraska and Iowa, Kansas and Missouri, with the Mississippi River forming the region's eastern boundary. The rocky skeleton of the country gradually appears on the Earth's surface as the rich soils of Oklahoma and Arkansas give way to the varied landscapes of Texas, and the deserts become increasingly arid as they reach toward the Mexican border.

Flowing toward its junction with the Mississippi, the Missouri waters the Dakotas and Nebraska. The Black Hills of Dakota are outriders of the Rockies, and the badlands of North and South Dakota are arid exceptions in a predominantly flat landscape that was once covered in the grass that fed huge bison herds. In the ecological system of the plains, countless millions of bison kept the grass growing vigorously with their grazing and trampling; they paid for their food with a steady supply of manure.

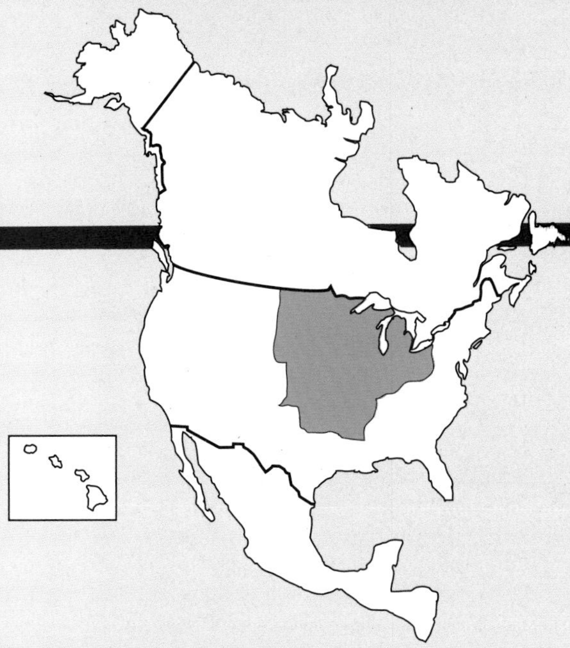

Today, protected parklands such as the Oglala National Grasslands in Nebraska preserve the grass species that once nourished the bison, and small herds have been re-established in refuges such as the Badlands National Monument along South Dakota's White River. East of the plains, the Mississippi runs its north-south course through the continent, swelling mightily as it passes the border of Missouri and Arkansas and receives the tributaries of those watery states.

Despite the growth of industrial cities, this great swath of country between the Rockies and the Mississippi is still the heartland of the country, its greatest watershed, and its richest source of produce. Through its parks and wildlife refuges it also provides a portrait of the natural power of water and land and the processes they set in motion before the days of plows and dams.

NORTH AND SOUTH DAKOTA

# BADLANDS

In the 18th century, the French-Canadian fur trappers who were traveling south on the Missouri River in search of pelts and trade came upon a region north of the White River which sorely tried even their adventurous spirits. Stretching in a wide band from the Missouri to the Black Hills in the west, the tortuous, arid terrain of deep gullies, razor-back ridges, and crumbling peaks was oven-hot and treacherous underfoot. The summer rain brought them no relief, since it turned the clay surface of the jagged landscape into a slick layer of soft mud that made every step of the way an ordeal.

The trappers called the area *les mauvaises terres pour traverser*—bad lands to cross. This echoed the name already given to the region by the Sioux Indians, who called it simply *mako pata*—bad land.

The present Badlands National Park in South Dakota occupies about an eighth of the total White River Badlands. In 1939, President Franklin D. Roosevelt urged that the area be classified as a national monument so that some of the wildlife that had been decimated by hunters could be restored to the region.

Among the bare bones of the Badlands are grassy valleys, basins, and uplands, and the edges of the Badlands merge into the fringes of the prairie. Plants such as prairie gold pea and buffalo grass flourish; they once provided grazing for the immense herds of bison that lived on the plains, as well as for deer and pronghorn antelope. The herds were the lifeblood of such Indian tribes as the Arikara and Sioux. However, white settlers moving across the land hunted the animals and invaded their terrain until they virtually disappeared from the White River lands.

Badlands National Park was established in 1978. Bison and pronghorn antelope have been successfully reintroduced to the area and have settled into manageable herds on the limited grazing now available to them, which is only a fragment of the enormous range they once covered.

The rocky wilderness of the White River Badlands is the final result of a process that began with a gradual accumulation of thick

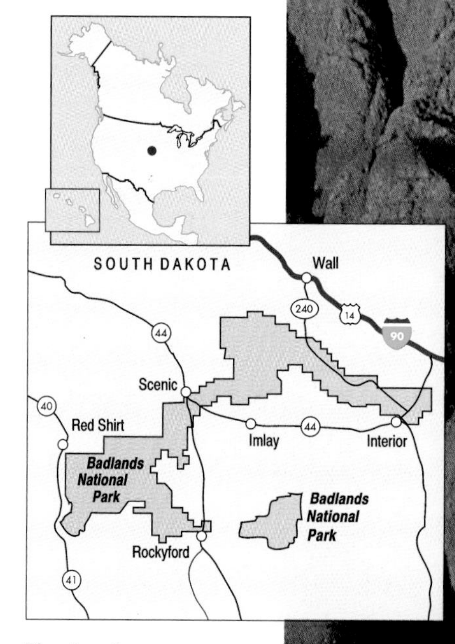


***The deeply worn furrows and valleys*** *of the Badlands glow with vibrant color in the fall light (right). Despite this barren appearance, the Badlands support a wide variety of plants and animals.*

marine sediment. After the layered seabed rose—along with the Rocky Mountains and the nearby Black Hills—streams and runoff from the Black Hills covered the original sediment with fresh mud from the high ground. Carried on winds from the west, volcanic ash joined the new deposits. What remains now are bare, upright slabs of this gigantic layer cake, cut through and revealed by several million years of water, wind, and ice.

Approached from the plateau to the north, the White River Badlands appear with startling abruptness, since they extend along a strip of land directly beneath it. The terrain descends so sharply and suddenly that the eerie moonscape of the Badlands remains invisible until the visitor has nearly reached the lip of the plateau. At sunset and sunrise, the horizontal strata glow with pastel colors.

The process of erosion that built the Badlands is still eating small canyons and gullies into the plateau. Rainfall here has a low annual average, and what rain there is often arrives in brief deluges, instantly creating streams and runoff that carry a heavy load of mud down to the White River, and onward to the Missouri.

As the elements pare away the Badlands' surface, they reveal evidence of an earlier age, no less than 30 million years ago, when the region was part of a huge, subtropical floodplain. The Sioux who foraged through the Badlands were amazed by the fossilized bones of unknown creatures that emerged from the eroding clay and shale.

Giant pig fossils, standing over 5 feet high, have been found, as well as huge, carnivorous, wolflike hyenaedons. The remains of the most famous prehistoric predator, the saber-toothed tiger, are also found in the Badlands. The region is the richest Oligocene fossil bed in the world, and a paleontologist's place of pilgrimage.

Today, the Badlands is home to a surprising diversity of plant and animal life. Apart from the bison and pronghorns, animal inhabitants include coyotes, prairie dogs, badgers, and jackrabbits.

Prairie rattlesnakes and bullsnakes glide through the dry gullies, and birdlife between the brackets of tiny rock wrens and golden eagles ranges from turkey vultures to rock doves, cliff swallows, white-throated swifts, and western meadowlarks.

Although sparsely wooded, the region does support trees like juniper, red cedar, cottonwood, and yellow willow.

North Dakota's Badlands lie alongside the Little Missouri River in the northwest of the state, within Theodore Roosevelt National Park. Created in the same way as South Dakota's Badlands, the territory is similarly split by water into a series of clefts and fissures.

Having bought a cabin here early in his political career, Theodore Roosevelt began to develop the passion for the wilderness that would influence him all his life and make him a major crusader for conservation. The Theodore Roosevelt National Park covers 70,416 acres and is divided into a North Unit and a South Unit, roughly 35 miles apart, with Roosevelt's Elkhorn Ranch site between them.

***A scenic drive through the park** passes these bright red and gold shale deposits near Dillon Pass (left). They built up about 65 million years ago when a shallow sea covered the Badlands, and although most are black-gray, a gradual oxidation here has given the iron in the shale its vibrant colors. The more subtle background rocks were formed by river sediment about 35 million years ago during the Oligocene epoch.*

Beneath the volcanic clays, called bentonite, that form the gray substrata of the Badlands are beds of soft coal, or lignite, which are the remains of tropical plants up to 70 million years old. Ignited by spontaneous combustion or prairie fires, lignite may smolder and burn underground for years, baking the clay beds above it to the hardness of brick and filling the air with acrid fumes that stunt nearby vegetation.

The lignite-baked clay is harder than most of the sedimentary layers of the North Dakota Badlands, and pieces of it sometimes act as capstones on top of banded pillars of softer material, protecting them from erosion. The South Unit also contains a region of petrified trees, fragments of which also appear as capstones on top of pinnacles.

The erosion rate of the Badlands within Theodore Roosevelt National Park is slowed by the natural qualities of bentonite, whose particles swell when they are wet and form a slippery, but waterproof, close-grained layer at the surface. Once bentonite reaches saturation point, water runs off its surface layer. This protects the immediate terrain, but it also leads to the erosion of non-volcanic clays and materials such as sandstone farther down the slopes.

**Badlands fossils**

Fossil beds rich with the remains of mammals from about 35 million years ago are scattered throughout the Badlands. Sometimes only parts of skeletons remain (inset; oreodont skull), while other specimens are whole, preserved in the sediment of periodic flooding exactly where they fell. Geologists have used these fossils to build up images of what life was like when the Badlands were covered with wood and grass during the Oligocene epoch, "the golden age of mammals."

Merycoidodons, usually called oreodonts (right), were typical of the creatures that roamed these plains. They had many of the characteristics now associated with pigs but with longer bodies and shorter legs. Unfused limb bones would have made it difficult for the beasts to run, making them easy prey for other animals. Scientists think a pit in the front of the head may have contained a gland similar to one used by modern deer to stake their territories with scent.

SOUTH DAKOTA

# THE BLACK HILLS

COVERING ABOUT 5,000 SQUARE MILES, the Black Hills of Dakota rise from plains on both sides of the Wyoming-South Dakota border, but most of their bulk lies in South Dakota. Roughly 125 miles long and 60 miles wide, the hills form an elongated dome that contrasts with the flat immensity of the plains. Harney Peak, the highest point in South Dakota, is part of the Black Hills range and stands 7,242 feet above sea level at its summit. Other major Black Hills mountains are Terry Peak (7,064 feet) and Thunderhead Mountain (6,567 feet). The Black Hills National Forest, which blankets most of the area, contains a number of designated parks and monuments.

Volcanic pressures that never resolved themselves into full-scale eruptions thrust the Black Hills above the plains. Bear Butte, northeast of the national forest, rises 1,400 feet above the prairie. This towering landmark, a sacred place for the Cheyenne Indians and for the Sioux who displaced them, is what geologists call a laccolith. A narrow chimney of lava pushed the crust above it into a steep dome. As the dome eroded away over millions of years, it left behind a tall, exposed lava cone, now covered with ponderosa pines.

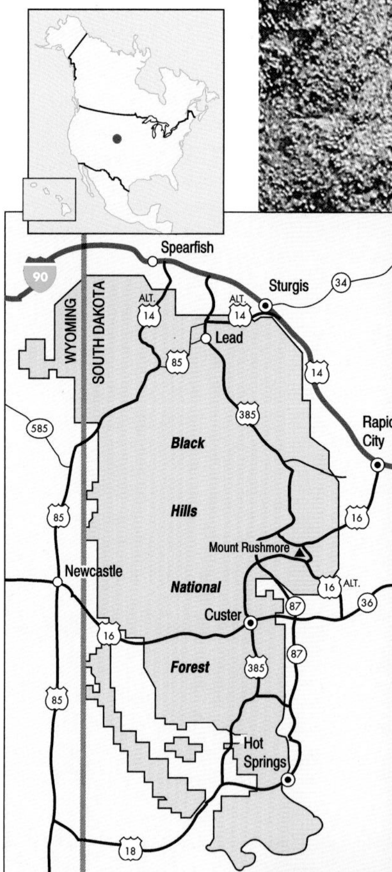


Similar developments shaped the Black Hills. The granite core of the elongated dome was overlaid with sedimentary strata of sandstone, limestone, shale, and gypsum. Pressures beneath the Earth raised it, and water, wind, and ice combined to erode the layers at the top of the dome and bare the granite center, which was surrounded by concentric ridges of the sedimentary layers.

According to Sioux legend, the Great Spirit stood on top of Bear Butte and declared that the Black Hills formed a sacred area—a sort of halfway house filled with gems—where the souls of dead warriors could prepare themselves for the heavenly wonders that lay ahead in the Happy Hunting Grounds. The Sioux named the mountains Paha Sapa, or Black Hills, because of their dark pines and considered the area taboo. They could hunt

***Pinnacles of granite*** *(right) flank the Needles Highway. Some 500 million years ago, shale and sandstone layers were pierced by molten rock, which hardened into granite. The surrounding rock eroded, leaving free-standing pinnacles.*

there and cut the straight pine trunks they needed for lodge poles, but they were forbidden, on pain of death by lightning bolt, to settle there. The 1868 Treaty of Laramie made the Teton Sioux the legal owners of the Black Hills region, but once gold was discovered there, the treaty became worthless.

Hot Springs, which is in the canyon of the Fall River in the south of the Black Hills, was a spa town at the turn of the century but has become more famous recently for its fossils. In 1974, builders discovered the Mammoth Site, a steep-sided drinking hole used by mammoths in the Pleistocene age up to 26,000 years ago. Many of the creatures became trapped in the sinkhole, and the fossilized remains of a large number have been excavated.

Wind Cave National Park, in the southeast of the Black Hills, is a limestone terrain of about 44 square miles. The wind cave after which this park is named was discovered in 1881, when a hunter heard air whistling from a 10-inch gap in the rock. The entrance has been enlarged to give access to visitors, but the phenomenon of the rushing air remains unchanged.

In common with other wind caves, this one exhales when the air pressure outside it falls and inhales when the outside air pressure rises. The wind cave is a maze of passages, decorated with a delicate tracery of interleaved calcite fins that create a sort of boxwork. The calcite formed initially in limestone crevices and was left intact when acidic water, working its way through the rock, dissolved the limestone around it.

The 28,000 acres of Wind Cave National Park that lie above ground form a protected habitat for bison, elk, deer, and antelope. They are also inhabited by colonies of prairie dogs that have been all but exterminated in other parts of the country by deliberate poisoning. There is also a remnant of original open prairie preserved here in its natural state.

Not far from Wind Cave National Park is Jewel Cave National Monument. The cave here was discovered by a pair of brothers prospecting for gold, and this one, too, gave its presence away by its noisy whistling. In fact this cave system is the fourth longest known in the world, with more than 73 miles of twisting labyrinths. Calcite crystals grow inside the cave in a form known as dogtooth

***Hordes of buffalo*** *(above) sweep majestically across the plains of Custer State Park.*

*The presidents' heads on Mount Rushmore (left) stand proud above the treeline. Carving the granite monument began in 1927 and, with interruptions, took 14 years to complete.*

spar. The long, delicate dogtooth crystals that cover some of the cavern walls in a dense mantle reflect a wide variety of browns and greens from their facets.

Many of the underground formations in Jewel Cave are especially rare and unusual. One such oddity is a formation called helictite which is only a few inches long. It twists and turns in all directions with no regard for gravity. Outside the cave is a forest of rare virgin ponderosa pines.

Mount Rushmore National Memorial is probably the most famous feature of the Black Hills. Gutzon Borglum, sculptor of the giant heads of four American presidents, had the privilege afforded few sculptors of working on a truly monumental scale. He and his assistants shaped the granite outcrop with dynamite, jackhammers, and drills, roughing out the features of George Washington, Thomas Jefferson, Abraham Lincoln, and Theodore Roosevelt.

Work began August 10, 1927, but it was not completed for another 14 years, with many delays due to bad weather and lack of funds. In March 1941, Borglum died and his son Lincoln took over until the money ran out later that year. Since then, nothing has been done to the monument.

In 1939, the Sioux tribe commissioned its own monumental sculpture, of Chief Crazy Horse, victor of the Little Big Horn battle. Korkzak Ziolkowski's figure is 641 feet long and 563 feet high. Still unfinished, it depicts the Oglala Sioux Chief charging out of the granite on his horse.

The Black Hills themselves far outshine any man-made monument, and the magnificent living terrain, the mountains, forests, and animals, are ultimately more valuable than all the gold that has been hacked out of the ground.

NEBRASKA

# OGLALA NATIONAL GRASSLAND

ADMINISTERED BY THE U.S. FOREST SERVICE, the national grasslands are a reminder to all who earn their living from the Great Plains of the importance of grasses to the ecology of this immense terrain. Tucked up against the borders of South Dakota and Wyoming, the Oglala National Grassland in northwest Nebraska is the smallest of the seven national grasslands in the Forest Service's five-state Rocky Mountain region.

Since Nebraska's statehood was declared in 1867, the grasses on its rich prairies have been replaced by crops, such as sorghum, sugar beet, wheat, soybeans, and corn. Prime beef cattle graze where bison herds once roamed. The Oglala National Grassland preserves about 94,334 acres of prairie roughly as it was when the sodbuster settlers first arrived following the passage of the 1862 Homestead Act.

The settlers' plows and long periods of drought stripped the topsoil from huge areas of the Great Plains and transformed the region into a dust bowl. The federal government eventually bought the ruined land of many failed homesteaders and began to restore it. Finally, the Forest Service took over the responsibility for this land, which was designated national grasslands in 1960.

Although it is subject to extremes of temperature, this is a cool, dry region for much of the year. The Oglala National Grassland is at an average altitude of around 3,300 feet above sea level. It is part of the Pine Ridge district, which has an average annual precipitation of slightly more than 17 inches, and temperatures swing to extremes, from highs of 110°F to lows in winter of −37°F.

Forests of ponderosa pine lie in the south of the Oglala National Grassland, close to Fort Robinson where Chief Crazy Horse surrendered his people to the U.S. army and died at the hands of its soldiers; and stands of hardwoods such as elm and ash grow in shallow valleys. These areas are

***There are several contrasting terrains within** Oglala National Grassland (right). The rolling hills of an upland prairie are its characteristic feature. Here, native grasses hold the fragile topsoil in place with their dense root systems, protecting it from the erosive effects of drought and wind.*

interlaced with patches of typical badlands, deeply riven and shaped by water and largely bare of vegetation. Mule deer flourish in this mix of forest and badlands.

Toadstool Geologic Park, within the Oglala National Grassland boundaries, contains world-famous deposits of mammal fossils, including those of many ancestors of animals familiar today, such as pigs, camels, horses, dogs, and deer. Two skeletons of mammoths which lived during the most recent Ice Age, about 12,000 years ago, have also been excavated here. Fossils may not be removed from the area, but visitors are allowed to collect rock specimens, which include petrified wood, chalcedony, and Fairburn agates.

The prairie of the Oglala National Grassland is mainly shortgrass, reflecting low rainfall. The eastern Great Plains, where the rainfall is higher, were once covered in tallgrasses such as big bluestem, which can reach heights of over 7 feet and put down a root system that can plunge 6 feet into the ground.

To the west and north, midgrass prairies dominated the central Great Plains with grasses such as little bluestem and needlegrass, which are half the height of the long-stemmed varieties and utilize moisture efficiently. Shortgrass prairies, like those in the Oglala National Grassland contain varieties like buffalo grass and blue grama,

***Toadstool Geologic Park** (above), within Oglala National Grassland boundaries, is a badlands site covering 800 acres and decorated by columns of fine-grained Brule clay. Caps of a kind of rock known as Arikaree sandstone perch above the soft columns, protecting them like umbrellas from the rain that shapes them.*

which are seldom more than 10 inches high although their roots can sink to 3 feet.

The shortgrasses curl their leaves to reduce moisture loss from evaporation and grow dense hair on their roots. They can also survive the heavy grazing and trampling they receive from herds of ruminants like bison. Close-cropped and densely rooted, the shortgrass prairies posed a problem for the settlers, who had enormous difficulty cutting through the tough mat to the soil underneath. Having learned to use the sods they removed from the land surface as building material, they produced the sod houses typical of many homesteads. One example of these sod houses has been preserved in Toadstool Geologic Park.

The Forest Service manages the national grasslands such as Oglala under a multi-use principle that provides for private grazing land as well as open prairie, and unspoiled recreation areas as well as productive livestock ranges. Conservation practices help maintain a natural balance between wildlife, plants, and water, and sustain yields of renewable resources.

# Tornado Territory

DEVASTATING TORNADOES, or twisters, are born out of thunderstorms. Only a few thunderstorms, however, actually become full-blown tornadoes, with the rotating black funnel-like vortex that characterizes them. Certain conditions have to be present to create the rotating updraft, which can occur when there is an intense low-pressure area under the storm clouds and the surrounding winds are traveling at varying speeds. The United States experiences more tornadoes a year than other countries, mostly in the central plains.

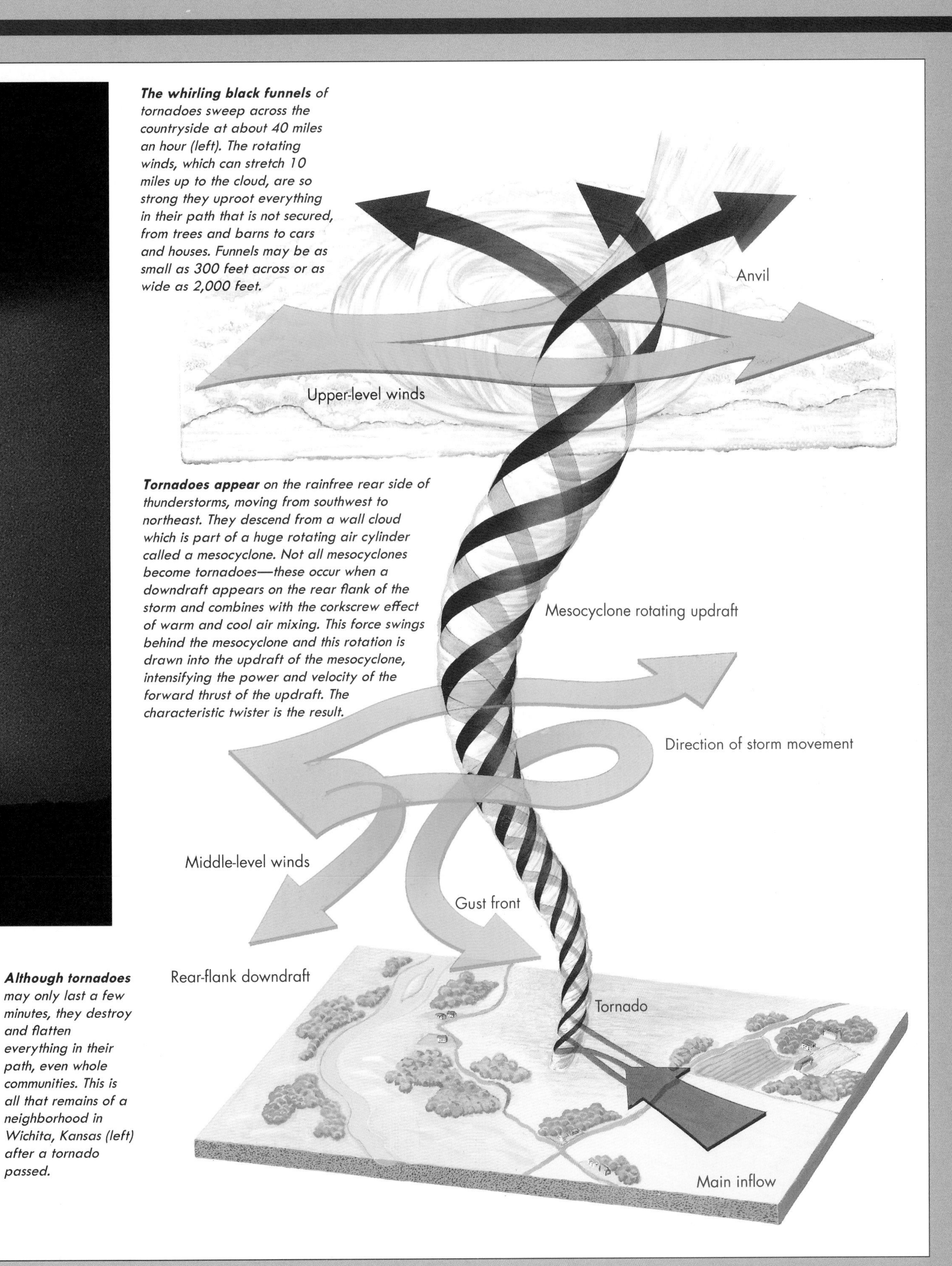


***The whirling black funnels*** *of tornadoes sweep across the countryside at about 40 miles an hour (left). The rotating winds, which can stretch 10 miles up to the cloud, are so strong they uproot everything in their path that is not secured, from trees and barns to cars and houses. Funnels may be as small as 300 feet across or as wide as 2,000 feet.*

***Tornadoes appear*** *on the rainfree rear side of thunderstorms, moving from southwest to northeast. They descend from a wall cloud which is part of a huge rotating air cylinder called a mesocyclone. Not all mesocyclones become tornadoes—these occur when a downdraft appears on the rear flank of the storm and combines with the corkscrew effect of warm and cool air mixing. This force swings behind the mesocyclone and this rotation is drawn into the updraft of the mesocyclone, intensifying the power and velocity of the forward thrust of the updraft. The characteristic twister is the result.*

***Although tornadoes*** *may only last a few minutes, they destroy and flatten everything in their path, even whole communities. This is all that remains of a neighborhood in Wichita, Kansas (left) after a tornado passed.*

MISSOURI, ARKANSAS

# THE OZARKS

THE OZARK PLATEAU IS A YOUNGSTER GEOLOGICALLY, a block of highlands that rose from the plains a million years ago. It consists of thick layers of limestone, sandstone, shale, and dolomite that between 400 and 500 million years ago were the floor of a sea. The region known as the Ozarks spans the Missouri-Arkansas border, reaching deep into both states. Countless springs and rushing streams water its lush, hilly forests and rocky outcrops.

Missouri is a state of rivers and lakes, and the Ozark National Scenic Riverways in the southeast of the state includes 100 miles of the Current River and 34 miles of the Jacks Fork River, both of which are undammed and free-flowing. These rivers run between forested banks that were covered with pines until the lumber industry leveled them. The pines were succeeded by oak and hickory seedlings, which have now grown into mature hardwood forests. Between the trees and along the riverbanks, dogwood and redbud blaze in spring, while summer brings carpets of wild geranium, sweet william, oxeye daisy, and goldenrod.

Bobcats, squirrels, and deer live alongside the rivers, and the rare red wolf has also been sighted. Red foxes are common in the woodlands. Apart from indigenous birds such as barred owls, whip-poor-wills, and green herons, large numbers of waterbirds also visit the region. They migrate annually along the broad swath of the Mississippi Flyway, stopping over in the protected refuges of the parks, which include the many units of the Mark Twain National Forest that surround the Ozark National Scenic Riverways area.

The waters of both the Current and the Jacks Fork rivers are swollen by springs as well as natural precipitation. On the Current River, cold, subterranean water wells up at Welch Spring and Blue Spring; Alley Spring feeds the Jacks Fork River. The Red Mill watermill, which was built in the last century to harness Alley Spring's power, still stands, and 81 million gallons of water flow daily from the spring. One of the greatest springs in the region is known simply as Big Spring; it boils sensationally out of a limestone outcrop, producing up to

***Eroded and striated limestone bluffs*** *line the Buffalo National River as its clear waters wind through the lush, hilly Ozarks. Along the river's 148-mile length, it flows both gently, as here, and much more forcefully over steep rapids.*

840 million gallons of water a day.

Flanking the rivers in this 81,000-acre waterways park, the limestone terrain sits on a bed of granite. Limestone bluffs overlooking the rivers break through the forest cover, and there are many caverns and sinkholes where the rain has seeped down through the porous limestone, eating away at crevices and faults to produce cave systems decorated with dripstone features.

One of Missouri's great recreational waterways is the huge Lake of the Ozarks, which took shape as a direct result of the damming of the Osage River. The Bagnell Dam was constructed as part of a hydroelectric scheme to provide power for the St. Louis area. When the dam was completed in 1931, the river backed up along its course and into its tributaries and side valleys, creating a winding waterway with many branches and inlets. Although its central channel is only 125 miles long, the shoreline of the Lake of the Ozarks measures over 1,300 miles.

The lake is set in a landscape of steep ridges and deep valleys cloaked with oak, hickory, pine, and cedar forests. Fishing is one of the great attractions, and the lake, from the deep water at the center to the shallow inlets serrating the shore, provides a variety of fish that includes striped bass, black bass, crappie, catfish, and paddlefish.

Like Missouri, Arkansas is crammed with the limestone formations and brimming rivers and streams that typify the Ozarks. In all, the state has nearly 10,000

***Unspoiled scenery***—*much as it was when Indians ruled the Ozarks—surrounds the Ozark National Scenic Riverways. Blue Springs (right), along the Current River, gets its name, not surprisingly, from the crystal-clear water with its deep blue color. The smooth surface here conceals an active spring pumping out 72 million gallons of water each day.*

*Wild turkeys (below), distinguished by leaner bodies than farm breeds, have been saved from near total extinction and now roam freely along the rivers. They roost in trees but feed off the ground.*

**The striped bass**

Also called the rockfish, rock bass, and striper, the striped bass is a fine fighting fish, prized by sport fishermen at the Lake of the Ozarks and other enclosed waters. A migratory fish native to the East Coast, the striper is a member of the sea bass family, with up to eight sharply defined black stripes on its silvery-bronze sides; it often has bright yellow markings on its fins and head.

In its natural environment, it moves upriver in spring and summer to spawn in fresh water and then returns to the sea. Over the years, newly constructed dams have trapped stripers in freshwater lakes and reservoirs, but the species has survived the loss of the sea and adapted to a more limited migratory life, still moving up the streams in the spring and returning to the lakes after spawning.

The adaptable fish has been deliberately introduced to enclosed waters to provide an exciting angling quarry that can reach an impressive size. Females are usually larger than males and can weigh up to 100 pounds. During breeding, females are courted by a number of males and spawn several million eggs, which drift on the currents and start to hatch three days later.

In the winter, when lake water is uniformly cold at nearly every depth, the striped bass sinks to the midwater zones and eats very little. As the surface zones warm up in the summer, the striper stays above the thermocline—the region where there is an abrupt change from cold to warm water.

miles of stream and 58,000 acres of lake.

The Ozark National Forest lies north of the Arkansas River in the Boston Mountains at the southern end of the Ozark Plateau and covers well over a million acres between Fayetteville, Fort Smith, and Russellville. A small separate unit south of the Arkansas River contains Magazine Mountain, the highest point in Arkansas at 2,753 feet.

In the main portion of the park, Blanchard Springs Caverns tunnel deep into the limestone. It is possible to explore up to 6 miles of corridors and caves on two levels that are linked by a 216-foot elevator shaft. The Cathedral Room, on the lower level, is 1,200 feet long and 180 feet wide and festooned with curtains of stalactites that seem to cascade from its lofty ceiling; it is dominated by a magnificent stalactite-stalagmite pillar.

The Ozark National Forest also contains two natural sandstone bridges, at Alum Cove and Hurricane Creek. The national forest is a rich wilderness of trees and ferns, cliffs and ravines, rocks and springs. Abundant water flows from streams into deep pools and pours over spectacular waterfalls. Buckeye Hollow boasts a total of seven waterfalls, while Falling Water Creek is a 5-mile stretch of continuous cascades and boulders.

The Buffalo River was designated North America's first national river in 1972, after conservationists waged a long, hard fight to keep the U.S. Army's engineers from damming it. Lined with deep woods and frequently walled by limestone bluffs 400 feet high, the Buffalo National River stretches for 148 miles between its source in the Boston Mountains and its junction with the White River, close to Buffalo City.

A broad corridor of land, created by a 96,000-acre subunit of Ozark National Park, protects the Buffalo River from waterside development. Now that it is a national river, the Buffalo is secure forever from every encroachment except that of visitors intent on enjoying the beauty of the Ozark wilderness.

MICHIGAN

# ISLE ROYALE

Moose first swam across the 15-mile stretch of Lake Superior between Canada and Isle Royale around 1900. Well nourished on the luxuriant vegetation, they soon displaced the woodland caribou, which had settled on the island previously. The last caribou disappeared in 1926. In 1949, during a winter so severe that much of the lake froze, timber wolves came trotting across the ice from Canada for the first time. These two immigrant species are now part of a dynamic ecological balance that keeps them both healthy and limits their numbers to what the terrain can bear.

Named by French missionaries during the 17th century in honor of Louis XIV, Isle Royale is the largest island in Lake Superior. Although only 15 miles from the Canadian shore, it is part of the state of Michigan, whose nearest point on the mainland is about 50 miles away.

Isle Royale and its smaller attendant islands make up Isle Royale National Park, which was established in 1940. Here the moose and the wolves are safe from hunters, but even in this unique environment, cut off by a natural water barrier and the park service regulations from the encroachments of the outside world, they are subject to the harshness of nature.

The island's highlands run in long parallel ridges along its 45-mile length and slope down to enter the water at the island's eastern end, to form long narrow peninsulas and islands divided by deep channels. Isle Royale is between 4 and 8 miles wide and contains 27 lakes, of which the largest is Siskiwit Lake.

Moose favor the summer months when they revel in the ideal terrain of swamps and bogs, rich in the water plants they devour and bordered by forested uplands where they can shelter and graze on twigs and leaves. Natural swimmers, moose have splayed hooves and long legs that enable them to move easily through bogs. Wolves will not follow them into deep water, and in the warm, wet season can only capture their calves as food, so at that time the wolves' diet includes beavers.

Once the northern winter hardens the ground and begins to put ice on the swamps

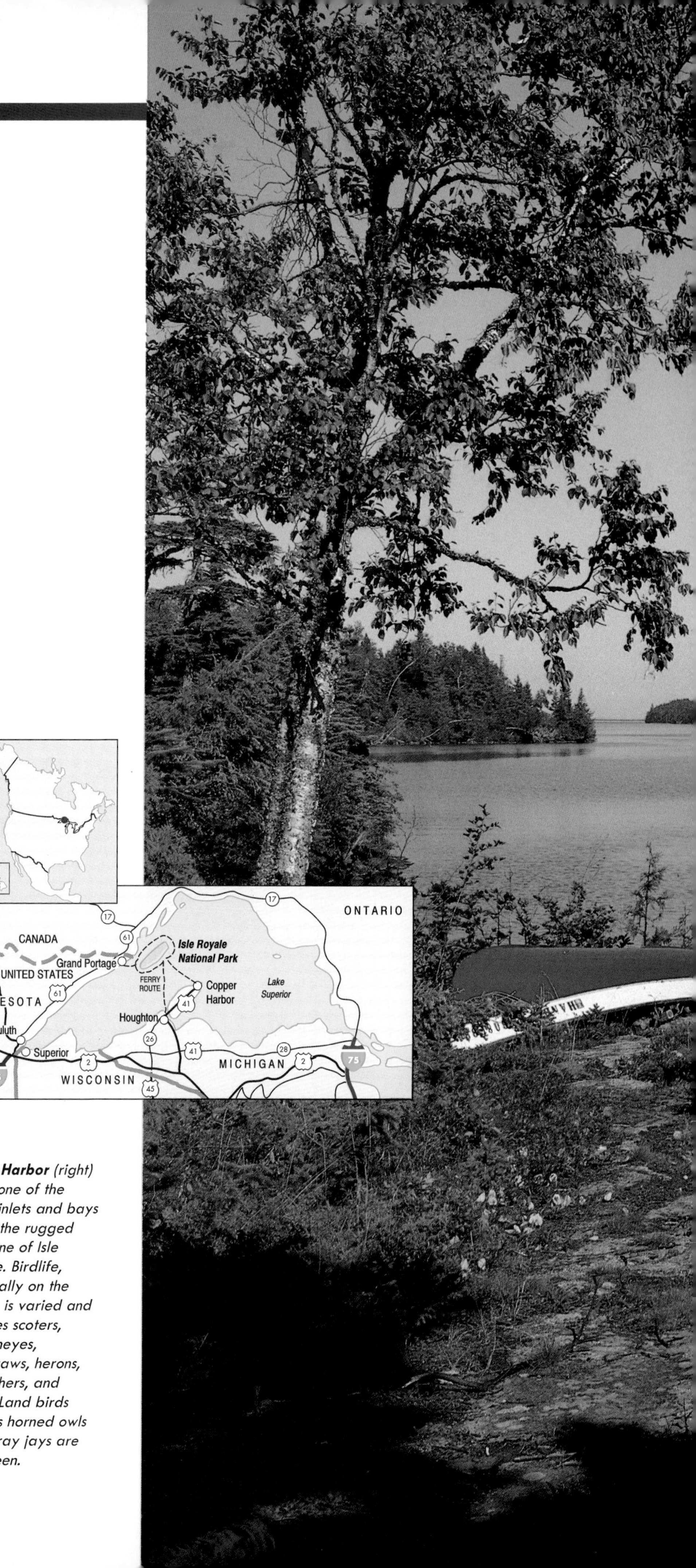


***Tobin Harbor*** *(right) is just one of the many inlets and bays along the rugged coastline of Isle Royale. Birdlife, especially on the water, is varied and includes scoters, goldeneyes, oldsquaws, herons, kingfishers, and loons. Land birds such as horned owls and gray jays are also seen.*

and lakes, the natural advantage swings to the wolves, which can follow their prey virtually anywhere over the frozen landscape. Hunting in packs of up to 20 animals, the wolves test a large number of moose without making a kill. If the prey defends itself or its calf aggressively, the wolves abandon it and seek an easier victim, usually hunting down isolated or weak calves and sick or aging adults.

The wolves perform an efficient culling that ensures the survival of only the strongest and healthiest moose. The reverse side of the process is that when the moose are lean and strong, wolves kill far fewer of them, and the weaker wolves fall by the wayside. In the first half of the 20th century, the moose population grew to 3,000 and more. Now they usually number under 1,000, and there are between 25 and 50 wolves, in three or four packs.

Spruce and balsam fir predominate in most upland forests, with hardwoods such as maples, birch, and red oak on the ridges. In spring and summer, the island brightens with flowers, and its famous range of at least 34 species of wild orchids features calypsos, lady's slippers, and ladies' tresses.

At Isle Royale, scientists and students examine the seasonal workings of a classic northwoods environment and the delicate and complex interactions of animals and plants untouched by humans.

***This bright-eyed marten** (below) is an agile, acrobatic creature that spends much of its time in trees where it preys on squirrels. Martens also hunt on the ground for small insects, fruit, and nuts. They den in hollow trees and produce a yearly litter of one to five young.*

# THE MISSISSIPPI RIVER

EVERY HUNDRED YEARS, the delta peninsula of the Mississippi River advances another 6 miles into the Gulf of Mexico. This extraordinary progress is caused by the river's depositing half a million tons of sediment into the sea annually. The components of the sediment, which has traveled from as far north as Canada and the Great Lakes, are the product of countless streams and rivulets as well as the many full-blown rivers that eventually merge in the waters of the Mississippi.

The Mississippi River—"Big Water" in the language of the Algonkian Indians—is the major drainage channel of the North American continent. Its catchment area includes 31 U.S. states and two Canadian provinces and covers 1,244,000 square miles that form a funnel defined by the Rocky Mountains in the west and the Adirondack Mountains in the east.

Measured from the headwaters of the Mississippi itself, the river's length is about 2,348 miles. Measured from the headwaters of its longest tributary, the Missouri, the river's length is around 3,740 miles. No one can provide an accurate figure for its length, because it changes from day to day as the river takes a short cut across a narrow neck of land and isolates an oxbow lake, or widens a bend by shifting a sandbank, or adds to the length of its own delta peninsula. With 45 of its tributaries navigable for at least 50 miles, the Mississippi navigable waterways system totals more than 15,000 miles.

The Mississippi itself represents three distinct stages of river development. From its source to the locks at St. Anthony's Falls in Minneapolis-St. Paul, where it becomes fully navigable for large craft, the river is youthful. From Minneapolis-St. Paul to the junction with the Ohio River at Cairo, Illinois, it is a powerful, mature river. From Cairo to the Gulf of Mexico, it is an ancient waterway, meandering erratically through its wide floodplain.

The Mississippi begins as a shallow brook, sparkling between the stepping

***The 500-foot bluff*** *at Pikes Peak State Park (right) provides a spectacular view over the hazy Mississippi River, with its islands merging into the open country beyond. The landscape in this northeastern corner of Iowa, with its limestone ridges and hills, is quite different from that in the south.*

***This aerial view** of the mighty Mississippi (above) shows the river in its lower stages, or old age. Because of the flat nature of the landscape, the river meanders across the plain, far from the exuberant start of its journey at Lake Itasca, Minnesota.*

*In the lower half of the photograph, it is possible to see where the meanders are accentuated, causing the two arms to meet and form oxbow lakes. The river has broken through the loop to adopt a new, more direct, course south.*

***The wild rice marshes of Minnesota*** *(above) provide both food and shelter for a variety of waterbirds. The rice itself has always been an important food source for native Americans, and is now considered a delicacy. It grows abundantly in the slow, shallow waters, often reaching between 3 and 10 feet tall, and has a large flower cluster.*

***Part of the 2,348-mile journey*** *of the Mississippi takes in the hardwood swamps of Wisconsin (above). One variety of fish here is the catfish, which lives on the river bottom and navigates with the aid of the fleshy whiskers that inspired its name.*

stones that mark its exit from the forest-fringed Lake Itasca in northern Minnesota, 100 miles from the Canadian border. About 9 feet across and only inches deep, it slides over its clear, gravel bed between low banks lush with reeds and marshy woods. It is difficult to believe that by the time this gentle stream reaches the sea it will be carrying 350 billion gallons of silt-laden water past a given point every day.

Early in its course, the river wanders northwest from Lake Itasca through a watery countryside of lakes, birch woods, and marshes, and then describes an irregular, sweeping arc through a series of lakes, including Leech, Cass, and Winnibigoshish in the Chippewa National Forest region of northern Minnesota. Gradually it turns south and then southwest, past Grand Rapids and Brainerd, finally leaving the lake country behind as it curves southeast. At the cities of Minneapolis and St. Paul, which are as close to each other as Siamese twins, it drops through double locks at St. Anthony Falls and takes on a totally new character.

From Lake Itasca, 1,670 feet above sea level, the Mississippi descends 700 feet in the 500 miles it covers on the way to Minneapolis. Over that distance, the river wanders through swamps bright with lilies and shallows green with wild rice, through

***Sandhill cranes*** *(above), shown here at Avery Island Bird City sanctuary in Louisiana, form small resident populations in Mississippi and Florida. They are large, long-necked, long-legged birds with white or gray plumage. One of the subspecies, the Mississippi sandhill crane, is now endangered.*

*This bird uses the wet pine savannas for nesting and feeding during the summer breeding season. Nests are usually found in shallow water.*

sudden whitewater rapids and high-banked chutes, under fallen trees that easily span its width, and through watered woods of birch, alder, and fir that are home to beaver, deer, muskrat, and black bear.

From Minneapolis, the Mississippi becomes a working river, wide, powerful, and deep—50 to 100 feet deep in the main channel. Twenty-nine massive locks, large enough to accommodate huge towboat rigs dragging acres of barges, lie between the start of this stretch and the city of St. Louis, near where the Missouri joins the Mississippi; beyond St. Louis, there are no more locks. At Cairo, the Mississippi is joined by the mighty Ohio River, which more than doubles its volume, pouring more water into the channel than the Mississippi and the Missouri combined.

For the 860-mile journey from Minneapolis to Cairo, the river progresses in a series of long, sweeping curves. Sometimes it narrows to run fast and deep between the steep sides of forested ravines. More frequently, it widens into long pools that are studded with islands.

At this stage, the river passes through hundreds of miles of black-earthed agricultural land, enriched by thousands of years of floods and river silt. Soybeans, barley, wheat, and corn grow alongside the river on the great, flat tracts of farmland; after harvesting, these same crops travel downstream in the barges.

South of Minneapolis, the river widens, then narrows again to run beneath high bluffs, where the forest comes down to the water's edge. Limestone ribs alternate with the smooth green of the foliage. The town of Red Wing sits on a bluff high above the river, and 5 miles farther south, Lake Pepin forms the Mississippi's longest and widest pool. Lake Pepin's expanse, 23 miles long and 4 miles wide, makes it vulnerable to winds and sudden storms that have been responsible for many sunken streamboats and lost lives.

Beyond Lake Pepin, forests and swamps mingle on the edges of the river near the town of Wabasha. Snakes and snapping turtles inhabit the swamplands, and beavers build their dams here. Ducks and egrets forage and fish on the tangled waterways where overhanging branches form leafy tunnels. The river widens for much of its passage along the Iowa border, where its eastern bank flanks Wisconsin and then Illinois.

From the enormous lock at Keokuk, the western bank touches Missouri, and at the town of Hannibal, the river reaches a region forever associated with the former river pilot and writer Mark Twain, the creator of *Huckleberry Finn.* Huck's adventures fleeing down the river on a raft with a runaway slave have imprinted the Mississippi on the imaginations of millions of readers.

About 10 miles north of St. Louis, the Mississippi is joined by the Missouri River. The headwaters of the Missouri reach as far as Canada and to the northern Rocky Mountains on the U.S. side of the Canadian border. The Missouri and its many tributaries drain the eastern flanks of the Rockies and the northern reaches of the Great Plains, bringing their waters, together with a heavy burden of muddy silt, into the Mississippi at St. Louis.

The muddy-yellow Missouri and the blue-green Mississippi run in the same channel for several miles, with a sharply defined line between them, before they eventually merge. The Ohio River joins the ever-swelling Mississippi at the city of Cairo, 200 miles beyond St. Louis.

From the junction with the Ohio to its bird-foot delta peninsula in the Gulf of Mexico, the Mississippi assumes the characteristics of an ancient river. It meanders southward through a floodplain that is up to 80 miles wide in places, twisting and turning in a long series of loops and bends.

South of Natchez, the Red River pours its muddy water into the Mississippi; just before it does so, it sends a spur southward known as the Atchafalaya River, which eventually joins Lake Fausse Pointe at the coast. The Atchafalaya drains a large basin west of the Mississippi River, and the whole area is one of watery bayous, dense with plant and animal life. The region is also a major refuge for the waterbirds that travel south and north along the Mississippi Flyway, one of the country's major migratory routes.

The Mississippi itself passes through New Orleans, through the salt marshes, and along the peninsula that it has built for itself out of sediment, finally emptying into the Gulf of Mexico from several mouths.

***The romantic landscape of the Louisiana bayous*** *(left) sees the last stages of the Mississippi River before it pours into the Gulf of Mexico. A familiar sight in these backwaters is the abundant duckweed (far left), a free-floating plant that acts as a natural purifier by oxygenating the water. It is a rampant grower and provides food for fish, waterfowl, and the occasional frog.*

*On the riverbank, a flash of scarlet reveals the presence of the ubiquitous male red-winged blackbird (above). The female builds her cup-shaped grass nest over or near the water, while the male sings from exposed perches and flashes his colorful wings to defend his breeding territory.*

# The East and Southeast

## Rushing river to river of grass

he eastern United States contains no scenic splendors that equal Yosemite or the Grand Canyon, no great deserts or ranges of snow-capped peaks. Perhaps understandably, the movement to protect America's threatened wilderness concentrated in its early years on the West. Yellowstone had been a national park for 37 years before any site in the East gained that status.

Yet the most frequently visited national park in the country is Great Smoky Mountains Park near the southern end of the Appalachians; and New York's state park in the Adirondacks, which was established in 1892, is larger than the four largest Western national parks put together. The forested mountains, great rivers, and long, sandy shores and lagoons along the east coast offer millions of city dwellers space, calm, and opportunities for recreation that few other places can rival.

Mammoth Cave in Kentucky, the largest cave system in the world, is a unique marvel, but what is most remarkable about these eastern regions is the rich variety of their trees, wild flowers, and birds. Between Maine and the Everglades, the climate ranges from subarctic to subtropical, and the vegetation includes both mangrove swamps and blueberry barrens. Throughout the year, the birdlife tends to change with the seasons, making the Appalachian ridges and valleys and the coastal lagoons some of the world's busiest avian thoroughfares. In a number of places, as many as 200 to 250 species of birds can be counted in the space of a year.

Knowing there is so much to see is one thing, of course; actually seeing it is often more difficult. But reserves like the Everglades and the Okefenokee Swamp have dedicated themselves both to protecting their wildlife and to enabling visitors to enjoy it at their own pace. Those who go to these and other parks for the scenery and fresh air will enjoy themselves, but those who take the trouble to learn even a little about the natural life around them will get a deeper satisfaction.

FLORIDA

# THE EVERGLADES

FOR THOSE WHO REGARD THE BIRDS OF NORTH AMERICA'S east coast lagoons and swamps as one of the continent's zoological treasures, there is no better place than the southern edge of the Everglades. Everything that a water bird could want in the way of food and vegetation is there, including a habitat where humans are kept more or less under control.

Go, for instance, to Flamingo (oddly named, since the flamingo is not native to North America and only the occasional zoo escapee has been spotted in the Everglades) as the sun begins to drop. You may be privileged to see pelicans rise from the shallow waters in a great swirling flock—heads held well back so their long beaks can rest on their necks—with the sort of unexpected agility and grace that is sometimes found in portly dancers. The sentimental might regard this circling flight as a salute to the end of another perfect day, but it is more probably a muster of the pelican tribe before it moves off to its roost for the night.

There are other pleasures evident on the shore: Louisiana herons racing through the ripples on the water's edge, flocks of egrets, roseate spoonbills, perhaps a skein of ibises. And also bald eagles and ospreys, which fish these waters as assiduously as the pelicans. Inland, there is a different range of avian reminders that this is subtropical America, beyond the reach of the continental winter's march south, where the mean January temperature is in the region of 67°F.

The rare mangrove cuckoo has its only North American perch among, obviously, the mangrove forests, the ruby-throated hummingbird winters here, and migrants from across the Caribbean make their landfall in the forests before starting a remarkable annual journey that takes some of them as far north as Cape Breton Island.

Standing in these forests, where the peace is disturbed only by voracious mosquitoes and the sight of the occasional torpid alligator, it is easy to forget how narrowly the pristine Everglades at the tip

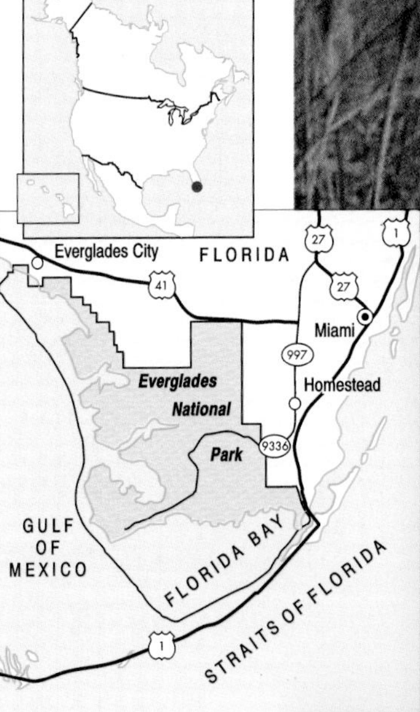

***A group of immature white ibises*** *(right) stands erect at the water's edge. Ibises and spoonbills are medium-sized waders with long necks, long wings, short tails, and webbed toes. Ibises have long, curved bills to search for insects and small aquatic animals.*

of Florida's bill have escaped extinction by agricultural and urban development. Today's population of birds may seem large, but it is nothing compared to the huge numbers which astounded visitors less than a century ago. Similarly, the swamps' population of black bears, pumas, and manatees has dwindled, but, like the birds, they survive and probably will continue to do so.

The national park protects the southernmost two-thirds of the Everglades, a 5,000-square-mile region that extends 100 miles southward from Lake Okeechobee. This was once, in its full extent, the "grassy water," the *pa-hay-okee* of the Seminole Indians, which the first European visitors considered a troublesome mixture of swamp and prairie full of saw grass and rough-edged palmetto.

A gentle flow of water, just a few inches deep but 50 miles wide, moved southward down the barely measurable gradient from the lake, as if it were really downhill all the way to the equator. In all of Florida there is no hill higher than 345 feet above sea level, and in the Everglades a 3-foot-high elevation has to be regarded as a natural feature.

A relatively new adjunct to the North American landmass, Florida joined it as the seas receded during the last Ice Age. Deep beneath the ground lie what were once the foothills of the Appalachian Mountains. On these have been deposited, layer upon layer, the tiny skeletons of the marine animals which form the limestone shelf that supports the Everglades' fauna and flora.

The nearest similar formation of any size is the Yucatan peninsula of Mexico. Here, as there, sinkholes are a feature, and so are hurricanes. The Everglades can expect to suffer severe damage at least once every five years in the hurricane season between July and November. The mangrove forests have been among the worst victims: the course of Hurricane Donna in 1960 can still be traced through them, and the experienced eye can even discern the path of the 1935 Labor Day hurricane.

As might be expected, the trees of the coastal forests, the thousands of islandlike hammocks found amid the interior's saw grass prairie, and the stretches of slightly higher rocky terrain have a mixture of origins. Hurricanes twisting across the Caribbean before they hit Florida brought the seeds of most of the plants found on the shore and on the hammocks. Trees in the swamps have often come from low-lying regions on the northern edge of the Gulf of Mexico. Pines and palms flourish in the drier conditions among the rocks. Other trees are more recent arrivals: coconut palms, feathery casuarinas from Australia, Brazilian peppers, sappodillas (the source of chicle for chewing gum), and many tropical fruit trees.

Some native species of trees have been sadly depleted. The Spanish, who first

***Mile after mile of saw grass** (left) covers the glades and gives rise to the Indian name of "grassy water." It is not, in fact, a true grass, but a sharp-edged reed that stands with its roots deep in the water. The reeds can grow to a height of 10 to 15 feet.*

*The saw grass marshland on the northern and eastern plains of the Everglades is dotted with salt prairies and low islands, or hammocks, where palms, pines, live oaks, and cypresses grow. Despite heavy rainfall between June and October, winter and spring can be so dry that water disappears into the underlying porous rock.*

settled Florida, logged the tallest mahogany trees for their highly prized furniture wood. Buttonwood (so-called because of the shape of its seeds) was cut and burned for charcoal, and pines and black ironwood were valued for their durability as building material in the insect-rich swamps.

Humans, hurricanes, dry season fires, and the prospect of rising sea levels all present dangers to the Everglades. Of these, humans are certainly the most immediate threat. Henry Flagler's remarkable railroad along Florida's east coast, which was completed when it reached Key West in 1912, encouraged the region's development and transformed the Florida Keys by linking them to the mainland.

The Spanish, who arrived in the 16th century, had been the first to plant the orange trees that have become Florida's vegetable gold, but apart from a change of ownership and Flagler's railroad, development in the four centuries since then had

## The mangroves

Mangrove forests are the natural protectors of muddy tropical coastlines. Their unusual above-ground root system allows them to tolerate the badly oxygenated soils and also helps to anchor them on Florida's hurricane-ravaged coast. There are three types of mangrove—red, black, and white—and each has its own particular place in the shoreline ecology.

The red mangrove likes shallow salt water and spreads out into the sea. Its curving aerial prop roots guarantee the aeration of the entire root system. The roots also form a tough web which traps silt and, in time, creates a barrier against the sea behind which other plants can grow. The reddish color of the roots gives this tree its name.

The black variety of mangrove grows in the tidal zones. This tree displays the well-known clusters of breathing pores which project into the air from the roots so the tree can breathe during high tides and floods. As the name suggests, the trunks are black.

The white mangrove is the least addicted to salt water of the three varieties and usually grows farther inland. It has few breathing pores and no prop roots. It gets its name from the light color of the bark.

The mangrove region supports raccoons, which feed on the coon oyster, roundtail muskrats, snakes, sea turtles, and tree snails, as well as the rarely seen manatee, a gentle walruslike animal also called a sea cow (left).

This harmless creature, which can be up to 15 feet long, feeds at night, foraging by touch and smell. Its diet is quite varied since it eats any sort of vegetation, often taking in small invertebrate animals with the plants. Pink shrimp, crab, snapper, redfish, and trout also share the watery habitat.

been as sluggish as the summer climate.

Even as late as the 1960s, Florida was still considered an economic loser when set beside the richer states farther north. But as North Americans became more and more addicted to orange juice and winter sunshine, the nation's rapidly growing cities provided markets for growers who could produce all year round.

By the 1980s, Florida was producing three-fourths of North America's oranges and grapefruit. South of Lake Okeechobee, canals drained the rich peaty soil to allow the large-scale production of tomatoes, sugar cane, and vegetables.

During the first half of the 1980s, the Fort Myers-Cape Coral metropolitan area, due west of Lake Okeechobee, was the fastest-growing urban conglomeration in the United States. North of Miami, unbroken urban development stretched for 100 miles, much of it catering for an aging generation who wanted a view of the sunrise (and sunshine to follow) for the rest of their days. Between 1970 and 1985, Florida watched its population grow by more than 40 percent.

None of this growth was good news for alligators and the arboreal inhabitants of the "grassy water." The influx of people and crops of vegetables and orange trees needed water as much as they did, and, moreover, had first call on it.

Marjorie Stoneman Douglas's 1947 book on the Everglades awakened Americans to the fact that these tropical swamps were a unique and priceless ecological jewel. The threat to this precious habitat inspired President Truman to declare the southern end a park in 1947. The protected area was enlarged when the 570,000-acre Big Cypress National Preserve was created on the northwest boundary of the park in 1974.

So far, the Everglades have managed to maintain a substantial part of their integrity as a wilderness. They will continue to do so only as long as their human neighbors value them more as a natural asset than as potential real estate.

***This sleepy alligator*** *(below) is a powerful amphibious carnivore that can grow up to 18 feet long. Tender in its mating habits, the male will stay with the female for several days, stroking her body with his forelimbs.*

*The female then finds a nest site near water and scrapes up plant material with sweeping movements of her body and tail. She packs the vegetation into a mound with a cavity for the eggs, which she guards while they incubate. The hatching young call out to her when they are ready to be freed from their nest.*

***The stunning zebra butterfly*** *(above) belongs to the* Heliconius *genus, more usually found in Central and South America. These delicate insects fly in and around dense forest areas, and their caterpillars feed on the foliage of passion flowers.*

***Steamy swamps*** *(left) evoke a mysterious atmosphere of prehistoric times. The dense, moist forests provide a perfect environment for aerial gardens of ferns and orchids. Air plants, or epiphytes, grow on host trees, but draw their moisture from the surrounding atmosphere. Rooting plants have only a thin mantle of marl and peat above the limestone basin on which to support themselves.*

# Hurricane Power

***Awesome North Atlantic hurricanes*** *begin as simple rainstorms in the Trade Winds off the West African coast when the ocean temperature exceeds 80.6°F. As a storm travels westward, its winds turn in on themselves and funnel upward, creating the characteristic swirling pattern of a hurricane.*

***The force of Hurricane Hugo*** *was so great when it swept through Charleston, South Carolina, that sailboats were picked up from a sales lot and dropped in the center of a road (left).*

*Coastal properties are battered with the full force of hurricane winds when the mighty storms make land (right). As well as the destruction to property, trees that have survived hundreds of years are uprooted with apparently effortless ease.*

*These rotating storms about 500 miles across have a distinctive cloud-free eye some 10 to 25 miles in diameter, around which blow violent winds. Roughly 80 to 100 of these storms form over the oceans each year, causing about $10 billion worth of damage.*

SWIRLING TROPICAL CYCLONES over the Atlantic Ocean with winds of at least 75 miles an hour are called hurricanes. Only a small percentage of the ocean storms ever develop enough speed and force to reach land, but when they do, they leave behind a trail of death and destruction worth billions of dollars. Similar storms have different names around the world. Over the western Pacific Ocean they are called typhoons, while over the Indian Ocean and around Australia the term is cyclones. It is difficult to predict hurricanes' behavior patterns.

KENTUCKY

# MAMMOTH CAVE

LIMESTONE CAVES HAVE A BEAUTY and mystery which make caves in other rock formations seem like murky holes in the ground. They twist and wind endlessly, varying in size from aircraft hangars to rabbit holes, mimicking both nature and art with frozen waterfalls, organ pipes, and stone flowers. Their rivers—an essential part of them—are as calm and pure as any water on Earth, and the caves' intricacy challenges the mapmaker's stamina as well as his skill. Mammoth Cave, 90 miles south of Louisville, Kentucky, is the largest of these labyrinths, twice the size of its nearest rival, the Holloch System in Switzerland.

Since limestone cave systems are so complex and difficult to explore, Mammoth's claim to being the biggest carried a cautionary question mark for many years. Then in 1972, an extremely slim spelunker, Patricia Crowther, answered the question by squeezing through a tight little tunnel that proved that the neighboring Flint Ridge system was joined to the Mammoth.

Since then, other intrepid explorers have found numerous new passages and crevices. The total length of the known system is now around 225 miles, and another 500 miles may still await exploration. Bob Houchins, the hunter who stumbled across the entrance around 1797 while pursuing a wounded bear, discovered a great deal more than he might ever have imagined.

Like so many modern discoverers of the world's wonders, Houchins was really a rediscoverer. The Indians beat him to the caves, probably by more than 3,200 years. Some ventured more than 2 miles from the entrance, leaving traces of soot and the charred remains of the canes and weed-stalks they used as torches as evidence of their presence.

Several mummified Indian bodies have been found in the caves. In 1875, the leader of the discovery party inscribed on the rock nearby: "Sir, I have found one of the grat wonders of the world in this cave, whitch is a muma . . . [*sic*]" An outraged contemporary scratched his response: "How are you grave robbers . . . They is nothing too mean for you to do. You low down scoundrels . . . P.S. Call again you honest fellows when you get hard up for a few dimes or call at some other grave yard [*sic*]." Another mummy, "Lost John," discovered in 1935 two miles from the entrance, had been killed by a falling rock.

Miners next became interested in Mammoth because of the nitrate deposits created over the course of millennia from the droppings of the caves' four bat species. The British blockade of American ports in the war of 1812 caused a serious shortage of

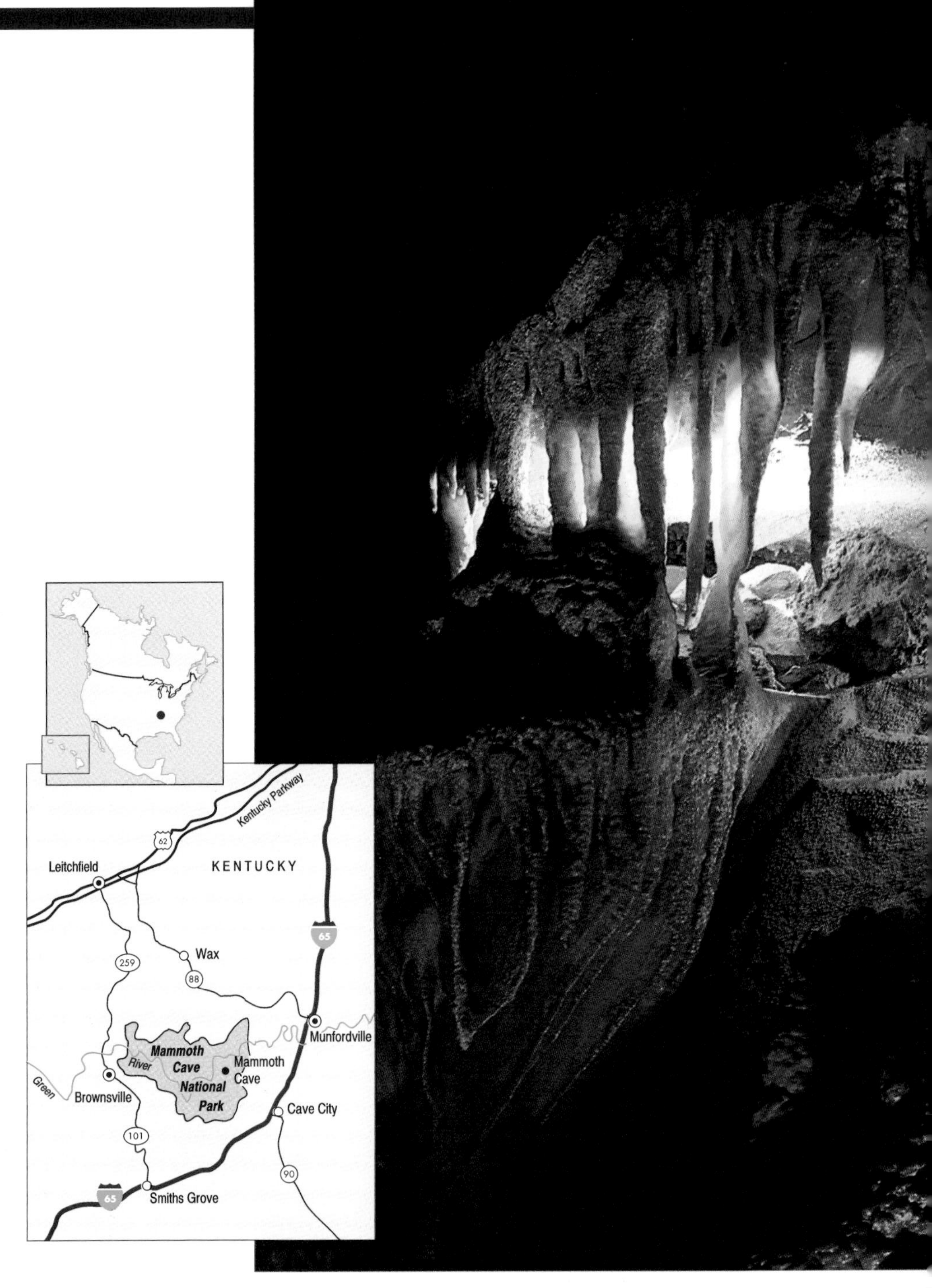


***Mother Nature's glorious sculptures*** *of limestone stalactites (hanging downward) and stalagmites (growing upward) dazzle visitors to Mammoth Cave (right). They take millions of years to form; rainwater seeping through the cave roof leaves small amounts of minerals which gradually build up.*

***Shimmering white gypsum crystal formations*** *are one of the spectacles adorning the cave's drier walls, ceilings, and floors. Some crystals develop flowerlike petals (left) or delicate spokes that resemble needles. Part of the wonder of these formations is in appreciating that no two are alike.*

saltpeter, which was needed for the manufacture of gunpowder. Mammoth's contribution of nitrates was transformed into almost half the saltpeter used in the war. The leaching vats, pipes, and other equipment are displayed. The caves have also been used for weddings and the staging of plays, concerts, and opera. Jenny Lind, the Swedish soprano, sang here, and Edwin Booth, the famous Shakespearean actor, performed here, too.

Visitors can choose from a number of tours of varying lengths. The Historic Cave Tour, which covers past and modern uses of the caves, is led by guides who are themselves part of the cave's tradition. When Mammoth was opened to paying tourists in 1838, its first guide was a black slave, 17-year-old Stephen Bishop. Two other slaves replaced him when he died in 1859, and since then each generation of guides has passed its unique knowledge of the caves to its successors.

Few visitors want to miss the cruise on Echo River, 360 feet below ground, which is as close to a trip down the mythical Styx as can be found in the 20th century. The river's crayfish share the waters with remarkable blind fish. These fish are finger-length and almost transparent, and their vestigial eyes have become mere lumps on their heads. They have large, almost winglike fins and use their senses like radar to guide them toward food. In the cave's sterile environment, food arrives courtesy of the spring floods, which raise the water level by 30 to 40 feet and carry a modest amount of edible debris.

Mammoth's spectacles include well-lit grottoes of stalactites (hanging downward) and stalagmites (growing upward); Mammoth Dome (a superb example of cave architecture) and the Rotunda; and Frozen Niagara, where the calcium carbonate carried in the water that seeps across the tumbled rock has been fossilized into fringed sheets of flowstone. Snowball Room owes its name and attraction to the crust of gypsum on the rock that has thickened in places into "snowballs." Some of these eventually break open into petals.

Privately owned caves near Mammoth, such as Cave City, feature onyx formations of great beauty and variety. Kentucky Diamond Caverns and Jesse James Cave, where the fugitive outlaw and his gang lived—unknowingly—with the occupants of an ancient Indian burial ground discovered in 1963 are also nearby.

Mammoth Cave National Park, which

***Well-lit giant vertical shafts,*** *called pits (right), show how the cave's limestone walls have been carved and shaped by groundwater seeping downward.*

*Mammoth's natural mystery is palpably evident to visitors (left), and the size and beauty of some of the caverns is awe-inspiring. Certainly the early Indians explored these caves, perhaps out of curiosity, perhaps for some religious reason, or perhaps to extract minerals. They extracted gypsum from the caves to trade with other communities which may have been used to make paint and plaster. They also extracted mirabilite and epsomite. But they stopped using the caves more than a thousand years ago.*

941, covers 51,000 set in the biggest the United States. l structure, known as estone with streams it and sinkholes like ave collapsed below the surface are two estone; the older Ste. kin is topped by Big en rain, which con-, sinks through the mestone, it forms a nic acid that over the k fissures and carves

running for 20 miles e valley it has cut, the places by water that the plateau.

**Subterranean dwellers**

After thousands of years in total darkness, fish, shrimp, crayfish, crickets, spiders, and beetles in Mammoth Cave have evolved differently from their aboveground relations. These underground creatures no longer have eyes; instead they use extra-sensitive organs to navigate their way through the cool, dark waterways and to find food.

The eerie transparent appearance of the crayfish (left) and eyeless fish (right) is because their color pigments ceased to exist centuries ago, as a result of living in total darkness.

GEORGIA, FLORIDA

# OKEFENOKEE SWAMP

ALLIGATORS ARE OFF the Okefenokee Swamp's endangered species list, which is good news for conservationists, but not exactly encouraging for beavers and otters. The beavers appeared on the records here for the first time in 1969, but vanished later; the U.S. Fish and Wildlife Service thinks they were devoured by the alligators. The otters still survive, but visitors are unlikely to see much of them unless they visit the swamp in winter, when the cold makes the alligators torpid and the otters relax a little.

As for the likelihood of *Alligator mississippiensis* snatching two-legged prey paddling a canoe on the waterways or enjoying the nature trails (swimming is prohibited), the wildlife service is reassuring: visitors need not worry about alligators or snakes (of which there are 37 species in the swamp), if they take normal precautions, stay on approved paths, and avoid disturbing the creatures and their nests. In any case, alligators feed mainly on fish, turtles, and other aquatic life.

The Okefenokee Swamp is 600 square miles or roughly the size of Rhode Island, and the four-fifths of it protected by the Department of the Interior constitutes the largest wildlife refuge in the eastern United States. Visitors are welcome—about 350,000 come here every year—but, except for fishermen and seasonal deer hunters, they are strictly confined to observer status by an administration whose declared mission is to provide an "optimum habitat" for the wildlife it protects.

The emphasis is on education rather than recreation. Visitors cannot go anywhere they wish at any time (apart from other considerations, it is easy to get lost), and camping within the refuge is permitted only on overnight canoe trips, which must have authorization. Those who wish to camp overnight should try the 82-acre Stephen C. Foster State Park next to the refuge's west entrance.

Substantial stretches of the refuge's dry land form islands (70 of them larger than 20 acres), but they make up only 8 percent of an area measuring 38 miles from north to

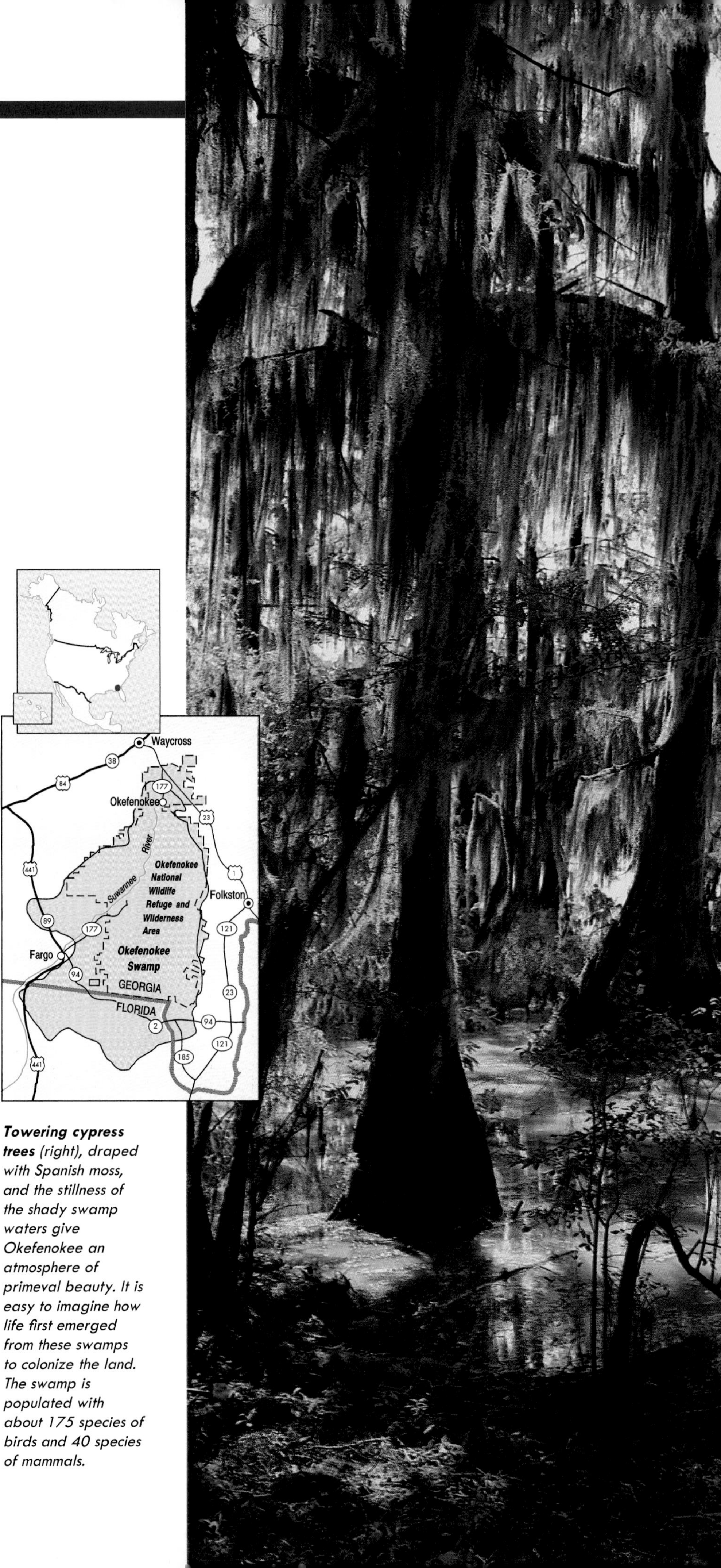


***Towering cypress trees*** *(right), draped with Spanish moss, and the stillness of the shady swamp waters give Okefenokee an atmosphere of primeval beauty. It is easy to imagine how life first emerged from these swamps to colonize the land. The swamp is populated with about 175 species of birds and 40 species of mammals.*

south and 25 miles east to west. Walking trails are short, and most people get to know the swamp by taking a guided boat tour, either by day or night.

Stephen C. Foster was a composer, but he never saw the Swanee (properly, Suwannee) River, much less its source, the Okefenokee Swamp. He wrote his songs in Pennsylvania and Ohio and only visited the South once, in 1852. He chose the river for "Way down upon the Swanee River" because the name fitted his music so well.

The Suwannee is the principal outlet for the swamp, whose gentle tilt guides its flow to the Gulf of Mexico and directs the smaller St. Marys River toward the Atlantic. The tilt amounts to a 25-foot drop from the northeast to the southwest, so the water moves easily through the reedy prairies and channels.

Nowhere is the swamp water much more than 8 feet deep; its average depth is about 2 feet. The swamp can dry out, but the construction of a low earthen dam across the Suwannee near the point where it leaves the refuge has helped maintain the water level as well as reducing the number of serious fires.

The bed of the swamp is part of the ancient seabed created when the shoreline of the Gulf of Mexico was north of the present Florida-Georgia state line. The ocean retreated, and fresh water filled the shallow depression that over the years had accumulated peat deep enough for substantial trees to root in it.

The peat islands gave the swamp its Choctaw name, Okefenokee, which means Land of the Trembling Earth. The average thickness of the peat is between 5 and 10 feet, but in places its depth is more than 15 feet. It grows at the rate of about 2 inches a century. In places, gases caused by decomposing vegetable matter have forced the peat above the water level in what are known locally as "blow-ups."

People once believed that the swamp received a substantial amount of its water from springs, but 95 percent of it is now thought to come from rain—60 inches in an average year. Some 80 percent of it returns to the atmosphere through evaporation and transpiration from the vegetation; the rest leaves through the Suwannee and St. Marys rivers.

Deeper patches of water known as lakes account for 500 acres of the swamp; marshy prairies make up another 60,500 acres, 21 percent of the total. The prairies were forested until drought fires devastated them, burning the top layers of the peat as well as the trees and bushes. Nature's checks and balances swung into action: woodpeckers lost their homes, but the prairies became great places for seeing wading birds, especially cranes, ibises, herons, and, with luck, bitterns. Sandhill cranes are numerous; some nest in the swamp, while others are winter visitors that nest in the north. Wood storks, considered an endangered species, are common in the summer and fall.

Winters can be cold, but essentially the swamp is subtropical. Shrub swamp covers a third of the area and forests of black gum, bay, and pond cypress nearly half. In the

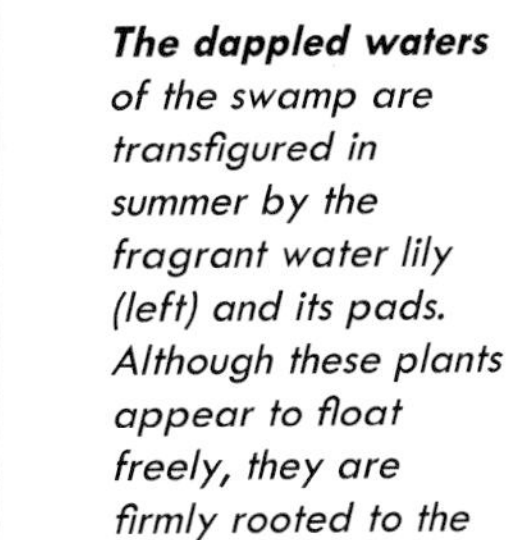

***The bony plates*** *along the backs of these alligators (above) show clearly above the swamp water. The large teeth near the front of the jaw, used for grasping prey, fit neatly into bony pits in the upper jaw.*

***The dappled waters*** *of the swamp are transfigured in summer by the fragrant water lily (left) and its pads. Although these plants appear to float freely, they are firmly rooted to the peat of the swamp floor.*

forests, the red-cockaded woodpecker, one of the more exotic rarities on the endangered list, can sometimes be spotted. It is the cypresses that put their stamp on the scene—tall, elongated pyramids lifting themselves above the blackish water.

At the beginning of this century, their value as timber led to the reign of the "cypress kings," the Hebard family, who between 1909 and 1927 exhausted the best forest and cut trees over 900 years old to build an estimated 42,000 houses. They did considerably better financially than their immediate predecessors, the proprietors of the Suwannee Canal Company, who lost a fortune in the 1890s trying to drain the swamp for agriculture.

The eastern entrance of the refuge gives access to an 11-mile length of the canal, which, along with the lumbering operations, eventually revealed the swamp's resilience and its ability to regenerate itself quickly. The Hebards converted their property into a private hunting and fishing reserve and, in 1936, sold it to the federal government, which established it as a wildlife refuge the following year.

The lake and ponds—the latter are known as "gator holes"—support sizable fish, including largemouth bass, pickerel, and gar. But among the 36 species of fish found in the swamp, the great majority are extremely small. The killifish, the smallest fish in North America, grows hardly more than an inch long, and the swamp holds huge numbers of pygmy sunfish, topminnows, and mosquito fish as well.

Island homes of the vanished race of swampers are open to visitors, who can discover what it must have been like to live in the swamp. Billys Island was named for the last Indian chief in the swamp, Billy Bow-Legs, and farmed in the last half of the 19th century by the Lee family. It was also the railhead and administrative center for the Hebards' lumbering operation.

Chesser Island provides a more detailed, homespun account of a swamper's life. The island is named for the last family to own it privately before the United States government bought it. Visitors to their house, built at the end of the 1920s, can watch demonstrations of beekeeping, meat-smoking, and chair-caning. The Chesser family moved to the more modern comforts of nearby Folkston in 1958.

TENNESSEE, NORTH CAROLINA

# GREAT SMOKY MOUNTAINS

NEAR THE SOUTHERN END OF THEIR RANGE, the hazy, slumbering mountains of Appalachia stretch and exert themselves a little to form the Great Smokies. Although they can boast 16 summits of more than 6,000 feet, the Smokies' charm rests less on grandeur than on their restful serenity. The forest softens the ridges, the mist is opalescent and unthreatening, and the rise to the top of the highest point, Clingman's Dome, is gentle.

The Smokies may lack the bare-rock magnificence of the West, but they are nevertheless the most popular national park in the United States. Around nine million visitors arrive every year to enjoy their cascading streams, lofty slopes, and—perhaps above all—the peace and tranquillity of their forests.

Nine million people in automobiles and campers might not sound very peaceful, but the Great Smoky Mountains are 60 miles long by 20 miles wide, and 95 percent of the visitors stick close to their vehicles and the 170 miles of paved road. You do not have to be exceptionally adventurous or athletic to leave your car and find solitude and silence on the hundreds of miles of walking and riding trails, including the Appalachian Trail.

The Smokies lay claim to being the largest virgin forest in the eastern United States. About 40 percent of the park has never been touched by loggers, whose damage to the remainder is being steadily repaired, and it has been designated an International Biosphere Reserve. It is probably North America's most varied natural arboretum. Nourished by generous rainfall and subtropical warmth in summer, nature has spread itself with more than usual generosity on these slopes, and there are more tree species to be seen here than in all of northern Europe.

In the East, the types of trees generally change with the latitude. So, visitors who do not have four months to spend hiking the Appalachian Trail from Georgia to

*The soft haze that hangs over the Great Smoky Mountains (right) speaks gently of its rich interior. Transpiration from the huge variety of trees is thought to account for the misty character for which the area is named. Under the cathedral-like canopy, nature reigns supreme.*

***In their eagerness to find food,*** *black bears (left), which weigh between 265 and 330 pounds, climb up trees and out onto the branches. It was recently discovered that bears sometimes make their dens in hollow trees 20 to 50 feet above ground.*

*Most bears sleep from December to March, emerging in April to search for squawroot, grass, and insect grubs. In summer, they seek blackberries and blueberries in the oak and pine woods.*

***The cascades and waterfalls*** *of the Smokies (right) provide a perfect environment for salamanders and aquatic insects. At night, raccoons search the streams in the hope of finding a tasty green frog, crayfish, or mussel.*

Maine can cover the same arboreal ground by walking from Cades Cove to the top of Clingman's Dome. They start with the magnolias and work up to a northern spruce forest without even taking a backpack.

The famous mists give the mountains their name. A convergence of warm and cold airstreams produces the condensation, but the trees contribute by exhaling their own hydrocarbonic breath full of aromatic terpenes, the gases drawn from their oils and resins.

Among the Smokies' chief delights are the coves, sheltered hollows or flattish stretches of land where the soil is deeper and more fertile, and its moisture content more stable, than elsewhere. In them, a great number of trees can live happily side by side. You know you are in a cove, say the botanists, when you find 20 to 25 species of hardwood trees mingling their leaves in the canopy overhead.

Coves are sometimes created out of abandoned farmland, but many may be far older. The tree species certainly are; some are found as fossils in rocks of the Cretaceous age, during which magnolias and beeches made their first appearance. The geology of the Smokies is complex and dominated by faults, with Precambrian rocks from the first span of geologic time thrusting northward over relatively latecomer Paleozoics. The first comprehensive geological history of the region was not produced until the 1960s.

A hiker climbing from the coves toward the mountaintops will soon find the forest changing. The shortleaf and pitch pines which thrive in hot, dry parts of the lower slopes thin out and eventually disappear. The buckeyes and maples become scarcer, magnolias get smaller. Hickories and oaks take over, along with thickets of mountain laurel and clumps of rhododendron, and in

### The first land vertebrates

Salamanders were the first group of vertebrates to colonize the land. Perhaps 200 million years ago, lobed-fin fishes began to move out of their water habitats and onto the land. The development of amphibians had begun. Salamanders are modern amphibians that have kept their fishlike swimming movements in water. On land, the body is lifted off the ground and supported on four limbs.

The most successful group of living salamanders includes lungless salamanders such as the dusky (top left) and spring (below) salamanders. They obtain oxygen across their moist skin or through the inside of their mouth, both of which are generously supplied with blood vessels. Dusky salamanders have pairs of yellow or red spots on the back, but these fade as they grow older. Spring salamanders are some of the largest and have various color and pattern combinations.

The marbled salamander (bottom left) is part of the mole salamander family. They are ground-living and rarely seen outside the breeding season.

some places there are stretches of fairly open oak forest.

The mountainside is rich in mosses and ferns. Eventually, on the slopes above 4,000 feet, the domain of spruce and fir is reached—the black, glum forest familiar to northerners, but scented and cool and immensely quiet except where the wind rushes through its branches on the ridges.

Animals, like vegetables, favor warm, well-watered places and leave the austere heights to species hardy enough to survive on them. On ancient farmland there are meadowlarks, with their startling yellow breasts, and bobwhites, endearing birds, particularly when they whistle their bob-bob-white at an intruder. Occasionally, there are wild turkeys, lean, limber birds in contrast to their domesticated relatives.

There are acrobatic chickadees to be found at all levels, ovenbirds singing their uninspiring song in the shrubs, warblers, woodpeckers in profusion (including, sometimes, the red-crested pileated variety, which feels happiest in large tracts of deciduous forest), red-eyed vireos, veerys, and Carolina wrens.

The birds here do not differ from the birds found anywhere else in the south. But the salamanders do. The Smokies are a salamander metropolis in a country which contains 82 species, a world record. No fewer than 30 varieties live on the Appalachian plateau, a region as near to paradise as a salamander can find, and some of them, like the black-bellied, the pygmy, Jordan's, and the yonahlossee, are found only in and around the Smokies. Salamanders live in trees, on cliffsides, in streams, wells, caves, and at altitudes of over 6,000 feet. Some are blind, and some species are lungless.

Salamanders (unlike lizards) are amphibious, so searching for them usually entails lifting rocks and logs in damp places. Like the beech trees, they are long established residents of the Smokies, having been around since the Cretaceous period. Those who study salamanders grow lyrical when writing of them: ". . . dryads, naiads and oreads the Greeks would have called them," declares one authority in the course of lamenting their neglect by the public.

In the streams and rivers noted for their purity live more than 70 species of fish, including catfish, chubs, minnows, shiners, dace, suckers, sculpins, darters,

***The delicate phlox*** *(above) joins a host of about 200 species of wildflowers on display from spring onward. August sees wild clematis, monkshood, and blue gentian, while goldenrod, ironweed, and asters bloom right through to early October.*

***Meigs Overlook*** *(right) unfurls its most glorious colors. The presence of hardwood species, more often seen in northern areas, makes the fall even more fantastic. The reds of the maple, the yellow beech, and the deeper shades of oaks blend with the southern species to provide a many-hued blanket.*

and lamprey.But chief among them are the trout which thrive in fast-flowing, clean streams. Brook trout, in particular, can be used as an indicator of clean water levels, since they need the purest water to survive.

Humans have not been kind to many of the animal inhabitants of the Smokies. The Cherokee hunted the bison to extinction, and white men wiped out the elk, beaver, wolf, and cougar. Bears took a pounding, too. Beavers have been reintroduced, and there are occasional reports of cougars being sighted (as there are from practically every well-wooded region of the eastern United States).

The large animals that have done exceptionally well under the National Parks Service's regime are white-tailed deer and bears, which thrive on the berries, grasses, roots, and grubs which the Smokies provide in abundance.

An unwelcome European immigrant is the wild boar, which has been present in the park since several escaped from a game reserve in the early 1920s. The damage that they have caused by rooting up the soil in search of bulbs and tubers to eat has been blamed for reducing the number of wildflowers such as spring beauty and wake robin. Smaller creatures, which are plentiful, include gray and red squirrels, skunks, possums, and raccoons.

Like the wild boar, humankind has had a somewhat checkered career in the Smokies. The Cherokee were either bought out or chased out by Europeans and finally deported to Oklahoma (but they now have a reserve next to the park).

The farming introduced on the heels of the Indians' departure wasted the natural resources, but affected only a small part of the area. It was the logging, which began in earnest in 1900, that caused most damage and aroused the conservationists.

In the late 1920s, Tennessee and North Carolina, backed by John D. Rockefeller, who donated half the $10 million required, began buying out the loggers, the farmers, and the people who owned summer homes. The devastated mountainsides are covered with trees once more, and the Japanese magnolias have taken root in the old fields by the streams. The Smokies have become an accessible wilderness, and anyone who visits the park would be churlish not to be profoundly grateful.

GEORGIA

# STONE MOUNTAIN

Stone Mountain looks as if it was thrust into the world exactly as it appears today, as a great bubble of molten magma that was blown through the Earth's crust and cooled amid the green foam of the trees. However, geologists have a different explanation. Forced toward the surface 300 million years ago by tremendous pressure, the molten rock of Stone Mountain cooled while still buried beneath a 2-mile overlay of the Earth. Gradually the overlay was eroded, and the world's largest dome of exposed granite emerged into the sunlight.

By turning surface moisture into explosive steam, lightning has pitted its smoothness in places. Quarrymen have chipped away its granite (to build Tokyo's Imperial Hotel and the locks of the Panama Canal among other things), and rain and the feet of thousands of tourists have left their mark. But since the surrounding plateau is still eroding, Stone Mountain's looming bulk grows more dominant all the time. At present, it rises 700 feet above the plateau and is 7 miles in circumference.

Its first European visitor was a Spaniard, Captain Juan Pardo, who arrived in 1567. The dome's glittering quartz impressed Pardo so much that he thought he had found a new El Dorado. He named the place Crystal Mountain and reported that it was littered with diamonds and rubies, but since he did not bring back any samples, no one rushed to stake a claim. The dome received no further publicity until a British officer published an account of its natural splendor in London in 1788. It quickly became a regional landmark, and two years later George Washington's emissary summoned the chiefs of the Creek Indians there to arrange for the signing of a peace treaty.

By the 1820s, the surrounding land had been settled by white farmers, and Stone Mountain had come to be regarded as "the great natural curiosity of the neighborhood." All were impressed by the breast-high stone wall that encircled the summit, which had probably outlined a sacred precinct of an ancient Indian culture. However, local residents took to rolling the

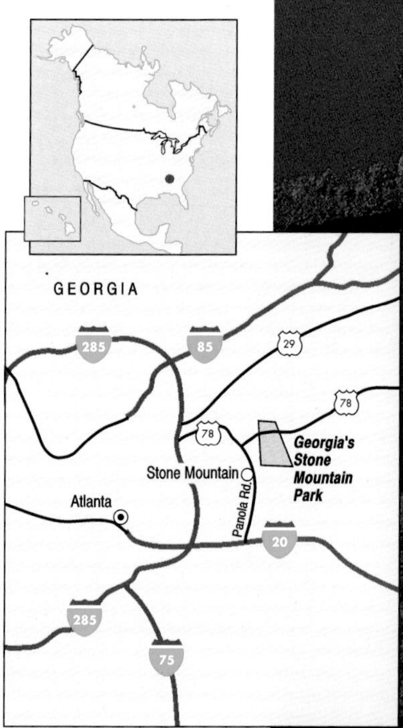


***Stone Mountain** (above) holds many a surprise; the dark gray color of the mountain is not granite, but lichens which grow over the weathered stone. During the rainy season, fairy shrimp live in freshwater pools that collect in eroded depressions on the mountainside.*

**Battle of stone**

Atlanta has always reveled in outsized gestures, so it is not surprising that in 1915 the United Daughters of the Confederacy chose Stone Mountain as the site for a memorial to the Old South. Finishing the project, however, turned into a battle of a different kind.

From the start, no one could agree on the design. The sculptor, Gutzon Borglum, began work in 1923 on the mounted figure of General Lee leading his army. The owners of the mountain, the Venables family, set a deadline of 1928. By 1925, at odds with his patrons, Borglum's contract

was canceled, whereupon he smashed his models and left. His successor, Augustus Lukeman, began work on his own designs, but with valuable time lost, the deadline arrived, and the Venables reclaimed their mountain.

For 36 years, no further work was done until 1963 when Walter Kirtland Hancock, whose family roots reached back to the Confederacy, was commissioned to finish the monument. Carved 400 feet up the mountainside, the scene measures 90 by 190 feet and, where it is most deeply carved, reaches a depth of 11 feet 6 inches into the stone.

wall's rocks down the dome for fun, so what remained of the wall was completely removed in 1923.

One of Stone Mountain's flowers, *Amphianthus pusillus*, a member of the snapdragon family, has a an erratic existence, vanishing in drought and blooming when rain falls. The yellow confederate daisy, which grows wherever the soil in the rock's crevices is deep enough to give it a foothold, is even more spectacular, and *Hypericum splendens*, a waist-high shrub, is unique to the mountain.

GEORGIA, NORTH CAROLINA, VIRGINIA, PENNSYLVANIA

# BLUE RIDGE MOUNTAINS

GEOLOGISTS STATE THAT THE OLD APPALACHIANS are a clearly defined ridge 1.1 billion years old. It runs southwest and northeast, from 50 miles north of Atlanta at one end to near Carlisle, Pennsylvania, at the other, with Roanoke more or less in the middle.

Along the ridge runs the world's longest scenic drive, an acme of automotive pleasure stretching from the Great Smokies to Shenandoah National Park along 470 miles of the Blue Ridge Parkway and 105 miles of the Skyline Drive through the Shenandoah. Even if the road was built as a sort of linear viewing station, it still provides the feeling of being on top of the world, of wandering along the ridgepole of eastern North America.

Commonly thought of as the backbone of the eastern United States, the Blue Ridge Mountains start on a modest scale, rising out of Pennsylvania in a long, low ridge. As they travel south, they rise steadily, reaching their peak, 5,983 feet, at Grandfather Mountain in North Carolina. In the Black Mountains part of the Blue Ridge stands majestic Mount Mitchell, at 6,684 feet the highest peak east of the Mississippi River.

Like much of the Appalachian chain, the Blue Ridge was created in gigantic folds when movement in the Earth's crust crumpled the sedimentary rock. Their uplift continued until about 280 million years ago; since then, the effects of erosion have greatly reduced the range.

It was, of course, the first frontier for the English-speaking settlers of North America, a barrier to westward expansion that offered their wagon trains no convenient water gaps south of Roanoke. The delectable valley of the Shenandoah remains as the pioneers found it, with fold upon fold of green crests melting into the Alleghenies. The scene is unchanged today, but feelings about it have been shaped, perhaps sentimentalized, by a mixture of myth and history. It has become the domain of American folklore, of fiddles and quilting bees and drift mines.

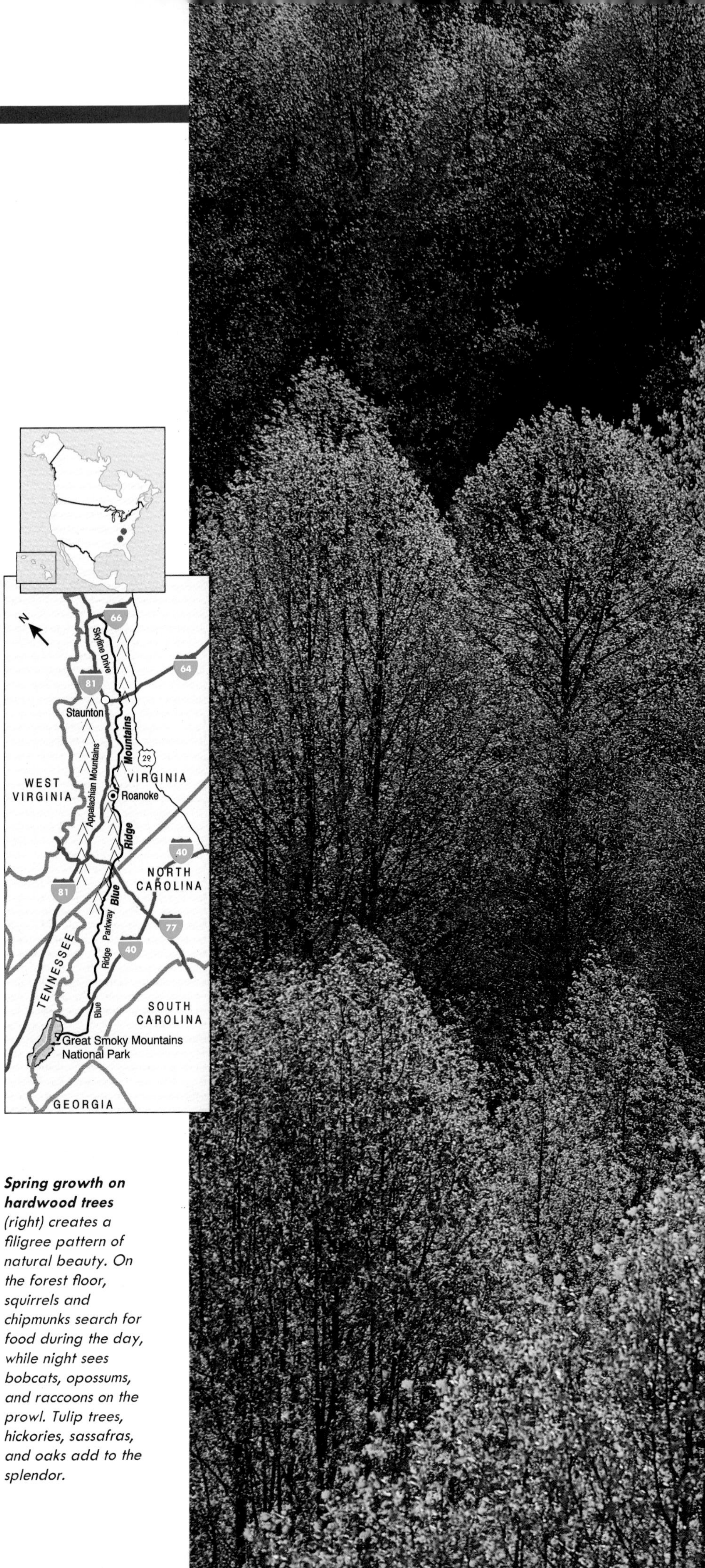


***Spring growth on hardwood trees*** *(right) creates a filigree pattern of natural beauty. On the forest floor, squirrels and chipmunks search for food during the day, while night sees bobcats, opossums, and raccoons on the prowl. Tulip trees, hickories, sassafras, and oaks add to the splendor.*

Looking across the Piedmont provides a view of a very different world, one that holds bureaucratic Washington, Richmond, tobacco fields, and great chemical industries. That way lies the heartland of the old Confederate South and Monticello, the home designed for himself by the economy-minded Thomas Jefferson, third president of the United States.

Harper's Ferry is the place where the Potomac River is joined by the Shenandoah and breaks through the ridge to flow down to Chesapeake Bay and the Atlantic. The river races through the gorge at such a pace here that George Washington used its force to power the new republic's first arms factory. During the Civil War, its strategic importance caused it to change hands several times. The abolitionist John Brown made an abortive attempt to seize weapons from the Harper's Ferry Armory in 1859; he was captured by Colonel Robert E. Lee and later hanged.

Front Royal is the gateway to Shenandoah National Park and Skyline Drive, which was built by unemployed mountain men during the Depression. Life was harsh for them, and the land had taken a buffeting from their scratch-farming methods, as it had from logging. The chestnut blight that had come from Asia took its toll, too, and by the 1920s the trees that had once been the glory of the mountains had shriveled to a forlorn army of dead trunks.

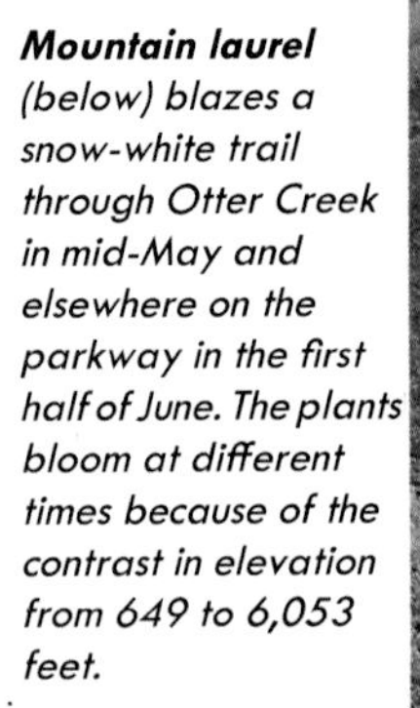

***Mountain laurel*** *(below) blazes a snow-white trail through Otter Creek in mid-May and elsewhere on the parkway in the first half of June. The plants bloom at different times because of the contrast in elevation from 649 to 6,053 feet.*

***Mount Pisgah,*** *(right) once part of the George Vanderbilt estate, now forms the 5,721-foot focus of Pisgah National Forest. Foliage is at its most glorious in October, when the leaves range from vivid red and orange to subtle russet and maroon.*

*In the spring, flowering shrubs compete with the memory of the fall display. Flame azalea bushes, heads of purple catawba rhododendron, and white blooms of mountain laurel harmonize with wild bergamot, lilies, and black-eyed Susan.*

**Ringtailed bandit**

With its dark black eye "mask" and its ringed tail, the raccoon is an ever-popular character with cartoonists and children's storybook writers. Familiar to residents throughout continental United States, the raccoon can be seen in its natural habitat all along the Blue Ridge Mountains.

The abundance of fish in the rivers and lakes and the fruits, berries, and other plant food means these endearing little animals thrive in these heavily wooded parts. Unlike many wild animals, raccoons adapt well to humans and can often be viewed up close. In other parts of the country, where food is not always so plentiful, raccoons have been found in cities in search of something to eat.

A stocky but agile nocturnal animal, the raccoon has thick, gray-black fur. Adults can grow up to 40 inches long, including their bushy tail, and often weigh up to 10 pounds. They are skilled swimmers, and their clawed paws which can grip bark make them adept at climbing trees.

These intelligent creatures seem to be obsessive about cleanliness and may appear to be "washing" fresh fish before eating them. In fact, these rubbing, feeling, and dunking actions, using their highly dextrous and sensitive front paws, are associated with the location and capture of aquatic prey, such as frogs. It is not known whether these actions are simply investigative or intended to rid the prey of distasteful skin secretions.

Raccoons give birth to a litter of one to six young. Their eyes open at about three weeks, and they start to explore with their mother at about two months, remaining with her for another ten months, during which time they learn to scavenge for food.

Fortunately, Henry Ford, with his mass-production techniques, had introduced the automobile to the world and created a taste for scenic highways. Between the road and the Shenandoah National Park which was created in 1926, the forest was revitalized. Trees grow fast in the eastern United States, and the locust tree and white pine quickly revived, even if the American chestnut did not.

The 500-year-old hemlocks of Limberlost somehow escaped the woodman's ax and can be reached on foot. The flowers are a particularly wonderful spectacle when spring drifts slowly up the slopes. Trillium lilies, once a favorite for Civil War graves, can be found, as can arbutus and serviceberries—if the bears have left any behind.

This is Thomas Jefferson country, and he loved Dark Hollow Falls, close to Big Meadow in the middle of the park. South of the park, near Lexington, is Natural Bridge, 90 feet long and up to 150 feet wide. Jefferson declared it "the most sublime of Nature's work" and before the Revolutionary War began, bought it from the Crown—which was clearly not so impressed—for 20 shillings.

The Blue Ridge is the watershed for some of the great rivers of the southeast—the Roanoke, James, and Potomac among them—and in the streams there are brown, brook, and rainbow trout, and pike, crappie, bream, and even striped bass where the water is deeper and moves more slowly.

During the fall along the parkway the brilliant colors and crisp air herald a seasonal event: the southward migration of birds along the Blue Ridge. Heading for the lands beside the Gulf of Mexico and for South America, hawks are the most noticeable and spectacular of these migrants. Smaller birds are on the move, too, but they tend to creep slowly through the woods, feeding as they go and keeping just one hop ahead of winter.

NORTH CAROLINA

# CAPE HATTERAS

ON A QUIET, HOT DAY, North Carolina's Outer Banks must be among the most tranquil places on Earth. The dunes slumber, and the waves dab almost listlessly at the shore. To the east, the first landfall is Bermuda, more than 600 miles away. To the west, from the middle stretches around Cape Hatteras, the low-lying land on the far side of Pamlico Sound is equally invisible. From below Nags Head in the north to Shackleford Banks in the southwest, the Cape Hatteras and Cape Lookout national seashores stretch for 125 miles, broken only by five inlets, a scattering of resorts, and the tallest lighthouse in the United States.

Nature is in dynamic form here, and the sea is winning, rising a foot every century and slowly rolling the dunes westward with the assistance of storms. Long smothered by the dunes, old peat bogs reappear on the seaward side of the shore, and new salt marshes develop landward.

The road to Cape Hatteras National Seashore runs from Bodie Island, and that route passes close to two national shrines. The first is Kill Devil Hills, where the Wright brothers made the first powered flight in 1903. The second, near-obligatory stop is the Fort Raleigh National Historical Site on the northern tip of Roanoke Island, settled by the first group of English settlers in the New World in 1585.

Cold northern currents and the Gulf Stream, warmed in the Caribbean, meet off Cape Hatteras, providing fishermen with the best of both worlds. The fishing is excellent from the beach, and those who charter boats can fish for marlin and sailfish. The birdlife is abundant throughout the Outer Banks, particularly on the landward side. Pea Island, in the Cape Hatteras Seashore, is the winter home of over half the world's greater snow geese, which migrate from the Arctic tundra.

No roads exist on the Cape Lookout National Seashore, which was authorized in 1966 to protect 58 miles of the lower Outer Banks, but the adventurous can reach it by ferry from the nearby mainland.

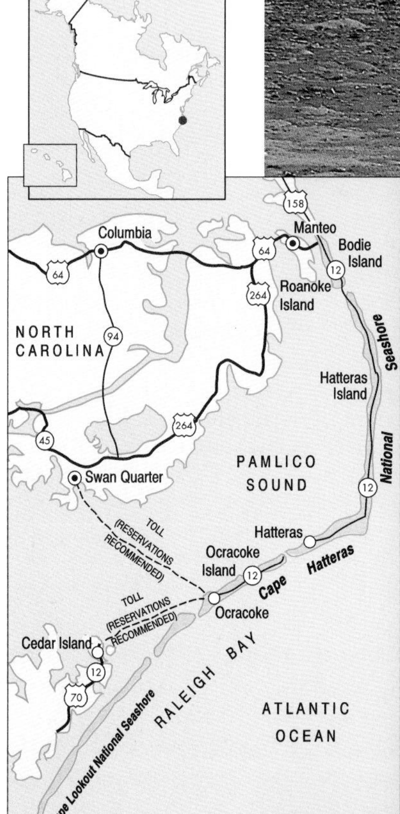

***The famous striped Cape Hatteras Lighthouse*** *(right) warns ships away from Diamond Shoals, a dangerous bank of sand ridges beneath the waves. Storms often batter these shores, leaving behind shells from other lands. Set back from the sea, holly berries and flowers contrast with the blue water.*

**Migrators' refuge**

Cape Hatteras National Seashore provides an idyllic environment for shore and wading birds, and a temporary winter home for migrating birds. Several types of heron, . silhouetted against the setting sun (below), can be seen here. There are great blue, green-backed, black-

crowned, and yellow-crowned night herons, as well as great and snowy egrets. Sandpipers, yellowlegs, and ruddy turnstones search the beach for a tasty crustacean meal.

Wintering snow geese (below) also populate the islands. From June to August, these geese nest and raise their young in the Arctic tundra of northeastern Siberia and Greenland, where there is little competition for space.

Snow geese are extremely sociable and nest in colonies that may number up to 150,000 pairs. As soon as the young can fly, the geese migrate south to spend the winter on open grass, preferably along the coast. They feed happily on grass, grain, berries, water plants, and insects.

MARYLAND, VIRGINIA

# ASSATEAGUE

SAILOR'S CHARTS OF ASSATEAGUE ISLAND omit the channel buoys marking the northern and southern entrance to Chincoteague Bay, the great lagoon behind it. Instead, notes warn navigators that the channels are constantly shifting. The sea is at work here, moving sand and shoals as it searches for a passage through the dunes that protect the mainland. In 1933, a hurricane helped it smash through just below Ocean City, Maryland's Atlantic resort.

So Assateague Island was severed from Ocean City and its holiday throngs. After another major storm and 32 years had passed, an Act of Congress awarded it to the birds, loggerhead turtles, and ponies which live there, and to anyone who enjoys unblemished dunes and sparkling sand stretching for mile after mile.

Assateague's mammalian life is restricted to otters, white-tailed deer, mink, and cottontails in addition to its ponies and Sika deer. But birdlife abounds; well over 200 species of birds have been seen on and around Assateague, and expert ornithologists conduct the Audubon Society's annual bird count at Christmas to capture all its rich detail.

Assateague is the largest stretch of undeveloped shoreline between Cape Cod and the Carolinas, and the birds have it more or less to themselves for much of the year. Its widely varied natural habitats include sea teeming with fish on the ocean side, sand dunes studded with wiry grass and stubby plants behind the beach, windblown oak and pine woods, and marshlands and lagoons.

These are the nurseries of many ocean-dwelling fish. The marshes and reedlands offer seclusion for nesting waterfowl in the spring and protection in the winter for the birds that flock to escape the cold and enjoy the mildness sustained by the Gulf Stream.

Approaching Chincoteague and Assateague by the causeways provides one of the East Coast's great sights: rafts of wintering Brent and Canada geese and a multitude of ducks resting on the reed-trimmed blue waters of the lagoon. Whistling swans are often here, and occasionally glossy ibises and even bitterns can be seen.

***Assateague Island National Seashore*** *(right) is a 37-mile-long barrier island built of sand that the waves have gradually raised from the ocean's sloping floor. On the surface, bluefish churn the water between the surf waves, while skimmers slice the water with their long lower beaks.*

***Two herds of wild ponies*** *(above) live on Assateague—the Maryland herd in the north, and the Virginia herd in the south. Each year, ponies from the Virginia herd are rounded up, and in a wild scene of tossing heads, splashing water, and thrashing hooves, the herd swims* $\frac{1}{4}$ *mile across the channel to Chincoteague where the foals are auctioned. The remaining ponies make the return swim to Assateague.*

*Smaller than horses—and ranging in color from solid brown to white or pinto—these sturdy ponies are well adapted to their harsh environment. They feed on marsh and dune grasses and find water in natural ponds. Their limited diet is thought to be responsible for their small size.*

NEW JERSEY, PENNSYLVANIA

# DELAWARE WATER GAP

THE APPALACHIANS have served both as a watercourse and a dam for two of the East Coast's great rivers, the Delaware and the Susquehanna. The rivers follow almost identical zigzags along the valleys until they find a way through the mountain barrier and at last flow unimpeded to the Atlantic.

The Delaware's struggle with the landscape left the Delaware Water Gap, a spectacular, welcoming wooded cleft through the long ridge known as Kittatinny Mountain. The gap is $2\frac{1}{2}$ miles long, 60 feet deep, and nearly a mile across at the top, and the river is 300 yards wide. Like other gaps, it played an important part in the westward expansion of the United States: the direct road from New York to Chicago runs through it.

The Delaware Water Gap National Recreation Area, created in 1965, covers much more than the gap itself, which is, in fact, the park's southern entrance. The park continues northward along the river valley for 35 miles. For most of the distance, it is 2 or 3 miles wide and never more than 5.

The snapping turtle is particularly common wherever the water is either still or moving slowly. Turtles are not adventurous swimmers. Eight species have been seen in the park, two of them—the spotted and bog—only very occasionally. The bog turtle (brown with a large orange earpatch) is regarded as an endangered species. Stinkpots, which defend themselves with an unpleasant smell, eastern painted, and wood turtles are fairly common.

Fishermen can choose between trout—brook, rainbow, and brown—in the side streams and panfish, pickerel, and bass in the ponds near the river. The river itself contains shad, walleye, and muskellunge, as well as other species.

The park also has a rich architectural inheritance: 83 buildings are either on or eligible for the National Register of Historic Places. The Aspinall Water Wheel, housed in a stone building built in 1915, once generated electricity for the neighboring countryside.

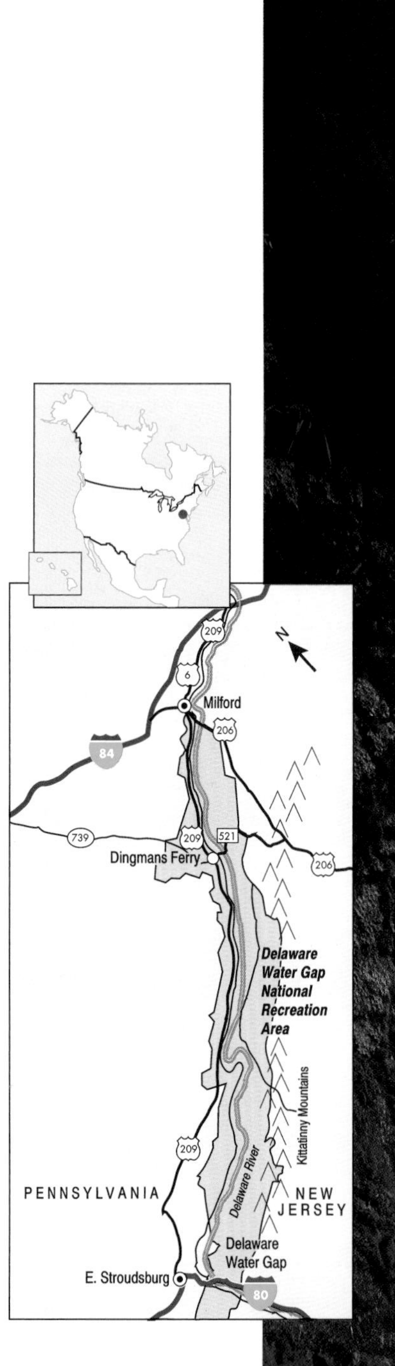

***This sparkling cascade** at Dingman's Falls (right) is typical of the refreshing beauty of the park. A rich variety of animals make their home in the forests and on the open hillsides. Woodchuck, flying squirrels, red foxes, and even the occasional black bear can be seen along the miles of hiking trails.*

***The bald eagle (above) is one of eight species in the genus* Haliaeetus*, all with a liking for fish—here provided by the Delaware River. Pairs of bald eagles remain together after breeding and re-establish bonds each year with spectacular courtship displays, when the birds lock talons in midair and somersault down together. Their nests are made of sticks and are sited in a large tree or on rocks. The nest is added to each year and can reach up to 8 feet across and 11½ feet deep.*

*The river is rich in birdlife, and ospreys can be seen fishing in the spring and fall, while red-tailed hawks and kestrels are common all year round. Other hawks, notably sharp-shinned, red-shouldered, and broad-winged, pass through the valley on their seasonal migrations. Between October and April, there are usually plenty of bufflehead and common goldeneye ducks, and ringtails appear in March and April.*

MASSACHUSETTS

# CAPE COD

CAPE COD'S BENT ARM MAKES A SKELETAL COME-HITHER GESTURE to the Atlantic's farther shore. The Pilgrim Fathers, whose first landing was at the Cape's tip, managed to reach this extension of Massachusetts, but an estimated 4,000 wrecks indicate that a very large number did not. Today's visitors usually make a successful landing by crossing the Cape Cod Canal on the Bourne and Sagamore bridges. Millions of them arrive during the summer, swelling the resident population of 165,000 three or four times over.

Luckily, Cape Cod is reasonably big—35 miles from the shoulder to the elbow and another 32 miles up the forearm to the knuckles—but the pressures imposed on it by visitors increase every year. The Cape Cod National Seashore was created in 1961, the first year of John F. Kennedy's administration. The seashore runs from Nauset Beach near the elbow (where some believe the Viking Leif Ericsson landed his longboat in 1003) up to Long Point Light at Provincetown, and in places the park extends right across the peninsula to include beaches on Cape Cod Bay.

Since the sea annually gnaws sand off the Atlantic side and compensates by piling it up on the other side of the peninsula, the park is a slowly shifting entity. The wide beaches are backed by dunes, freshwater ponds, stretches of heath, and sand cliffs that face the Atlantic in walls 175 feet high. The strong winter wind tends to bend the scrub pine and oak trees and stunt the crouched bushes of bayberry, shadbush, and beach plum. The ocean nourishes a rich assortment of edible creatures including oysters, clams, lobsters, crabs, and "the great stoare of codfish" which so delighted the English captain Bartholomew Gosnold and his men in 1602 that the Cape was named in their honor.

On the beach, throngs of plovers and sandpipers scuttle near the sea's edge, while behind the dunes march wrens and, in summer, nesting terns can be seen. They are nimble and exceptionally graceful fliers, best observed in the air but possessive mother birds can deliver a sharp peck to anyone who ventures too close.

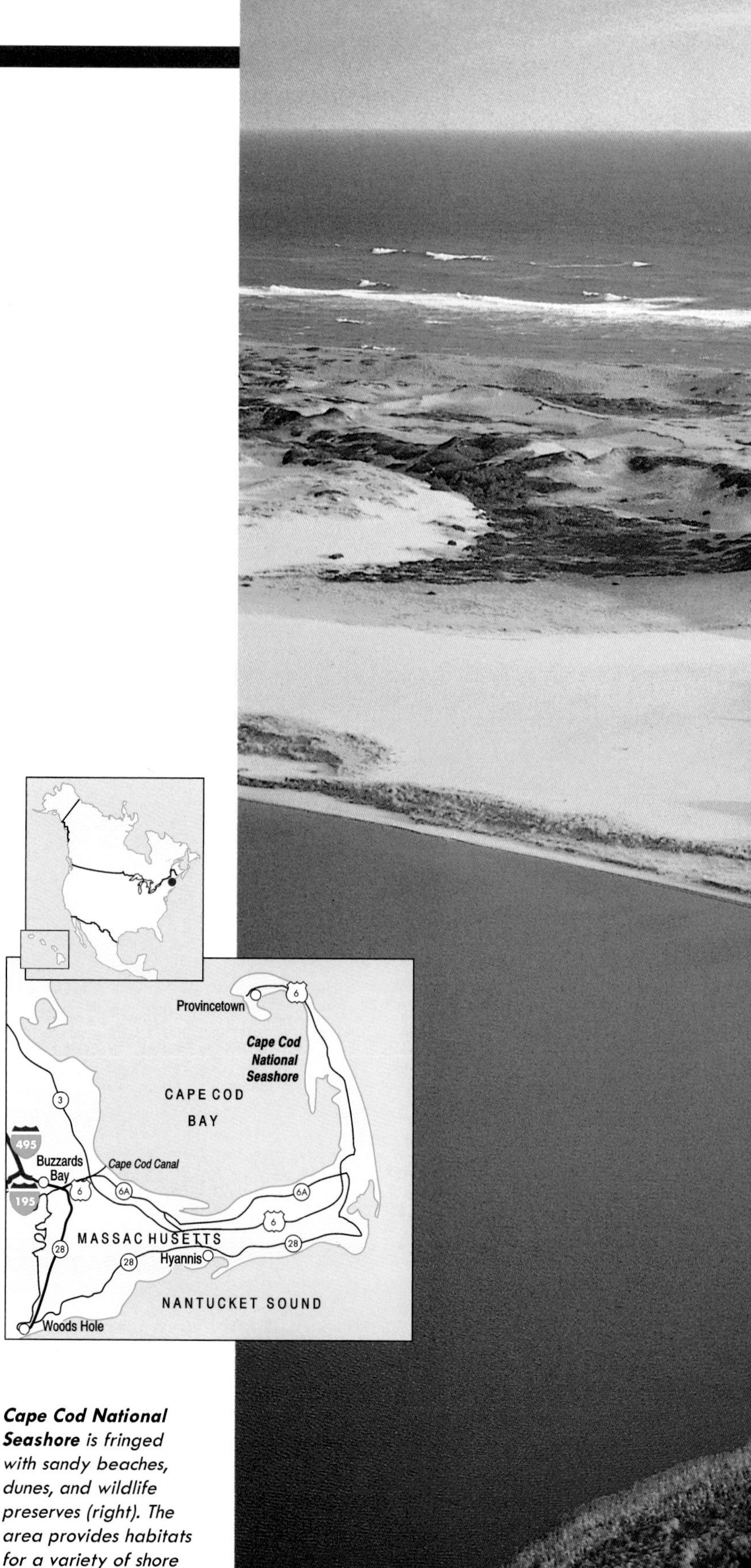


***Cape Cod National Seashore** is fringed with sandy beaches, dunes, and wildlife preserves (right). The area provides habitats for a variety of shore and sea birds, including the osprey. These birds plunge beneath the waves to grab fish, using the small spikes on the soles of their feet to "spear" them.*

***The Buttonbush Nature Trail** (above) has been specially laid out for the blind, with Braille signs that describe the scene and give details of the plants and animals along the way. Visitors are encouraged to stop and listen to the redwing blackbird—particularly vocal when chasing females—and to smell and touch the pretty white flowers of the beech plum.*

### The mighty cod

The cod, for which this area is named, is an extremely valuable food fish which has been exploited by people for centuries. Other members of the family include haddock and whiting. The cod is a stout-bodied fish which can be identified by its three dorsal and two anal fins, and by the single sensory barbel on its chin that is equipped with additional taste buds. Its mouth is large, containing many small teeth, and its mottled coloring is variable. Cod usually swim in schools in surface water, but will also search for crustaceans, worms, or other fish to eat at midwater depths or on the sea floor.

NEW YORK, VERMONT

# THE ADIRONDACKS

EVER SINCE GEOLOGIST Ebenezer Emmons made the first ascent of Mount Marcy in 1837 and told the public about it, the Adirondacks have held a special place in the hierarchy of American wilderness areas. Dr. Emmons's local guide, John Cheney, stood atop Marcy—at 5,344 feet, the highest point in the range—and said: "It makes a man feel what it is to have all creation placed beneath his feet."

Modern America's attempts to capture and enshrine Cheney's revelation have had mixed results. Over the past 150 years, the cultural life of the Adirondacks has developed with its natural heritage, and now the region is an amalgam of wilderness, ski slope, sanatorium, and playground.

It remains not only a state park but the biggest park, state or federal, in the United States—130 miles long and 90 miles across—which makes it bigger than Massachusetts and bigger than the four largest national parks in the West put together. On its western flank, the park has a heavier snowfall than anywhere in the United States east of the Mississippi, which helps to explain why this site was chosen for the 1980 Winter Olympics.

The Adirondacks were never of much use to farmers. By the time Dr. Emmons reached the summit of Mount Marcy, the trappers had no further use for them either, having exhausted the supply of fur-bearing animals. The most powerful tribe in the region, the Iroquois, hunted but never lived here and referred contemptuously to the Algonquin inhabitants as "bark-eaters," believing that they ate nothing else in winter. It was these poor Adirondack Algonquin who gave their name to the region where, by 1875, 200 hotels catered for affluent vacationers.

Today, some 2,800 lakes, ponds, and streams throw themselves down between mossy rocks to join the rivers, and their waters still sparkle. Mount Marcy is near the watershed which divides the rivers that flow into Lake Champlain and the St. Lawrence River from those like the Hudson that run south.

***Winter's white mantle*** *hugs the slopes and coats the trees of Algonquin Peak (right). Of the many mountains in the Adirondack Range, this is the second tallest (at 5,114 feet) after Mount Marcy. The sparkling slopes and accessible beauty of the area make it a favorite destination for winter sports enthusiasts.*

The mountains in whose creases the lakes lie are composed of anorthosite, an igneous rock composed largely of plagioclase feldspar. They are not, as is often supposed, an outcrop of the Appalachians; their parent is the Canadian Shield from which they hang, linked by the thin chain of the Thousand Islands in the St. Lawrence. Most of the summits are low, but more than 40 rise above 4,000 feet.

The mountain-building forces that raised the Adirondacks ceased work 25 million years ago. Since then, the Wisconsin Glacier has been chiseling away at the high cliff faces, smoothing down mountaintops and ridges, and damming the narrow lakes with its moraines. The last pockets of ice probably disappeared from the high ground about 9,000 years ago, but the mountains can still be bitterly cold. On the higher slopes, the snow usually lasts

***More than 2,800 lakes** and ponds dot the landscape, providing peaceful retreats like this one on Big Moose Lake (above) for many visitors. City dwellers, particularly those living in New York, have discovered with delight that untrammeled nature is alive and well right in their the backyard.*

*They also provide habitats for a variety of birds including loons. Large diving birds which may reach 24 to 36 inches long, loons nest in mounds of vegetation next to the water of many Adirondack lakes.*

through May, and there are only about 100 frost-free days a year.

The glacial molding of the Adirondacks is one of the area's more interesting aspects. Look around for kettleholes, drumlins, and eskers. The depressions created by detached blocks of ice as they melted are the kettleholes. Drumlins are the smooth elongated hills, sometimes over 100 feet high, formed by the rocks, gravel, and other materials deposited by the slowly moving glaciers. Formed from the deposits left by meltwater tunneling under the ice, eskers are narrow ridges resembling railroad cuts. Geology enthusiasts should also watch for kames, the rounded hillocks formed by the outwash of debris from melting ice on the retreating glacial fronts.

**Reintroducing the lynx**

Wild lynx once prowled through the Adirondacks like kings of the forest, but since the early years of the century, they have been virtually extinct here. They fell victim to the massive land clearances that fueled the local lumber industry, as well as to hunters, trappers, and the mightier bobcat, so there are no wild lynx left in these rugged, northern woods.

In the winter of 1989, however, conservationists began a program to reintroduce this cat to the area with imports from the Canadian Yukon; 18 lynx were released the first winter, and 32 and 42 were released the following two winters respectively. Capable of wandering over large areas, each lynx was fitted with a small radio transmitter so its movements could be monitored.

The automobile, however, has replaced the lumberjack's ax as the main modern-day threat to lynx, with about a third of the cats dying in accidents with cars. Because of this high mortality rate, the program's future is being reviewed.

A solitary cat, the lynx comes out at night to hunt its prey and feed on the much smaller snowshoe hare, as well as young deer and grouse. The lynx's fur acts as a camouflage while it patiently waits in low vegetation to make its kill.

***The action of retreating glaciers*** *during the last Ice Age left this area covered with glacial till, while also creating the amazing variety of gorges, waterfalls, lakes, and ponds for which the area is now famous. Heart Lake (left) is just one of the small, irregularly shaped lakes nestling in the soft swath of foliage.*

*Leaves from the silver birch and red maple (right) merge in this delicate woodland setting. The Adirondack mountainsides are thickly covered with spruce, white pine, and the fragrant hemlock, interspersed with hardwoods on the lower slopes. This open woodland is perfect territory for the wild coyote, whose howling can be heard far into the night. Its diet consists mostly of rodents and rabbits, although it will also eat snakes, fruit, and berries, and even enter the water to catch fish, frogs, and crustaceans.*

Sixteen wilderness areas cover 2.4 million acres with mile upon mile of mountainside trees; only the occasional peak pokes up above the timberline. On the whole, oaks and other deciduous trees like the maple, birch, beech, and black cherry are more common than conifers. However, spruce and fir take over higher up the mountainside, while above 4,500 feet the forest is almost wholly balsam fir, whose seeds are a favorite food of spruce grouse.

In the second half of the 19th century, the railroad brought the region within easy reach of millions. Writers like Rev. William Murray and Ralph Waldo Emerson were delighted by the mountains' pristine qualities, but Francis Parkman, author of *The Oregon Trail*, was not as enthusiastic. Surveying the increasingly developed shores of Lake George in the 1890s, he wrote, "The *nouveau riche*, who is one of the pests of this country, has now got possession of the lake and its islands." Vacation homes are still a problem for the Adirondacks.

A state forest preserve was created in 1885, largely as a result of concern about the effects of heavy logging. That was followed in 1892 by the creation of the state park—then about half its present size—and the forests were given "forever wild" status in the park's charter. By the beginning of this century, a quarter of a million visitors were pouring into the Adirondacks every summer. The private landowners in the park, many of whom were considerably less well off than the bulk of the visitors, faced the prospect of a bonanza from proposed development. Public concern over the nature of this development came to a head in the 1960s when plans for 20,000 vacation homes were presented.

At the time, there was no real authority to control private lands. Proposals for placing about half the park under federal control were dropped in favor of making it all a "greenline" park, an idea adopted from the British national park system where privately owned, undeveloped land is subject to strict planning controls intended to preserve the character of the area and open it up to the public. The park's new status was confirmed by the New York state legislature in 1973.

MAINE

# MOUNT DESERT AND ACADIA

THE MAINE COAST IS AN ICE AGE BATTLEGROUND where the glaciers and the sea joined forces against the land, fiercely holding much of it underwater until it drowned. The coast bears testimony to the ferocity of the struggle in the countless fragmented islands and rocky inlets where the land barely managed to keep its back above water as the glaciers retreated and the sea levels rose. Even the conifers crowding down to the water's edge give the impression that they are looking for survivors.

Mount Desert Island stands like a monument to resistance, the place where the glaciers met their match. Its main peak, Mount Cadillac, is, at 1,530 feet, the highest point anywhere on the eastern and southern seaboards of the United States from the Rio Grande to the Canadian border. Scratched out by a glacial finger which curled around the edge of the mountain, Somes Sound provides the island with another unique distinction: it is the only true fjord in the Lower 48 states.

The Labrador Current keeps the sea chilly, which is good for fish and lobsters, but not so congenial for swimmers and sunbathers. Yet that is part of Mount Desert's charm: it is a place to get away from the worst of the crowds, a place where nature maintains its integrity. Desert Island's aloof beauty found favor first with painters and then with millionaires who, driven north in the search for privacy, built their palatial "cottages" here in the late 19th and early 20th centuries. Many were destroyed in the forest fire of 1947.

The first artist to arrive, in 1844, was Thomas Cole, one of the leaders of the Hudson River School, who was enchanted by Bar Harbor, a fishing village perched on the edge of Frenchman Bay. No one followed him for years: the first summer home, Petunia Cottage, was not built until 1877. After that, the millionaires began to

***Mount Cadillac*** *(right) soars high above the surrounding landscape. Closer to the ground, the age-old rocks are covered with a green-gray coating of lichens, which provides food for caribou and reindeer in the far northern ranges. Fall foliage forms a stunning contrast.*

***Bright-eyed and bushy-tailed*** *is an apt description for the red squirrel (above). They are alert, social creatures that have evolved a complex system of signaling with their bushy tails. Their eyes are large, and vision, including color, is good. They are also highly vocal.*

*The red, or spruce, squirrel is reddish-brown and has white underparts, while its cousin, the Douglas squirrel, is slightly smaller and has reddish-brown underparts. These creatures undergo periods of dormancy in cold weather. This differs from true hibernation in that the animal wakes up every few days in order to eat pine cones collected during the fall.*

dominate the scene, and Bar Harbor rivaled Newport in the wealth of its inhabitants.

Millionaires are not always regarded as an environmental plus, but in Mount Desert's case their desire for exclusivity dovetailed with a passion for conservation early this century. John D. Rockefeller, Jr., took the lead in acquiring land that was eventually offered to the federal government. His gift and others became Acadia National Park, created in 1919, the first national park east of the Mississippi.

The park encompasses the larger part of the island, Schoodic Point on the mainland to the east, and Isle au Haut, 15 miles southwest. Mount Desert Island was discovered in 1604 by the French explorer, Samuel de Champlain, who was struck by the naked granite of its summits. The highest is named after the island's first owner, Antoine Laumet de la Mothe, Sieur de Cadillac. Given title to it in 1688 by Louis XIV, he is more often remembered as the founder of Detroit.

The name of the park is thought to have an Indian origin, but it also sounds like Arcadia, a place in ancient Greece famed for the rustic bliss reputedly enjoyed by its inhabitants. Like most of the other Maine coastal resorts, Bar Harbor is pleasantly

***The muted mists** off the Atlantic coast (above) offer gentle relief. An occasional seagull may swoop past to drop and crack open a sea urchin on the nearby rocks.*

*The name of the quaking aspen tree (left) refers to the sensitivity of its leaves, which tremble in the slightest breeze. The smooth white bark is eaten by rabbits, while grouse and quail feed on the winter buds.*

sophisticated rather than simple, but in high summer, Mount Desert Island's woods, shores, and lakes are as close to felicity as most mortals will ever get.

The days are often sunny, the breeze gentle, the shore low and rocky, with trees perched bravely on the tidemark. The harbor seals bask like slugs on the distant rocks, and even the red squirrels doze on the branches. Close offshore, where the sea begins to sparkle, there may be more activity; an osprey fishing, gulls screaming around a shoal of fish, even porpoises and whales. If there are humpbacks around, you may glimpse the remarkable sight of a whale breaking clear.

The pools and rocks uncovered at low tide may be muddy underfoot, but clams and bloodworms thrive in this habitat. This

part of the coast produces some of the world's most succulent seafood: unsurpassed lobsters, mussels, and several types of clam, ranging from the little nut to the larger quahog.

Seaweed abounds here. Dulse from the rock pools tastes of cod liver oil and is supposed to be good for growing children. Irish moss or carrageen, used in jellies and soups, is also somewhat medicinal. Whelks and periwinkles are both edible, but the local clams are hard to beat for flavor.

Away from the shore, there are flowers in the open spaces among the rocks and wherever meadows survive. Lupines flourish, as do heathers, bunchberries, blueberries, and fragrant little strawberries. Best of all is the wood lily, whose scarlet flower opens boldly toward the sky.

*__The flourishing birdlife__ of Maine's summer woods includes the mysterious waxwings (right), with their crested heads and bank-robber eyebands. There are also towhees, with their distinctive orange and white breasts, even though the park runs near the northern limit of their range. Kingbirds, phoebes, and other flycatchers abound, and their sad songs capture the mood of the northern woods.*

# Alaska and Hawaii

## Land of ice, land of fire

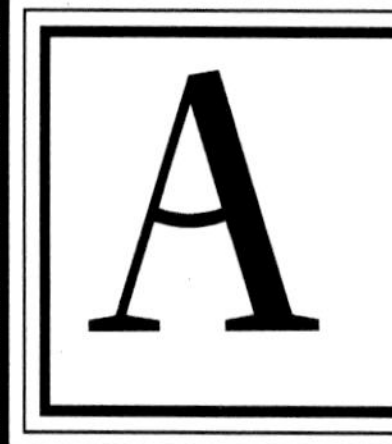

A huge rugged wilderness, one of the last on Earth, Alaska is a place that plucks at the heart. It is cold, vast, unfriendly; yet to anyone with a sense of how the world once was, and perhaps might be again, this northwestern edge of the American continent has a magnetic lure. A state since 1959, Alaska was long ignored, which helped keep the countryside unchanged. There is more wild land preserved here than in any of the other 49 states.

The crown of Mount McKinley, the highest mountain in North America, rises here in lofty isolation. Wild creatures share a largely unspoiled life, with bears, wolves, and deer in large numbers. Birds abound, and in the summer, the valley meadows are bright with a carpet of flowers.

Alaska has few urban centers, so much of the state is empty. Inland, the cruel cold and heavy snowfalls have prevented extensive exploitation and settlement. Still, humans will go to great extremes to mine for minerals or bore for oil, and whether Alaska can remain a pristine state into the 21st century remains uncertain. It still merits the description "untouched," but environmental issues and protection must never be set aside if this true wilderness is to survive.

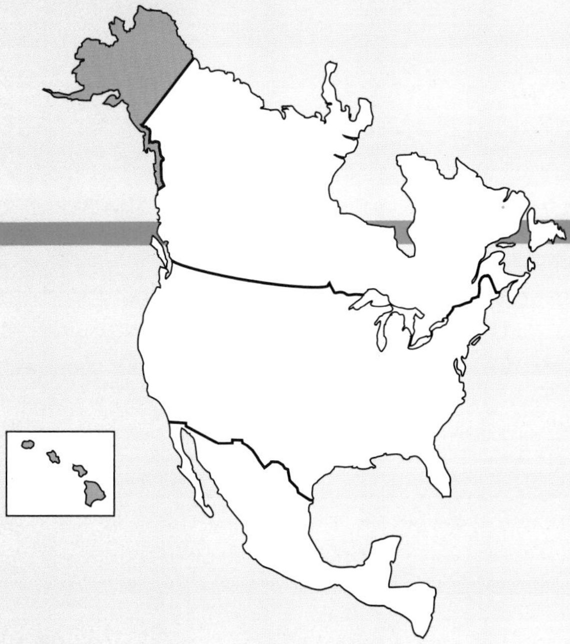

The first settlers of the beautiful islands of Hawaii arrived from the south in outrigger canoes 1,500 years ago. The string of islands and atolls trailing from a rift below the surface of the sea was the creation of still-active volcanoes. What the settlers first saw was an uninviting island exploding with fire. One island, Hawaii, was particularly prone to violent eruptions and still is. But they now occur sporadically, usually in the national park on the Big Island, as Hawaii is known locally, and Nature's firework display is considered a sight worth seeing.

ALASKA

# MOUNT MCKINLEY

The best-known feature of Alaska is Mount McKinley, already the tallest mountain in North America and still growing. The mountain, whose towering peak reaches 20,320 feet above sea level, is situated in the 400-mile-long Alaska Range in the central part of the state and is surrounded by Denali National Park and Preserve and neighboring Denali State Park. An area of 6,000,000 acres, Denali incorporates within its boundaries many other mountains, rising above the vast and varied expanses of Arctic terrain.

Mount McKinley provides the profile of the park. It was produced from the juxtaposition of the two plates that form the Denali Fault beneath the mountain. Perpetually shrouded in snow, this awesome pile was given its original name by the Athabascan Indians, who called it *Denali*, or the Great One. Did they know it was the highest mountain on the continent?

When it can be seen, which is not often, the mountain is one of the most impressive natural sights in all of North America. Its great snow-laden head rears up through the clouds, but unfortunately, this view is rarely seen from the park. From ground level, the peak is often hidden from view; mists and cloud usually cloak it, and even in summer it is only visible about 25 percent of the time. Indeed, the mass of the mountain range crowned by Denali is so immense that it virtually makes its own weather, which accounts for the nearly continuous cloud cover.

Mount McKinley is surrounded by a unique area of virgin land, a vast spread of valley meadows, taiga, and tundra reaching up the mountain flanks, all of which is preserved. Denali National Park was established in 1917, not because the land includes Mount McKinley, but for the benefit of the extraordinary range of wildlife it contains.

Many unusual mammals, birds, plants, and insects live within its boundaries, scattered through the wild contrasting countryside at the lower elevations. Easily approached by road and rail, the park is

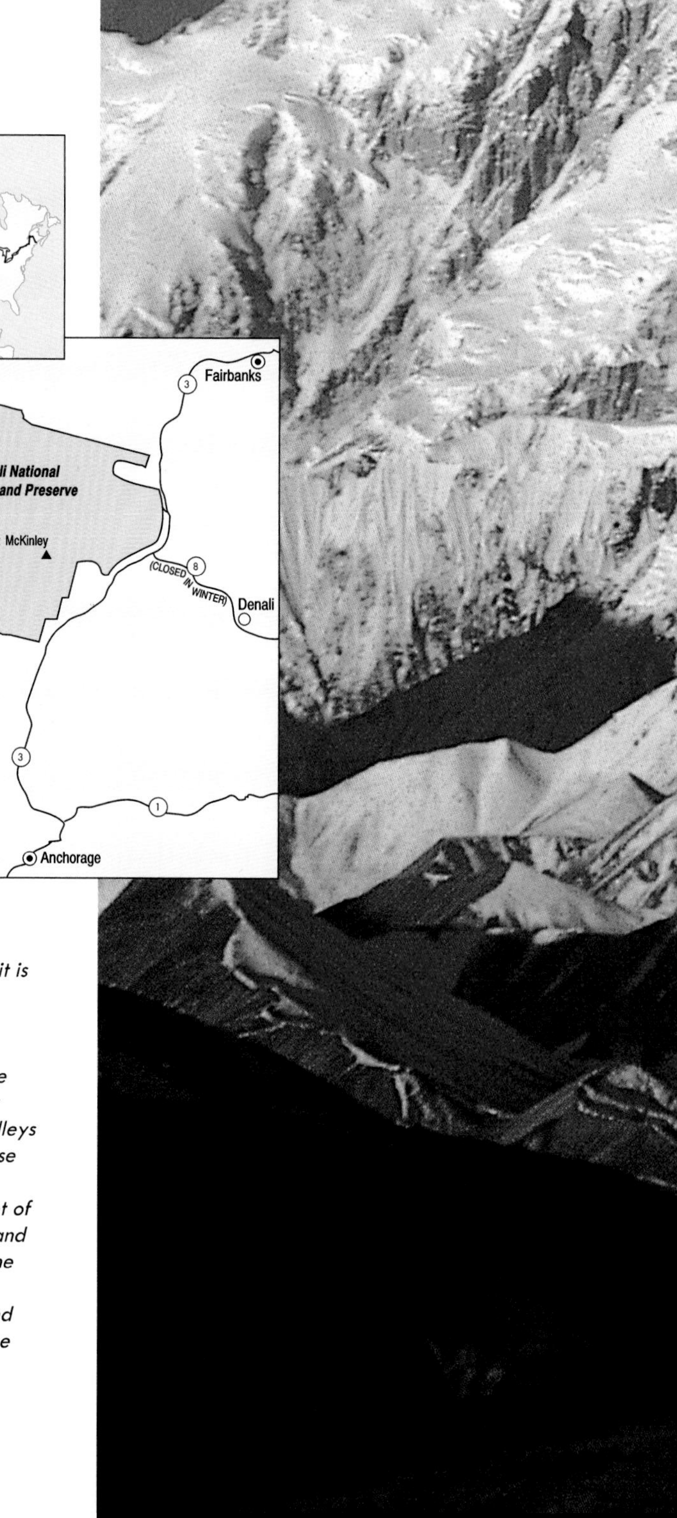


***On a clear day,*** *it is possible to see Mount McKinley (right) and the glaciers that have carved their way down into the valleys below. At the base of the mountains stretches a carpet of lichens, grasses, and dwarf shrubs—the tundra—which provides food and grazing for moose and caribou.*

most popular during the short summer months, but for the serious naturalist, the complex patterns of wildlife can be studied more effectively during the brief spring or fall periods, particularly during the courtship, mating, and birth cycles of many of the area's larger mammals.

***Brown bears that live near rivers*** *(above) will stand in the fast-moving waters to catch salmon as they swim upstream to their spawning ground. The paws of these big bears are wide and flat with long claws that help them to catch the fish. Fruits, berries, nuts, honey, and insects also form an important part of their diet.*

During the long, white winter, the moose, deer, and wolves that come down to the lower latitudes as the snow deepens are quite easily seen, but rabbits, snow hares, and willow ptarmigan develop white coats in November to blend with the snow. They revert to their summer coloring in April.

Of all the mammals in Denali National Park, the great grizzly bear—called grizzly because of the grizzled appearance of its gray flecked coat—is probably the best known. One of America's most formidable and grandest animals, it inhabits the park by the hundreds. The bears enter underground dens (usually caves) in the winter, from late October until April, and the females give birth to their young in January, during the hibernation period. When they emerge with the cubs, the mothers are among the most dangerous creatures to encounter—they are aptly named *Ursus arctos horribilis*. They have poor eyesight, but are so protective that they will readily charge at a hostile scent.

There are also black and brown bears in the park (although they are more common at Admiralty Island, south of Juneau), as well as moose. The Alaskan moose that roam freely here are the largest members of the deer family and are thought to have arrived in this wilderness during the Ice Age. A mammal of truly awe-inspiring proportions, a bull moose can weigh 1,600 pounds, stand 7 feet tall at the shoulder, and carry a rack of antlers that spread 7 feet and, by themselves, tilt the scale at up to 70 pounds. The species developed its massive body in order to store enough energy and conserve enough heat to survive the long, grueling winters.

***Northern white orchids** and silverweed combine with Indian paintbrush (left) for a colorful contrast to the icy peaks of Mount McKinley. The flame petals of the paintbrush are, in fact, modified leaves called bracts. The small, yellow flowers of this mountain meadow plant are found at the base of each bract; they bloom from spring to summer.*

The adult moose has a voracious appetite and can consume 40 to 60 pounds of forage in a single day. Willow shoots are a favorite meal, as are various shrubs left behind by retreating glaciers, and moose frequently wade into shallow ponds to feed on the sodium-rich plants that line their banks.

There are also large herds of caribou, whose males sport spreads of upcurving antlers. The white, short-tailed dall sheep, with its impressive curled horns, is easily spotted on the mountainsides.

Coyotes, shy foxes, and bolder wolves are also predators in the park. The majestic bald eagle is common in Alaska, setting up its territories in March. Its famous name is misleading, since a head of brilliant white feathers caps the bird's dark body. Golden eagles and peregrine falcons are among other local predators; the latter migrate from as far as Argentina and Brazil to nest in the park's interior.

Thanks in part to its long, savage winters, the sparsely settled area that encompasses Mount McKinley and the Denali Park is one of the world's last remaining regions of true wilderness. Luckily, this essential wilderness has been preserved for future generations through a far-sighted policy.

ALASKA

# GLACIER BAY

AN AREA OF SOME 14,135,269 ACRES OF MOUNTAINS AND GLACIERS set in southeastern Alaska, Glacier Bay National Park is one of the last untouched wildernesses of North America. The bay itself is backed by a rank of high and impressively craggy mountains from which the glaciers emanate and, like many other Alaskan bays, the glaciers terminate their downard flow abruptly at the waterline.

Glacier Bay gives a real sense of a river of ice, with its fantastic icy cliffs banked against the steel-blue water below. As the glaciers reach the water, majestic chunks of ice break away and sail off as icebergs. But at Glacier Bay the reverse is also happening, for here the glaciers are in retreat. As Mount McKinley is growing and altering, the parent glacier inland pulls back and enlarges a lake that was once probably crowned with ice. The runoff from this now enlarged lake in turn feeds and subsequently deepens the frigid waters of Glacier Bay.

Most of the time, the ice is moving in extremely slow motion—literally imperceptibly—but for short periods, a geological phenomenon called a surge can speed the movement dramatically, shifting the gigantic mass at 10 to 100 times its usual rate. Very few glaciers experience such surges, however, and their occurrence is completely unpredictable.

Perpetually pushed by gravity and the constant massing of snow in the area appropriately known as the accumulation zone, the ice flows ever downward. Both melting and evaporation lessen its bulk in the lower region, or ablation zone, which is divided from the upper region by an equilibrium line. A glacier is deemed stable if enough new snow is added at the top to balance the loss at the bottom. It will neither retreat nor advance until that delicate balance is shifted.

Flowing water beneath the glacier aids its progress, serving as the essential lubricant that allows it to slide over the underlying bedrock and gravel. In the open air, the water that seeps up from the depths of the

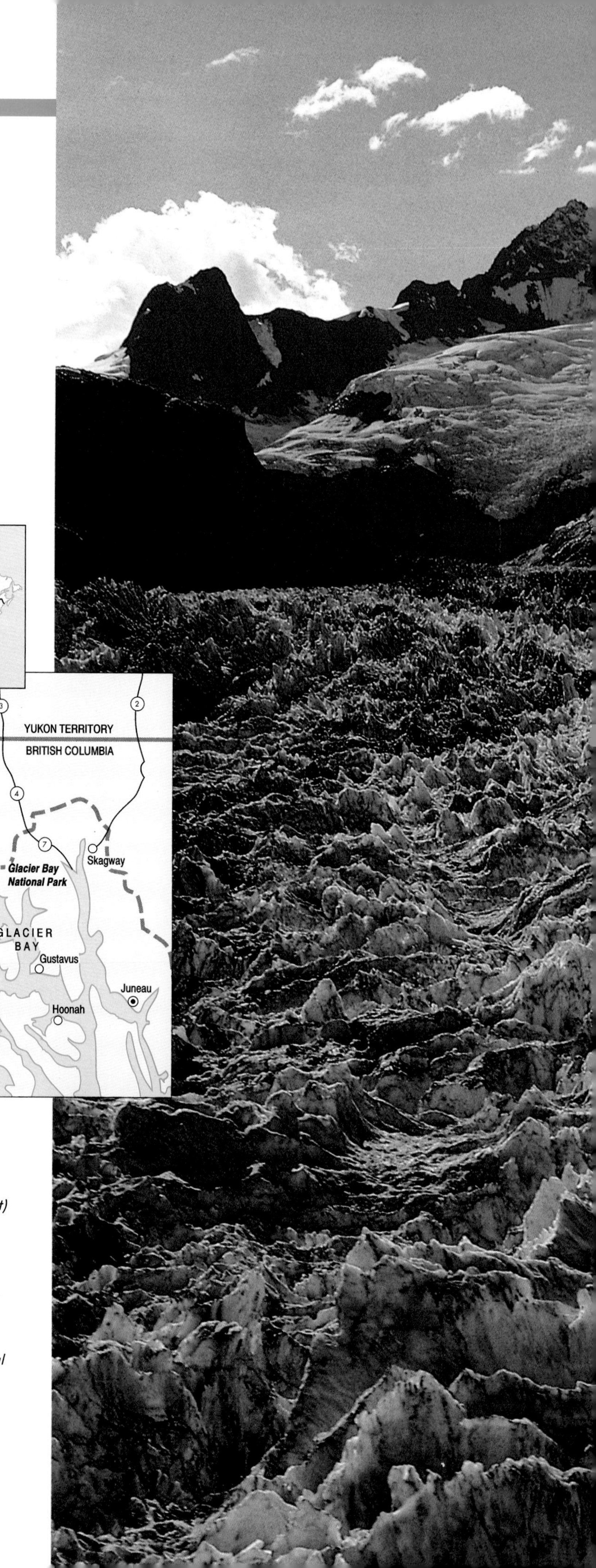


***Reid Glacier relentlessly carves the landscape*** *(right) from the forbidding Brady Icefield. Sediment carried along by glaciers is called moraine, and it usually travels on or near the surface of the ice. Subglacial moraines, however, move under the ice and are responsible for the scouring action of glaciers.*

accumulated snow freezes on the surface into so-called ice lenses, which lie horizontally, and glands, which form vertically. Both the lenses and the glands add to the weight of the accumulated snow and help compress it into densely packed ice.

Only a few Alaskan glaciers finally reach the sea, but as long as a glacier continues to accumulate more snow and ice than the amount that melts, it will continue to advance.

As the glaciers here continue their retreat, land is exposed at the mouth of the bay and along its shores, allowing the establishment of a temperate rain forest like that found all along the Pacific Northwest coast of North America. Its huge trees and richly diverse undergrowth make a dark green curtain against the great gray mountains,

***Bartlett Cove*** *(above), near the mouth of Glacier Bay, supports a unique 200-year-old rain forest. After the glacial retreat, plant recovery began with a covering of algae which stabilized silt and retained moisture. This was followed by moss, then scouring rush, fireweed, dryas, and alder, which helped add nitrogen to the soil. This enabled spruce and hemlock forests to complete the luxuriant new plant community.*

treeless and grim, that loom above the hulks of ice pushing down the valley.

This rain forest grows a rich base of moss and fern topped with Sitka spruce and Nootka cypress. The Indian tribes indigenous to this area have for centuries carved elaborate and beautiful totem poles from these woods.

The forests and the sea around Glacier Bay sustain rich and varied numbers of animal species as well. Birds of note include the horned puffin and the bald eagle. At nearby Chilkat State Park there is a Bald Eagle preserve along the Chilkat River. Over 3,000 birds flock here during November and January, feeding on the late running salmon. And there are bears, again attracted by the spawning and dying salmon which run up the rivers from the sea.

Several varieties of salmon are notable here, making their way up the steep mountain streams to the base of the glaciers to lay their eggs, then die, having ensured the continuity of their mysterious life cycle. Many species of trout inhabit the streams and are eagerly sought by anglers, and in the sea there are swarms of shrimp and herring as well as huge halibut and crab. The sea also sustains harbor seals, humpback whales, and killer whales which can be spotted in the inlets along the coasts.

Alaska contains an impressive collection of birds, mammals, fish, and plants, all of which have adapted to the extreme temperatures and the long, cold, and dark winter. The whole state can be seen as one enormous natural park of great diversity. It covers some 586,412 square miles or one-fifth of the entire area of the United States.

The state is a large-scale mosaic of huge mountains and vast open spaces filled with ice, snow, and permafrost, of volcanoes, deserts, rain forest, and tundra. It is surrounded on three sides by water, with the Pacific to the south, the Bering Sea to the west, and the Beaufort Sea to the north. Inevitably, much of the moisture is locked up in the form of ice that never melts, even during summer.

The only mositure that is channeled away from these ever-frozen areas comes down from the heights as runoff from the melted surfaces of glaciers and frozen rivers. These waters feed Glacier Bay and help create the beautiful fjords and dripping forests of Glacier Bay National Park.

***Northern fur seals,** sea lions, porpoises, and whales, use these coasts as a playground. Fur seals (above) are generally gregarious and haul themselves in their masses out of the water onto a breeding site, known as a rookery. The main features that distinguish them from other seals are the presence of external ears, and their ability to use their hind flippers to help them move on land.*

***Sixteen massive glaciers,*** *as well as several smaller ones, flow from the mountains into the waters of Glacier Bay. Several tidewater glaciers offer a spectacular show of geological forces in action when blocks of ice up to 200 feet high break loose and crash into the sea, filling the narrow inlets with massive icebergs. This cruise ship (left) looks dwarfed alongside the majestic Muir Glacier.*

# Earth Fire

***Volcanoes erupt*** *when pressure and intense heat deep inside the Earth cause part of the Earth's mantle to melt. This molten, or melted, rock is called magma. During an eruption, the magma in the form of lava breaks through the Earth's surface at a hole called a vent. Sometimes solid pieces of lava and lava ashes are thrown into the air (right), while in other explosions liquid lava flows for miles before cooling enough to solidify.*

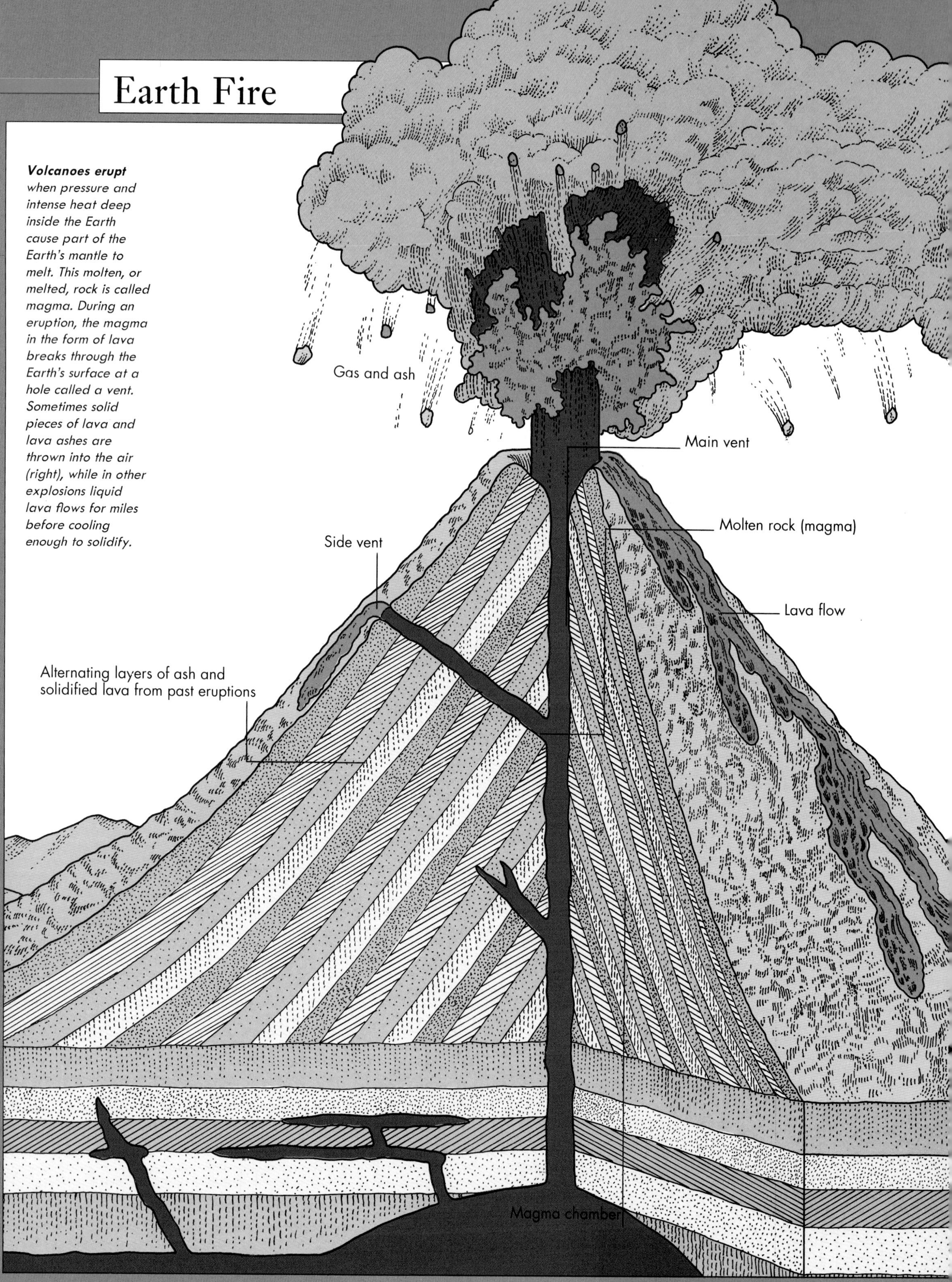

VOLCANOES ARE OPENINGS in the Earth's crust that spew out glowing red-hot molten lava, hot gases, and ashes when they erupt. Some volcanoes, like several on the Hawaiian islands, are continuously active, while others lie dormant for hundreds of years before suddenly becoming active and erupting. This was what happened in 1980 when Mount St. Helens in Washington state burst into action after 123 dormant years, destroying more than 100 square miles of forests and leaving a total of 62 people dead or missing. Volcanoes that geologists think will never erupt again are called extinct.

Mount St. Helens is an example of a central volcano, in which eruptions occur through a single cone, but more common are fissure volcanoes. In fissure volcanoes, the lava simply flows out of cracks along the Earth's surface.

***Like a spectacular natural fireworks display,*** *Kilauea Volcano on the island of Hawaii erupts with glowing molten lava dotting the mountainside (above). All of the Hawaiian islands are actually the tops of a chain of underground volcanoes.*

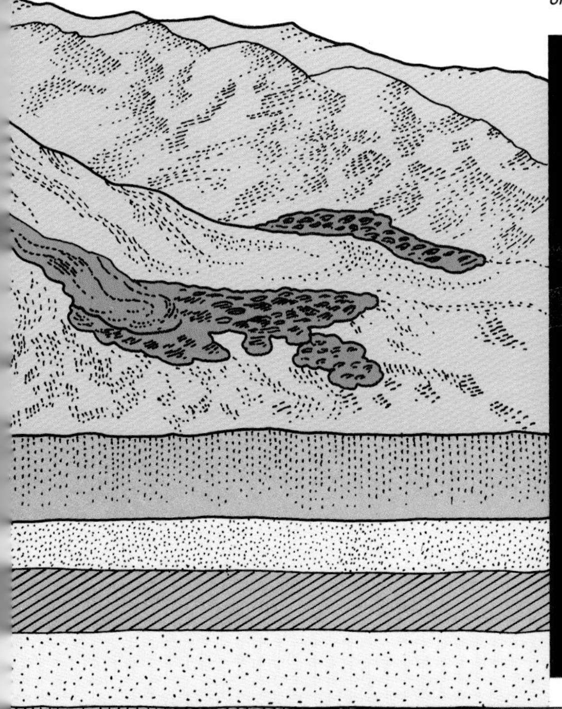

***Lava in a continuous stream (below) flows from Mauna Loa*** *on the island of Hawaii, the world's largest volcano, towering 13,677 feet above sea level. Smooth lava flows like this are called* pahoehoe, *while rough lava that looks like irregular cinder rocks is called* 'a'a.

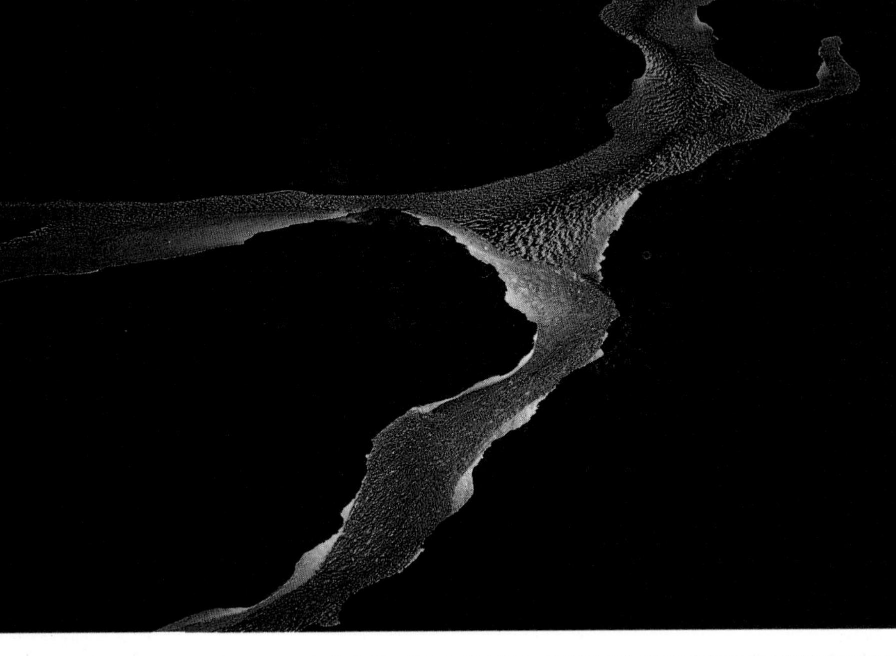

MAUI, HAWAII

# THE VOLCANOES OF HAWAII

CLOTHED AS THEY ARE IN DENSE VEGETATION and arising majestically out of the great blue of the Pacific, it is hard to imagine that the Hawaiian islands owe their birth to volcanoes, erupting over the millennia, building layer upon layer of lava to emerge from the sea.

In fact, the Hawaiian Islands are all volcanic mountains, and should the sea miraculously dry up, they would be the highest mountains on Earth, rising up to heights of more than 30,000 feet if measured from the sea floor. Hawaii, the Big Island, is the youngest and largest of the Hawaiian chain, with no material within it more than a million years old. Moving west, the islands are progressively older; Oahu is between 2.6 and 3.6 million years old and Kauai is about 8 million years old.

The ocean floor, however, is considerably older, dating from 80 to 120 million years. Under the sea floor is a site of intense volcanic activity—a hot spot, or plume, to geologists. It is this hot spot that is responsible for the birth of all the islands, islets, and seamounts of the Hawaiian series. Over the hot spot, the floor of the Pacific Ocean passes, becomes heated and swollen, and finally a rift forms in the rock, through which lava passes. As thousands of years elapse, the submarine volcano increases in size as the lava continues to spill out of the rift. Eventually the mound of lava breaks the surface of the sea to become a volcanic island.

As long as the island is over the hot spot it continues to grow; Hawaii itself is still over the hot spot and its southeastern volcanoes, Kilauea and Mauna Loa, still produce lava. As the islands on their Pacific Plate drift farther away from the hot spot, their volcanic activity will cease and the forces of rain, wind, and ocean waves will erode their mass until they once again disappear under the water. Then the process starts again; in fact, a new bulge of some 980 feet to the southeast of Hawaii is beginning the long march to the surface.

***The islands in the Hawaiian archipelago*** *(right) are the tops of mountains that have built up from the ocean floor over millions of years. The molten lava solidified, leaving a mix of black and gray rock, and the occasional beach of black volcanic sand bears witness to the island's origins.*

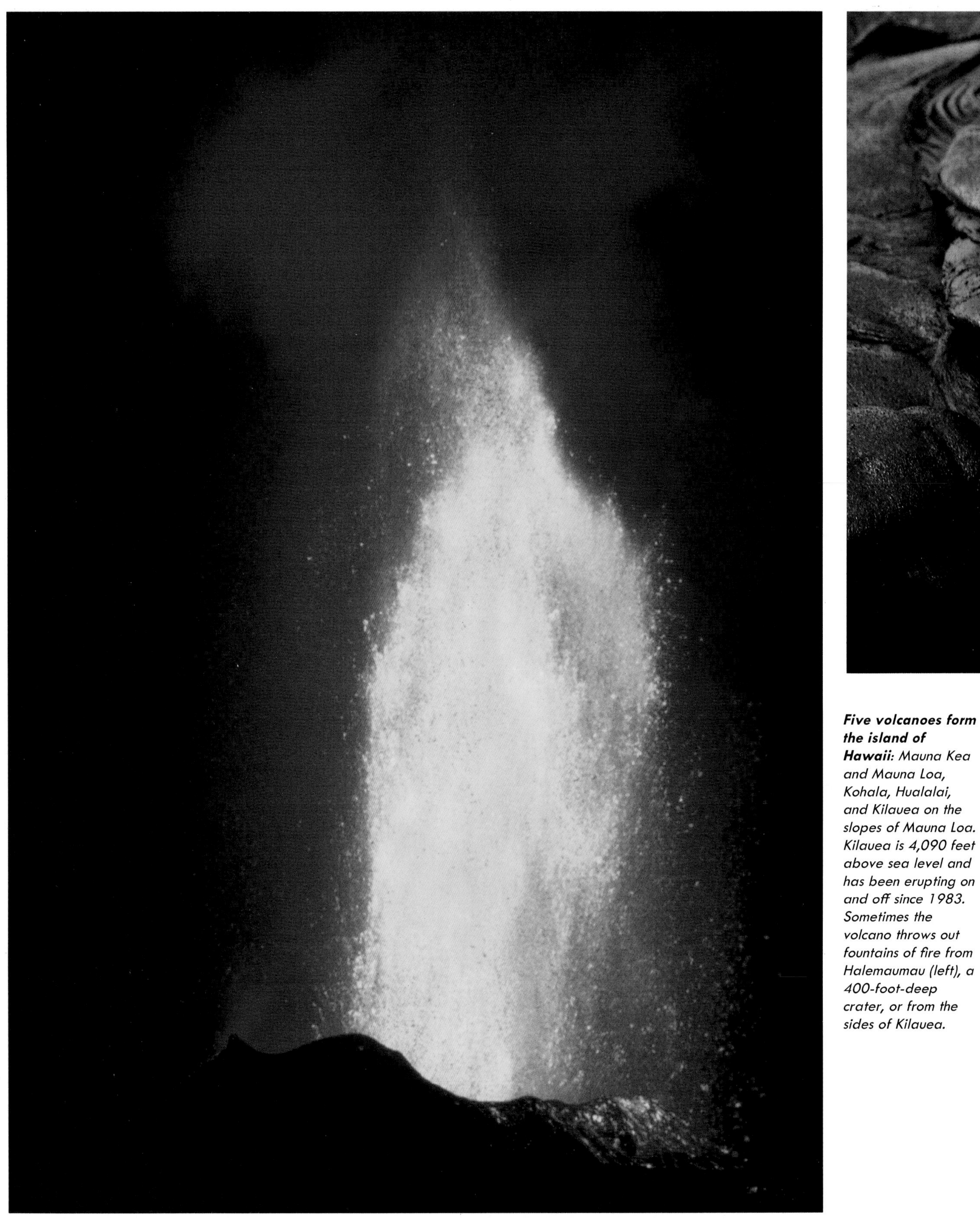

***Five volcanoes form the island of Hawaii:*** *Mauna Kea and Mauna Loa, Kohala, Hualalai, and Kilauea on the slopes of Mauna Loa. Kilauea is 4,090 feet above sea level and has been erupting on and off since 1983. Sometimes the volcano throws out fountains of fire from Halemaumau (left), a 400-foot-deep crater, or from the sides of Kilauea.*

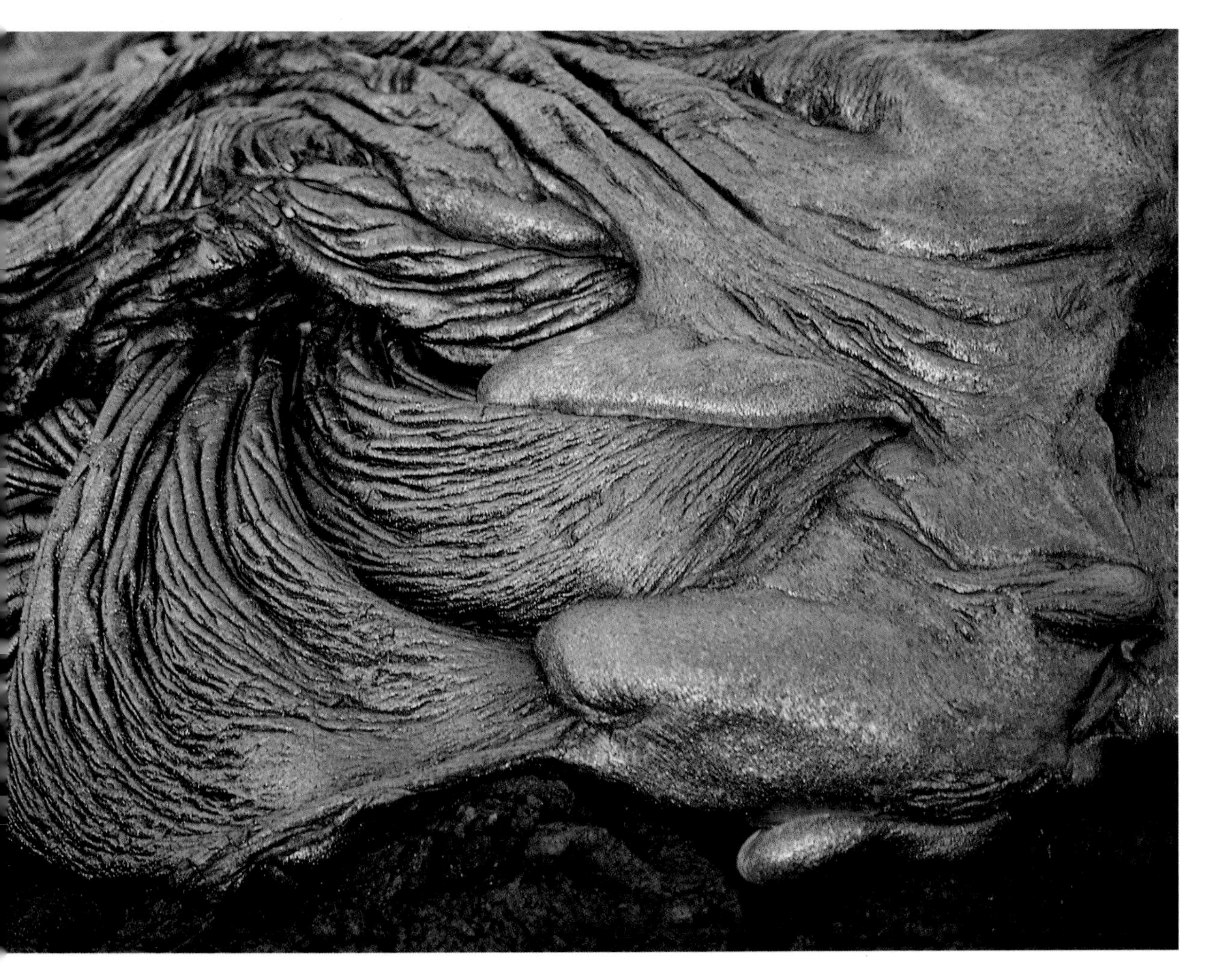

***Hawaiian volcanoes release two kinds of lava.*** *Geologists know them as either* pahoehoe *(left) or* 'a'a. *The former is generally smooth with wrinkles interrupting its surface like crinkled satin; the latter, because of its different gas content, solidifies into a mass of small, clinkerlike rocks with very rough surfaces.*

The Hawaiian volcanoes are not tall and cone-shaped, like Mount Hood in Washington, for example, nor do they erupt violently. Instead, the occasional eruption looks more like a spectacular, natural fireworks display. As the lava flows, it builds broad mountains with shallow craters that are known as calders here.

Hawaii National Park was designated by the United States Congress in August of 1916, taking in three volcanoes—Mauna Loa and Kilauea on Hawaii and the dormant Haleakala on Maui. But in 1961, the park was split in two to form Haleakala National Park and the Hawaii Volcanoes National Park. The two largest and most active volcanoes on Earth are contained in a unique ecosystem of stark, surprising beauty—the park also features giant fern groves, hardwood rain forests, and exotic bird and plant life. In addition to its spectacular fauna and flora, Hawaii Volcanoes National Park is one of the few places in the world where visitors can look into an active volcano.

The vast eroded landscape of Haleakala Crater is an extraordinary sight, made all the more startling at dawn when sunlight strikes the chemicals in the rocks and stains the hills and sides of the pit with a multitude of colors.

Volcanic products—the streams of molten rock from the Earth's interior—are composed for the most part of silicates and oxides mixed with abundant water vapor and various gases. The lava that makes up volcanic islands varies a great deal; two different flows have been identified in Hawaii. Their Hawaiian names *pahoehoe* and *'a'a* are universally used by geologists; *pahoehoe* is hotter, smoother, and holds more gas than *'a'a*, which has a rough exterior and is denser within. The material of the two types is virtually the same; the differences lie in their composition, gas content, and temperature.

The many small eruptions that have taken place on Hawaii over the past decades have usually been less violent than others around the world. Hawaiian lavas are more fluid, less viscous and hot than lava elsewhere because the average gas content is only about 0.5 to 1 percent of their weight. A high gas content produces very viscous, thick lava, and when combined with high temperatures, the trapped gases are tightly compressed, then build to a high pressure, and when they finally escape it is with considerable force.

Kilauea's last eruption was in 1960, but as Washington's Mount St. Helens demonstrated in 1980, even an apparently dormant cone can come alive with violent activity when least expected. But warnings of a build-up in subterranean pressure usually rumble beforehand; associated small earthquakes provide further warning and the volcano swells or inflates, which causes an outward tilting of its slopes. This tilt is measured by tilt-meters; the changes in inflating or deflating volcanoes are measured by a process called leveling.

Although the possibility of large eruptions still exists, it is not very likely, since Hawaii is moving away from the hot spot which generates the pressure and the molten lava. Although the great days of enormous activity for the Big Island's volcanoes are probably over, the marks of past activity are still visible.

Of particular note are the bleak, now cold prairies of cindery volcanic stone along Hawaii's Chain of Craters road, on the grim slopes west of the mountains, and in the area's oddities, like the lava tubes. Rushing lava streams cooled on the surface while molten magma continued to flow underneath. Once drained of magma, a long tunnel remained, like a stone tube with a rounded ceiling and flat floor.

On these mountaintops there is still a very real sense of being in a moonscape—the first astronauts trained here in a vast crater—while the coast is still linked to the mountains by a wide, barren expanse of once molten rock.

Mauna Kea, a dormant volcano north of the national park, rises 13,796 feet from the seabed and has the distinction of being the world's highest mountain. By contrast, Mount Everest, often cited as having that honor, is in fact only 32,130 feet tall. If Mauna Kea becomes active again, the 13,678 feet that are now visible above the ocean's surface could be augmented by molten lava.

Mauna Loa is the world's tallest active volcano. When it erupts—about once every three and a half years—lava flows from the central crater as well as out of openings on the sides, called fissures.

Mount Haleakala on Maui is a typical shield-type volcano, like its siblings on Hawaii. The mountain sits on the eastern side of the island and rises to a height of 10,023 feet, with a vast volcanic crater that is about 7½ miles long, 2½ miles wide and 3,000 feet deep. Haleakala last erupted in 1790; it is considered dormant but not extinct.

Haleakala's head is high above the treeline, yet within its crater flourishes the silversword, an odd plant, which grows only above 6,000 feet on this mountain and nowhere else on Earth. Botanists think this

***Spectacular fiery lava*** *flowing into the sea (left) gives a clear image of the forces at work on this tropical island. Although active, Hawaii's volcanoes are relatively gentle, and the Hawaii Volcanoes National Park was set up to preserve Mauna Loa and Kilauea in their natural settings.*

***The vivid green of new growth*** *shows how ferns (below) find a way to push through the dark lava flows from previous eruptions.*

*Among the best known of Hawaii's endemic plants are the ferns (right), the acacia koa, several species of hibiscus, alpine silverswords, and shrubby violets.*

spiky silver-gray plant, a member of the sunflower family, has evolved on the island from seeds carried by air currents across the Pacific.

After growing for up to 20 years, the silversword blooms once, producing a cluster of reddish-purple and yellow flowers, and then dies. Hundreds of seeds are produced by each flower, and as the seeds develop, the plant slowly deteriorates until all that is left is the dry "skeleton." Hawaiians know this plant as "gray-gray" because of the color of the plant when it is not in bloom.

The iiwi, a Hawaiian finch with vibrant red feathers and a long pointed curved beak, is one of the rare and exotic birds at home in the national park. The iiwi's colorful plumage was once used to make the ornate ceremonial robes worn by Hawaiian nobility. Iiwis are more likely to be heard before they are seen because of their shrill call. Bird watchers may also spot the elepaio, a flycatcher found only in the Hawaiian islands. This active bird is bold and curious by nature, and feeds on insects.

# KAUAI

THE ADJECTIVE "FANTASTIC" describes the landcape of Kauai better than most, for the island is an extraordinary mixture of geographical and geological features. Basically a mountaintop protruding from the sea, the island is bordered by cliffs of an awesome height, of which the steep and greatly indented palisades of the northwestern Na Pali Coast are the best example. The beaches at their feet are often composed of unusually colored silicate particles, resulting in miles of deserted strips of postcard-like golden, sandy beaches. Other beaches attract surfers challenged by the fast-breaking surf with waves that can tower up to 14 feet high.

Kauai's dazzling natural wonders in their lush, tropical settings draw hundreds of thousands of tourists each year, yet the island remains unspoiled. Compared to Maui or the heavily populated Oahu, this island feels like a backwater. It has no high buildings at all; its major settlement, Lihue, is small and simple; and, since few major roads exist, life for the residents is slow and quiet. It is still possible to appreciate the island's wonders in splendid isolation, or feel as if you are the first person to view sights that have captivated human attention for centuries.

Westernmost of the major Hawaiian islands, Kauai covers 555 square miles and has just over 90 miles of coastline. It is also the oldest of a group of eight volcanic islands that are several million years old. Kauai was formed by one huge volcano about eight million years ago, and all that remains of the ancient cone is 5,208-foot Mount Waialeale. Like all of Kauai's volcanoes, it has long been extinct. It is now threaded with waterfalls; the most spectacular, Wailua Falls near Kapaa, has an 80-foot drop. It was here that Hawaiian chiefs once proved their courage by diving into the pool at the foot of the falls; local legend maintained that only men with royal blood would be brave enough to attempt this death-defying feat. The Wailua River, on the eastern side of Kauai, is the island's only waterway that is navigable.

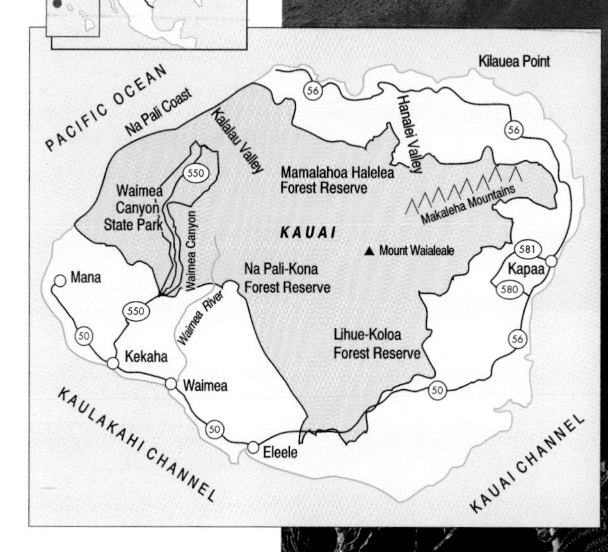


***Frilled native ferns*** *(right) add a timeless quality to the natural beauty of Kalalau Valley. Ferns were the most abundant form of land plant during the Carboniferous period, which began millions of years ago. Scientists sometimes call it The Age of Ferns.*

The heights of Kauai are a vivid green—unlike the snow-capped mountains of

***This small Pacific island*** *is a paradise for birds. A small blue heron (above) floats on a leaf while eyeing the water for food, which it will grasp with its powerful, dagger-shaped beak. All herons have patches of powder-down feathers on their breast and rump; the powder produced by these feathers is used to remove slime from the feathers when preening.*

Hawaii—due to the massive amount of rain which falls on this tiny island. It is not only the wettest of all the islands, but the wettest place on Earth, receiving the highest rainfall anywhere. Kauai's seven rivers emanate from the centrally located Mount Waialeale, the wettest spot on this whole wet island, where 500 inches of rain fall every year. The soaked terrain below has produced some of the world's most productive sugar cane fields, the backbone of the island's economy.

This rainfall provides for a remarkable number of habitats: Kauai's canyons, its steep and wooded cliffs, and its well-forested interior harbor a different range of animals, birds, and plants from the other Hawaiian islands. Fortunately for the wildlife, and unlike most of the other islands, Kauai remains relatively undeveloped, especially in its densely wooded interior, which is virtually inaccessible.

In the label-conscious 20th century, the island's nickname is the Garden Isle. Even given the fact that the flora of all the Hawaiian islands is amazingly rich and diverse, this title is peculiarly appropriate to Kauai, whose vegetation is truly extraordinary, lush, and varied. More than 200 endangered plant species are protected on the island.

As Kauai has not suffered as much at the hands of developers, the natural balance has not been lost, and much of the land remains wild and virgin. Kauai has preserved most of its species, some of them highly unusual. Among them is a violet that can grow over 6 feet tall; in Europe, the violet is a tiny plant, but in Kauai's moisture-laden climate it grows to enormous heights.

Birdlife, too, is particularly unusual here, although, sadly, some of the species are now extinct. Red-and-black honeycreepers are rarer than they once were but can still be seen, and in the higher levels of the island, iiwi and apapane still live in the treetops. Although clearly audible, they

***The humid, tropical climate of Kauai*** *is ideal for the banana plant (above), which can be grown all year round. The plant is, in fact, a gigantic herb that grows from an underground stem to form a false trunk up to 20 feet high. A plant only produces one bunch of fruit, grouped in hands of 10 to 20 bananas. After fruiting, the plant is cut down, and new shoots start to rise from the underground stem.*

***The cascading waters*** *of 80-foot Wailua Falls (left) add a sprinkling of moisture to the surrounding ferns, breadfruit, and fragrant ginger trees. Wailua, which means "twin waters," was important to the ancient Hawaiians.*

may not always be visible; the iiwi gurgles and makes humanlike whistles and reedy notes, often described as the sound of a child playing with a rusty harmonica. These birds drink nectar, often from the blooms of the lehua, with their slender, curved beaks. The iiwi is one of about six Hawaiian finches whose plumage was traditionally used to make colorful cloaks and other ornamentation for Hawaiian nobility; it is still possible to see some of the beautiful garments made from tufts of feathers in the island's museums. Hunting the bird for this purpose has been stopped, although it is still cited by some as the reason for the bird's near-extinction. Others, however, blame habitat destruction, the introduction of livestock, cats, rats, and non-native forest birds. Although the iiwi is still common on Kauai, it is extinct on Lanai, almost extinct on Molokai and rare on Oahu and Maui.

The akialoa, another Hawaiian finch, is a Kauai native, with its natural habitat being upper mountain rain forests. Like the iiwi and apapane, the akialoa feeds on flower nectar, particularly that of ohias and lobeliads, as well as insects. It uses its curved,

***The rugged beauty of Hanalei Bay*** *(left), in the north of the island, fronts the flat green patchwork of taro fields that lie in the valley behind the bay. Taro (also called eddo or dasheen) is an important cash crop for the island, and is cultivated in the rich, well-drained soil. The underground tubers of this herbaceous plant are harvested and eaten as cooked vegetables, or made into the local poi, while the leaves are more often stewed. Coconut, fruits, and macadamia nuts make up the other important island products.*

***The breathtaking gorge of Waimea Canyon*** *(left) coils across the south-western end of the island in spectacular fashion. Nimble-footed wild goats roam the cliffs, and the scarlet of birds and flowers flashes against the green landscape.*

*Many of the native trees of these Pacific islands served more than one purpose. Coconuts were used for eating, the fibers of the husk for making rope, and the fronds for shade. The bark from paper mulberry was made into cloth, and the thorny leaves of the pandanus were cleaned and woven into mats, sails for canoes, pillows, and sandals.*

slender, sharp beak for probing dense moss and tree bark to locate and then devour its small prey. The akialoa's loud and deep trilling song can quite easily be mistaken for that of a canary.

A migrant from the freezing Alaskan winters is the golden plover, which flies all the way to its warmer winter haunts in only 48 hours, many birds flying nonstop.

The eroded valley of Waimea Canyon which cuts across the western side of Kauai is the island's best-known natural feature. The canyon was created by wind and water gradually eroding the often soft volcanic rock and is inevitably labeled the Grand Canyon of the Pacific. A steep-sided gash, 10 miles long and 2,800 feet deep in places, it has a thickly forested floor along which runs the Waimea River.

Against a dark red and purple background, the walls of the canyon are striped in ocher, red, and yellow. The enormous variety of lush plant life includes red torch gingers that bloom year-round, wild lychee and guava, plum trees at Kokee, and many varieties of ferns—only the jagged peaks of the canyon are bare. In the thick vegetation clothing the canyon's sides, wild goats and the occasional pig can be seen grazing.

Lookout spots from roads along the length of the canyon culminate in a high point of 4,000 feet at Kalalau Valley which offers views down the often misty valley to the Na Pali coastline below and to the sea. A unique species of hibiscus tree flowers in the cliff pockets, while white tropicbirds and other exotic birds gracefully glide over the valley's canyon walls.

Perched on a 20-foot cliff at the northernmost point of Kauai, Kilauea Point National Wildlife Refuge is a habitat for a number of seabirds including red-footed boobies, albatrosses, and wedge-tailed shearwaters. The red-footed booby often captures the attention of natives, as well as visitors, because of its crash landings, which it manages to survive unscathed. Off the coast, groups of humpback whales, porpoises, and giant sea turtles frequently can be spotted in the sparkling azure ocean.

The Pacific's inviting, cooling waters are off limit for humans in January, when the baking sun is at its most intense, because of large populations of a deadly species of jellyfish. These transparent creatures can sting if stepped on, often resulting in death. It is then that the man-made wonders of swimming pools are most appreciated.

The sculpted canyons and remote cliffs of rainswept Kauai offer a different vision of the state of Hawaii, far removed from the beaches and tourist centers of the other islands. Kauai has kept its pristine, mysterious atmosphere, its primeval beauty, and has the air of a secret and very much unexplored island.

# Canada

## The last great North American wilderness

Canada is a vast country, occupying almost the entire northern half of the North American continent. Covering a total area of 3,849,673 square miles, it is the largest country in the western hemisphere and the second largest in the world. Much of the country is unspoiled wilderness, with an extraordinarily diverse assortment of topography, vegetation, and wildlife.

Arctic tundra, snow-fed glaciers, majestic mountains, dense forests, lush grasslands, rolling prairies, jagged coastlines, tumbling rivers, pristine lakes, and nurturing wetlands are all part of the rich variety of landscapes that make up Canada. Among its natural wonders are the world's most significant and extensive dinosaur bonebed, the highest tides, the largest free-roaming bison herd, the largest prehistoric ice sheet south of the Arctic Circle, one of the world's most spectacular waterfalls, and glacier-studded national parks.

Wildlife abounds in remote areas, as well as in parks and sanctuaries. Elk, antelope, mountain goats, moose, deer, grizzly bears, bighorn sheep, beavers, caribous, reindeers, bison, and polar bears are among the 163 species of terrestrial mammals found in Canada. Various whales, dolphins, porpoises, sea lions, seals, and walruses can be counted among Canada's 35 species of marine mammals. There are also more than 500 species of birds, 42 species of reptiles, 41 species of amphibians, and thousands of species each of fish and insects.

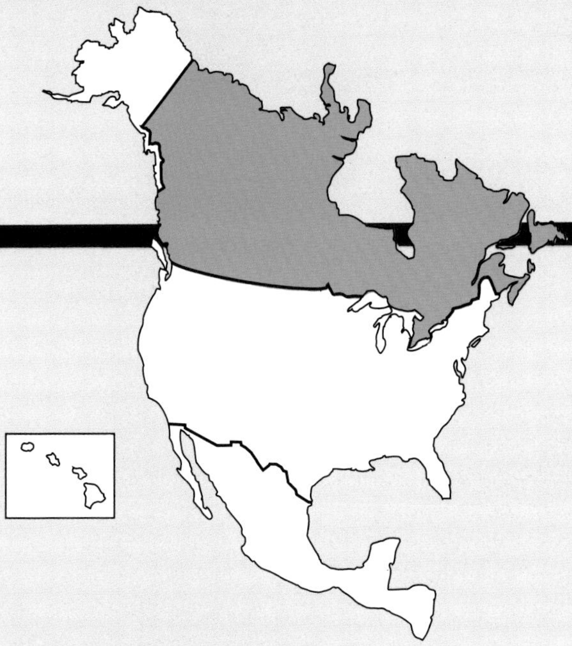

Some of Canada's magnificent landscapes, wildlife, and areas of historic interest are protected by its system of national parks, which was founded in 1885. There are currently 34 national parks, encompassing a total area of more than 72,587 square miles. Canada leads the world in the amount of designated parkland, and the government has expressed its intention of creating at least one national park to represent each of the 68 distinct natural regions thus far identified. Canada is also the leading federal agency in the UNESCO World Heritage Convention, which recognizes and safeguards the world's cultural and natural heritage for future generations. Of the more than 215 World Heritage Sites, 9 are in Canada. The country's natural heritage is its national legacy.

ONTARIO, NEW YORK

# NIAGARA FALLS

EACH SECOND, up to 700,000 gallons of water thunder down a cliff into the Niagara River, creating one of the largest and most impressive waterfalls in the world. Named *Onguiaahra*—"the thunderer of waters"—by the Neutral Indians, Niagara Falls has long been regarded as one of the world's great natural wonders, and its majestic power and beauty attract an estimated 15 million tourists each year.

The falls were formed about 12,000 years ago when melting and retreating glaciers caused the waters of Lake Erie to overflow at the end of the last Ice Age. The rushing waters ran north to Lake Ontario, carving a channel in the landscape; the ancient waterway is now the Niagara River, and the channel is now the Niagara Gorge. Erosion caused the riverbed to drop abruptly, creating a steep cliff. The water that rushes off the edge of the cliff forms one of the world's most spectacular waterfalls.

The Canadian-American international boundary bisects the Niagara River, separating the cities of Niagara Falls, Ontario, and Niagara Falls, New York, as well as the famous waterfalls. Partly in Canada and partly in the United States, Niagara Falls consists of two major waterfalls: Canadian, or Horseshoe, Falls and American Falls.

Canadian Falls is the larger and more spectacular of the two, measuring 176 feet high and more than 2,200 feet wide at its crest; the crest is characterized by a deep, horseshoe-shaped curve, from which the nickname derives. The depth of the river at the crest of the Canadian Falls is about 20 feet, compared with only about 39 inches at the crest of the American Falls. Ninety-four percent of the total volume of water at Niagara Falls crashes over the crestline of Horseshoe Falls, at a rate of almost 41 million gallons a minute.

Dividing Canadian Falls from American Falls is Goat Island. Unlike Canadian Falls, American Falls extends in a fairly straight line for about 1,075 feet, plummeting 184 feet. Luna Island separates it from the smaller Bridal Veil Falls. With a flow of almost 3.7 million gallons of water a

***A crowd of daffodils*** *(right) cheers this spectacular display at Horseshoe Falls. The Niagara Plateau is made up of layers of rocks, which are responsible for the vertical drop over which the Niagara River plunges. The clearness of the water enhances the drama of this natural wonder.*

minute, the American waterfalls carry only 10 percent of Niagara's total volume.

After rushing over the edge of the falls, the river's waters flow along for about 3.7 miles before reaching the dramatic Whirlpool Rapids, where the waters churn and plunge at a speed of more that 30 miles an hour. The river then winds through the Niagara Gorge, past Queenston Heights, Fort George, Lewiston, and Fort Niagara, and finally into Lake Ontario.

In the Table Rock Scenic Tunnels, an elevator descends to the base of the falls, where tunnels pass in front of and behind the falls, enabling visitors to see, hear, and feel the roar of the waters crashing around them. Another popular perspective is from the water: the "Maid of the Mist" boats, which have operated since 1846, carry sightseers directly in front of the falls for perhaps the best panorama of the cascading water, ever-present mist, and rainbows. One of the two observation towers has a deck that looms 775 feet above the falls, and helicopter flights offer another perspective.

Every evening, the falls are illuminated for a few hours by power generated by the river. Under certain nocturnal conditions, a lunar rainbow can appear above the falls. In winter, Niagara Falls is a spectacular sight, shrouded in ice and snow. Occasionally, an "ice bridge" forms which spans the river from shore to shore.

***The mist that shrouds the falls*** *(above) is particularly alluring on sunny days when rainbows dance above the waters. Legend has it that Indians would throw a girl into the mists as a sacrifice to the thunder god below.*

***Dressed in winter white*** *(right), Canadian, or Horseshoe, Falls seems even more mystical than in summer light. Ice and snow have taken their toll on American Falls, which has frozen over at least five times.*

At the brink of the falls, the underlying rock consists of hard dolomite limestone resting on softer layers of shale and sandstone. Over thousands of years, the impact of the rushing water striking the foot of the precipice has caused the softer rock to erode and undercut the harder cap rock. Periodically, the cap rock collapses, and the falls recede. Due to erosion, Niagara Falls is now 7 miles farther upstream than its original site.

However, joint efforts of the Canadian and American governments have slowed the erosion of the falls considerably. Since 1950, some of the rushing water has been diverted to hydroelectric power plants before it reaches the falls. Iron rods, bolts, and cables have been strategically placed to strengthen the underlying rock. By the turn of the century, geologists say erosion will be reduced to just over an inch a year.

NOVA SCOTIA, NEW BRUNSWICK

# BAY OF FUNDY

SANDWICHED BETWEEN THE COASTS of Nova Scotia and New Brunswick, the Bay of Fundy is remarkable for its dramatic tides, among the world's highest and the largest in volume. Twice daily, around 126.5 billion tons of water—the equivalent of the daily discharge of all the rivers in the world—surge in and out of the bay.

Tides are caused by the gravitational pull of the Sun and the Moon on bodies of water connected with an ocean. Two additional phenomena working together produce the giant tides at the Bay of Fundy. The first is the shape and size of the bay, which is funnel-shaped, with widths ranging from 30 to 50 miles along its 94-mile length. A large volume of water from the North Atlantic Ocean floods into the wide mouth of the Bay of Fundy. The bay narrows rapidly, and at its head, it splits into two smaller arms, Chignecto Bay and Minas Basin. As the water rushes up the narrowing bay, it piles up on itself, gathering momentum and velocity. Thus the highest tides occur at the head of the bay.

The second phenomenon is the stationary wave, which is caused by the tides sloshing in and out of the bay. By chance, the rhythm of the tides in the bay roughly echoes the rhythm of the tides of the North Atlantic: the Bay of Fundy-Gulf of Maine tidal system has a natural oscillation period of about 13 hours, and its tides respond to a push every $12\frac{1}{2}$ hours from the North Atlantic. The two movements combine and reinforce each other, driving the water to great heights in the Bay of Fundy.

High Fundy tides cause tidal bores and reversing falls. A tidal bore occurs when the incoming tide pushes upstream against the current, producing an effect in which the river appears to run backward. In North America, tidal bores are unique to the Bay of Fundy; they occur in many rivers around the head of the bay.

The Reversing Falls Rapids at Saint John, New Brunswick, are a series of rapids and whirlpools at the mouth of the Saint John River. Four times a day, when the bay tides rise higher than the river, the rapids

***The immense tides in the Bay of Fundy*** *(right) leave their mark along the coastal cliffs. The waves at Hopewell Rocks have undercut the cliffs, leaving huge, isolated stacks. In summer, more than 20 kinds of whales can be seen around the bay, including finback, minke, and humpback.*

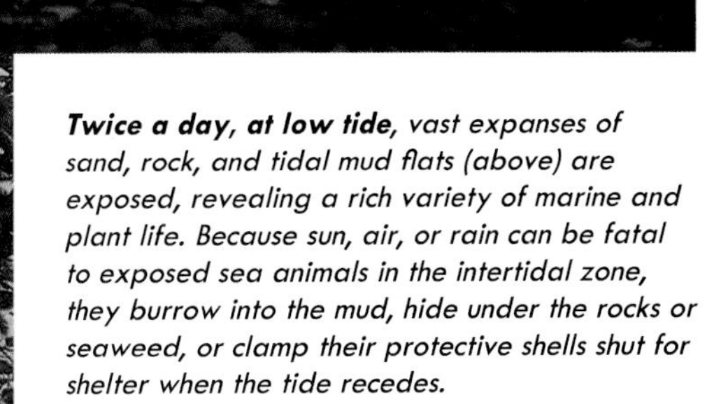

***Twice a day, at low tide,*** *vast expanses of sand, rock, and tidal mud flats (above) are exposed, revealing a rich variety of marine and plant life. Because sun, air, or rain can be fatal to exposed sea animals in the intertidal zone, they burrow into the mud, hide under the rocks or seaweed, or clamp their protective shells shut for shelter when the tide recedes.*

are forced to reverse their flow. When the tide ebbs, the river flows into the sea again.

New Brunswick's Fundy National Park skirts the bay for 8 miles and encompasses a total area of almost 80 square miles. Alma Beach is one of the best places to watch the incoming tide rising, at a rate of almost an inch per minute. With its phenomenal tides and their profound effects on the lowland and marine environments, the Bay of Fundy is quite unlike any other body of water in the world.

ALBERTA

# DINOSAUR PROVINCIAL PARK

BENEATH AN EERIE, SURREALISTIC LANDSCAPE in the southeastern corner of Alberta lies one of the world's most important and extensive deposits of dinosaur skeletons and fossilized bone. Dinosaur Provincial Park is a graveyard of the dinosaurs, reptiles, amphibians, birds, and mammals that inhabited the area some 75 million years ago.

At that time, what is now the Red Deer River Valley was covered in lush forests. Rivers flowed east across a coastal plain into Bearpaw Sea, a giant inland expanse that covered much of the western prairies. Numerous species of dinosaurs inhabited this warm, swampy, marshy region, and when they died, their bodies often floated downriver. The tons of sand, silt, and mud that were also carried by the rivers subsequently buried their remains, and the massive corpses were slowly fossilized.

The dinosaurs disappeared 63 million years ago, but more than 300 complete skeletons of 35 different species have been uncovered in the park. They range from the relatively small *Stegosaurus* to the large, ferocious *Albertosaurus*, which stood over 16 feet tall and weighed up to 2.7 tons. The Dinosaur Trail takes modern-day fossil hunters into the Valley of the Dinosaurs, where many important finds have been made. Hadrosaurs (duck-billed dinosaurs) and ceratopians (horned dinosaurs) are the most common fossil groups found in the park, and fossils of more than 80 species of other vertebrates—frogs, lizards, turtles, mammals, and birds—have been found.

Belying its apparently barren, harsh, and unforgiving terrain, Dinosaur Provincial Park nurtures a fragile and unique ecosystem, with a rich variety of plants and animals, many rare or endangered. The 16,380-acre park also protects Canada's largest and most spectacular tract of badlands. Because of its historic, scientific, and cultural significance, Dinosaur Provincial Park was designated a UNESCO World Heritage Site in 1980.

***Towering hoodoos,*** *or rock pillars (right), dot the landscape along the Red Deer River Valley. These sandstone sculptures were created by the same activity that formed the Rockies 70 million years ago. As the continent was being reshaped, the Red Deer River shifted eastward, cutting through fossil-rich layers of silt and sand to form the hoodoos.*

## Dinosaur treasure

Seventy-five million years ago, the swamplands that have become Dinosaur Provincial Park were home to a host of dinosaurs, including *Panoplosaurus* (above) and *Tyrannosaurus* (below).

The Late Cretaceous soil here contains a wealth of perfectly preserved fossils, including smaller reptiles and plants as well as the mighty dinosaurs. It has been popular with fossil hunters since the first remains were uncovered by American and Canadian museum scientists soon after the beginning of the century. Most geologists recognize this area as containing some of the world's most extensive fossil beds.

The armor-plated *Panoplosaurus* may not have been as large as some of the other dinosaurs of its time but it was well equipped to protect itself. Sharp, pointed spikes protruded from its sides along the length of its body, large square plates protected its neck and shoulders, and smaller, bony studs covered its back. If attacked, scientists believe, the *Panoplosaurus* simply lowered itself to the ground and used its armor plating to fend off the enemy. It could also have used the spikes to attack a smaller opponent.

The towering *Tyrannosaurus* could reach up to 50 feet long and weigh more than 8 tons. The creature's huge body has led to its reputation as the most terrifying of all reptiles. Scientists think that *Tyrannosaurus* attacked and devoured smaller dinosaurs by hiding in tall trees and pouncing on its unsuspecting victims.

BRITISH COLUMBIA

# GLACIER NATIONAL PARK

MORE THAN 100 YEARS AGO, when the Canadian Pacific railway was eager to find a pass through the wild, formidable mountains in the area that now contains Glacier National Park, general manager William Van Horne marveled at what he described as "the climax of mountain scenery."

One of Canada's oldest national parks, Glacier covers an area of 521 square miles in the rugged Selkirk and Purcell ranges of the Columbia Mountains, just west of the Rockies, halfway between Revelstoke and Golden in southeastern British Columbia.

Spectacular vistas are common in the park, which was named for its 400 glaciers and icefields. Glacier-fed rivers and streams tumble down the mountains where countless avalanches have scarred the sheer valley walls and cliff faces. Erosion caused by glacial waters and underground rivers has created enormous caves.

The park's two principal features and phenomena are glaciers and avalanches. In winter, heavy snowfalls can accumulate to a depth of 75 feet. The fresh snow maintains the park's many glaciers and contributes to its extensive avalanche activity.

Perhaps the most prominent glacier is the Illecillewaet, looming 6,561 feet above sea level. Scarred and punctuated with giant crevasses and seracs (tall columns of ice), the massive icefield falls a distance of more than 3,500 feet and covers an area of 10 square miles.

The best time to see glaciers here is late July through early September, since at other times of the year they are covered in a thick blanket of fresh snow. Several major glaciers and mountain peaks are visible from a viewpoint on the Trans-Canada Highway at the summit of Rogers Pass. Hikers can tackle the Abbott Ridge, Glacier Crest, Avalanche Crest, or the Great Glacier trails for a closer look at glacial ice.

Because of the sheer mountain walls, this is one of the world's most active avalanche areas. During the annual "snow wars" at Rogers Pass, the world's largest mobile

***Mount Bonney*** *(right) in the Selkirk Range is one of many peaks which is mantled by glaciers. Snow- and ice-covered peaks tower to heights of over 11,000 feet and 12 percent of the landscape is permanently capped in snow and ice.*

avalanche control program constantly monitors snow conditions and, when necessary, dislodges potential avalanches with howitzers to stabilize the slopes.

The Nakimu Caves in the Cougar Brook Valley, just southeast of Rogers Pass, are another natural phenomenon. Discovered in 1903, they are believed to be the longest caves in Canada. Three miles of underground passageways and several huge caverns (no longer accessible to the public) have been carved by the glacial waters and disappearing streams that eroded the valley's soft limestone bedrock.

With elevations rising from the Beaver River Valley at 2,798 feet to Mount Dawson at 11,122 feet, the park has three major zones of vegetation. All are affected by the heavy precipitation, over 58 inches annually with a 50 percent chance of rain in the summer and snowfall almost every day during the winter.

Mild temperatures, heavy precipitation, and a six-month growing season sustain the lush Columbia forest zone. Covering elevations between 1,968 and 4,265 feet, the forest is renowned for its abundant western red cedar and western hemlock, as well as its dense and diverse understory of devil's club, thimbleberry, false box, and ferns. The aptly named skunk cabbage proliferates in the valley wetlands in the spring.

A subalpine forest of Engelmann spruce, subalpine fir, and mountain hemlock, along with an understory of white rhododendron, black gooseberry, and mountain huckleberry, fills the interior subalpine forest zone at altitudes from 4,265 to 6,233 feet.

Above 6,233 feet, the forest thins into treeless alpine tundra, much of which is covered in glacial ice, poor soil, or bare rock. Only hardy, ground-hugging alpine plants such as moss campion and lichen can survive the cold temperatures, high winds, and hostile environment.

Another distinct vegetation zone is created by the avalanche paths that stretch from the craggy mountain peaks to the valleys. Typical vegetation includes slide alder, fern, blueberry, cow parsnip, and scrub willow.

Well adapted to the rugged mountain terrain, the mountain goat is the most common large mammal found in the park. Unlike bears, hoary marmots, ground squirrels, and other species that hibernate in winter, mountain goats can be seen year round foraging for food on the rocky mountain cliffs. The environment is generally too harsh for reptiles, and the only common amphibian is the western toad.

Roughly 180 bird species have been recorded in the park, 50 of which may be spotted on a good day in June. Few species are year-round residents; most leave by October for warmer climes. The Beaver River and Loop Brook trails offer excellent bird-watching opportunities. Golden eagles, white-tailed ptarmigans, water pipits, and rosy finches are found in the treeless alpine region. In winter, pine siskins, red crossbills, white-winged crossbills, and pygmy owls can be spotted from the Trans-Canada Highway.

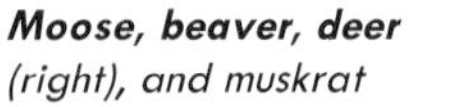

***Moose, beaver, deer*** *(right), and muskrat are common in the park, particularly along the wooded Beaver River Valley. But Glacier National Park is best known for its large population of black bear and has perhaps the country's highest density of grizzly bears.*

***Late July and early August*** *are the most colorful months in the upper subalpine meadows (left). Wildflowers such as glacier lily, mountain valerian, Indian paintbrush, lupine, mountain spiraea, and various heathers burst into flower, carpeting the meadows in a myriad of colors.*

***The Illecillewaet Glacier*** *feeds a fast-flowing river of the same name (above), as well as numerous streams that flow down through the valley. Since the early 1970s, the glacier has been advancing almost 33 feet a year. At this rate it will cross the Trans-Canada Highway in the year 2641. In the background brood the rugged peaks of Mount Sir Donald and the Selkirks.*

Prehistoric man, native people, and early explorers all regarded this unforgiving, mountainous region as a no-man's-land. Yet it played a pivotal role in the early history of the province; the dream of Canada's first prime minister, Sir John A. Macdonald, for a coast-to-coast railroad prompted the search for a pass through the mountains.

The promise of a trans-Canada railroad lured British Columbia, then a British colony, into confederation in 1871. It took the engineers and surveyors about 15 years to find a route through the towering, snow-covered peaks, the narrow valleys, and the hard metamorphic and igneous rock of the Selkirk Range. In 1881, Major A. B. Rogers, the engineer in charge of the mountain division of the Canadian Pacific Railway, discovered the pass which today bears his name.

With the railroad came tourism, which was further boosted when the Canadian Pacific Railway built Glacier House in 1886. Situated at the foot of Illecillewaet Glacier, with two professional climbing guides from Switzerland on the payroll to lead excursions, the hotel quickly became a focal point for recreational and professional mountaineering in North America, as well as one of Canada's first grand mountain resort hotels. (The hotel was closed in 1925 and demolished in 1929.)

To protect and preserve the region's unspoiled wilderness, Glacier National Park was created in 1886. The accessibility of the untamed mountains attracted alpinists from the United States, Britain, and Switzerland, who had mapped many of the park's peaks and glaciers by the turn of the century. To this day, the park is renowned for its mountaineering and various other recreational opportunities.

Although CPR passenger trains no longer run through historic Rogers Pass, a privately-owned tourist train operates in the region during the summer.

In 1962, construction of the Trans-Canada Highway via Rogers Pass, paralleling the original CPR line, was completed, making the park more accessible to the public. Flanked by awe-inspiring peaks and glaciers, the 25-mile stretch of the highway bisecting Glacier National Park is regarded as one of the world's most spectacular and scenic drives.

# Northern Lights

***A shimmering curtain*** *of red and pale golden lights (right) appears to hang across the polar sky during the aurora borealis. Alaska and northern Canada, with their vast dark skies over sparsely populated regions, are among the best locations in the northern hemisphere for viewing these magnificent light shows. The lights are most easily observed in February, when high barometric pressure remains stationary over the North Pole.*

***Magical looking,*** *this band of green (above) is part of the aurora borealis over an Alaskan forest. Some displays remain unchanged for hours, while others appear to dance across the polar skies. The most spectacular displays occur after periods of intense solar activity around the Sun, when charged particles are sent toward the Earth's atmosphere.*

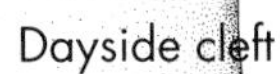


**The Equilibrium Model**

Scientists, attempting to understand why solar particles only enter the atmosphere at certain latitudes and why aurorae are only visible near the North and South poles, have developed this Equilibrium Model. The distorted shape of the magnetosphere (above right), where the Earth's magnetic fields extend into space, forces solar particles into beams, directed on the polar regions. Some particles enter the magnetosphere on the sunward side and penetrate the atmosphere through the dayside clefts. The inset (above) illustrates the main regions of the magnetosphere important in the formation of aurorae; the larger drawing is a detail of the yellow area of the inset.

***Auroral zones** that are oval are centered on magnetic poles and do not coincide with the Earth's circles of latitude.*

VISIBLE THROUGHOUT THE NORTHERN UNITED STATES AND CANADA, the aurora borealis, or northern lights, is a dazzling display that illuminates the whole night sky in the area surrounding the North Pole.

When solar winds carry charged particles from the Sun into the Earth's atmosphere, particles may be pulled into the pole's magnetic field. The particles vibrate the atmosphere's nitrogen and oxygen molecules to produce the colorful lights.

ALBERTA

# COLUMBIA ICEFIELD

THE LAST ICE AGE HAS YET TO RELINQUISH its grip on the vast Columbia Icefield, North America's largest sheet of prehistoric ice south of the Arctic Circle. Nestled in some of the highest mountains of the Canadian Rockies and spanning the Continental Divide, the icefield is the source of three of Canada's major river systems, which flow into three different oceans.

It is a spectacular, dramatic, and dynamic landscape, sculpted and scoured by great mountains and rivers of ice over thousands of years. The high elevation, low temperatures, and heavy snowfall combine to produce conditions that sustain the raw, rugged beauty of Columbia Icefield and its numerous glaciers.

A remnant of the great ice shield that blanketed most of Canada 10,000 to 15,000 years ago, the Columbia Icefield covers about 200 square miles with depths ranging from 420 to 1,200 feet. The icefield contains about 30 distinct glaciers, with several glacial tongues, or flows, extruding toward the lowlands. Perhaps the most impressive and most accessible of these is the Athabasca Glacier, a massive river of ice that is almost $1\frac{1}{2}$ square miles and reaches depths of 820 to 1,050 feet in some places. One-third of its area towers more than 8,530 feet above sea level—roughly the height of a 100-story building.

Due to the force of gravity and hydrostatic pressure, the glacial ice of the Columbia Icefield is constantly moving, transforming the landscape. Expanding and retreating ice snaps off enormous fragments of bedrock and drags them across the landscape, gouging valleys, vast basins, and steep cliffs and mountains as it travels.

Tons of glacial deposits and rock debris, called moraine, can be seen at the sides of glaciers, particularly Athabasca Glacier. Much of the scoured bedrock is pulverized into fine particles known as glacial flour, which gives the rivers their characteristic milky appearance and tints the glacial lakes brilliant aquamarine and turquoise hues.

Linking Lake Louise to Jasper is the 143-mile Icefield Parkway, one of the world's most scenic drives. Running parallel to the Continental Divide, the highway passes the spectacular icefields, glaciers, and mountains of the main eastern ranges of the Canadian Rockies, follows the headwaters of three major rivers, and crosses two major passes. En route, magnificent vistas unfold of snow-covered peaks, icy waterfalls, turquoise and emerald lakes, and alpine meadows.

The Columbia Icefield owes its grandeur to thousands of years of glaciation, a process that continues to this day.

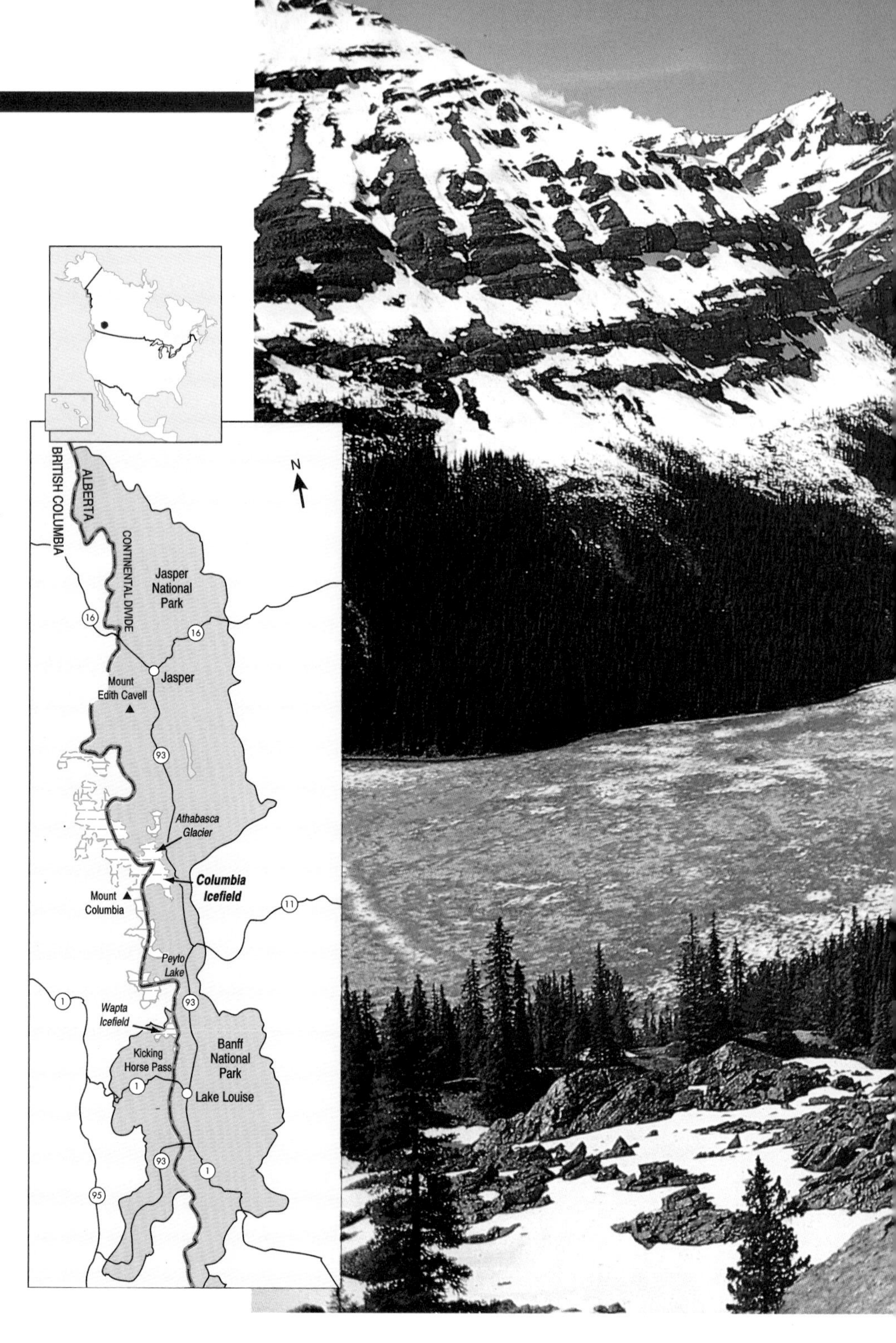


***The spring sun sparkles** on the surface of Peyto Lake (above) at the southern end of the 143-mile Icefield Parkway. The main glacial surface of the region drops off deeply into steep canyons. The Canadian lynx, with its large paws for moving over snow, is one of the few inhabitants here.*

***Glacial meltwater forms*** *when snow and ice melt in summer, and streams form on the surface of Athabasca Glacier. Streams start to flow (left) between hummocks of ice, cutting channels in the ice. The streams may run a long way over the surface before disappearing into tunnels within the ice.*

ALBERTA, NORTHWEST TERRITORIES

# WOOD BUFFALO NATIONAL PARK

IN A MEMORABLE SEQUENCE in the movie *Dances with Wolves*, vast herds of massive, shaggy bison, displaying surprising ability for their tremendous bulk, stampede across the open plains. The scene is a poignant reminder of the fact that some 50 to 60 million bison dominated the central plains of North America just a couple of centuries ago, before European settlers hunted them to the brink of extinction.

The more than 6,000 bison in the immense, unspoiled wilderness of Wood Buffalo National Park are the largest single remnant of that enormous population and now represent the world's largest free-roaming bison herd. Straddling Canada's 60th parallel, lying two-thirds in Alberta and one-third in the Northwest Territories, Wood Buffalo is a magnificent example of Canada's northern boreal plains, a rich mosaic of dense forests, meadows, muskegs, prairie, streams, lakes, and rivers. Covering 17,300 square miles, it is Canada's largest national park and one of the largest in the world.

The park was established in 1922 specifically to protect the last herd of wood bison, which then numbered about 1,500. A larger, darker subspecies of the plains bison, the wood bison is the largest herbivore on the North American continent.

Shortly after the park was created and the herd had begun to recover, a major error in wildlife management again threatened the wood bison with extinction. From 1925 to 1928, 6,673 plains bison from Buffalo National Park (which no longer exists) near Wainright, Alberta, were transferred to Wood Buffalo National Park. Plains bison interbred with the resident wood bison, creating a hybrid population that all but eradicated the indigenous species. This hybrid population remains in the park today.

Compounding the problem was the fact that most of the transplanted animals were infected with bovine brucellosis and tuberculosis, which they quickly transmitted to the healthy wood bison. Today, an estimated 30 to 50 percent of the bison population in Wood Buffalo is infected with these diseases. By the 1940s, wood bison were thought to be extinct in the area. However, in 1957, a herd of 200 purebred, healthy wood bison was discovered in a remote northwestern area of the park.

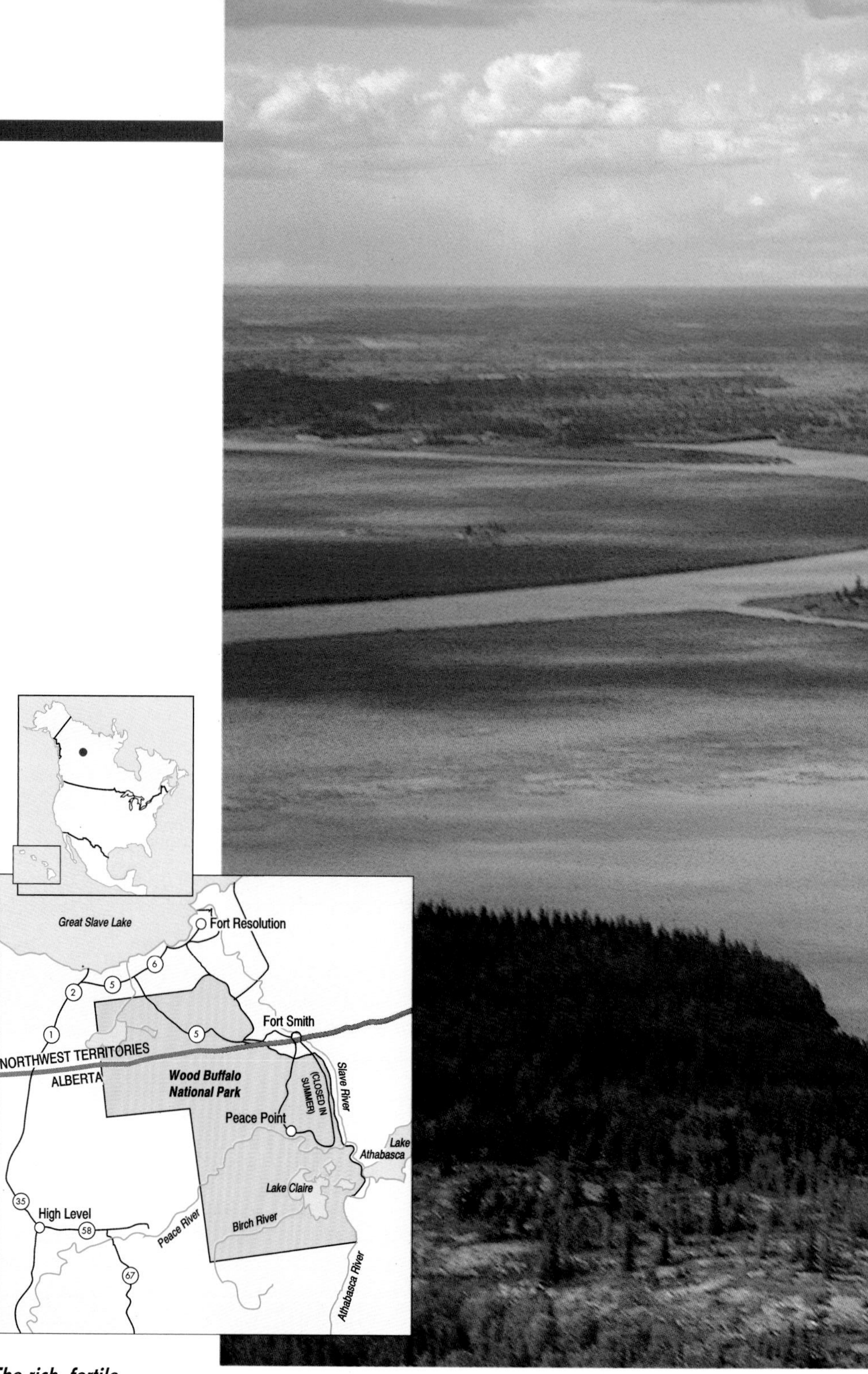


***The rich, fertile plains*** *of the Peace-Athabasca Delta (above) support many varieties of animals as well as providing grazing land for the national park's bison herds. During summer months, the park rangers provide insight into the diverse natural vegetation and wildlife with guided nature walks and illustrated lectures.*

The Peace-Athabasca Delta, created by the complex interplay between the waters of the Peace, Athabasca, and Birch rivers and Lake Athabasca, is a fertile oasis,

***The small Quatre Fourche River** (left) helped balance the region's ecosystem for centuries. During heavy rains, the river flowed backward, flooding the delta to keep shrubs at bay. Since the opening of a Peace River dam in 1968 floods rarely happen, and vegetation is changing with natural feeding grounds being lost.*

***The massive wood bison*** *(left) was saved from extinction by the creation of the national park. In 1790, an estimated 60 million plains, wood, and eastern bison roamed a vast area that stretched from the Northwest Territories to central Mexico and from the Rocky Mountains to New York.*

*European settlers soon learned what native tribes had long known—that bison were an excellent source of food, clothing, and shelter—and that knowledge marked the beginning of the decline of bisons in North America. Yet millions still roamed the open prairies in 1870. However, bison slaughter became so widespread that fewer than 2,000 were left by 1890.*

***This calliope hummingbird*** *(left), which grows to 3 inches long, is the smallest bird breeding in Canada and the United States. It is a territorial bird, and signals other birds to stay away by reflecting sunlight off its bright purple chin feathers.*

whose lakes, marshes, sedge meadows, and meandering streams support a rich variety of wildlife. Most of the park's bison graze here, on the largest undisturbed grass and sedge meadows in North America. The delta is also a habitat for black bears, lynxes, wolves, muskrats, beavers, moose, woodland caribous, and white-tailed deer.

A total of 230 species of birds frequents the delta, including rare peregrine falcons, bald eagles, and great blue herons, which nest here. Four important waterfowl flyways of North America intersect over the delta, resulting in a pageant of more than a million migrating ducks, geese, swans, and other waterfowl each spring and fall. The continent's most northerly colony of white pelicans feeds and nests on the islands of the Slave River near Fort Smith. In the spring, goldeye, pike, whitefish, and walleye return to spawn in the delta's lakes.

In the northeastern part of the park, the broad band of karst is regarded as the finest example of its kind in North America. Karst terrain is characterized by the underground caves that are created where seeping groundwater and rain dissolve the gypsum and limestone bedrock. The caves provide refuge for hibernating bats and reptiles, including the northernmost population of red-sided garter snakes.

When the underground caves grow too large, they eventually collapse under their own weight, creating depressions known as sinkholes. The park has thousands of these sinkholes, ranging from about 10 to 325 feet in diameter. When the sinkholes fall below the water table, sinkhole lakes are formed, which may draw small creeks underground.

***Acres of grassy wetlands*** *in the Peace-Athabasca Delta (left) provide homes for the park's wildlife population, including more than an estimated million ducks and geese each summer.*

*The rare whooping cranes (below) lay eggs and nest here after their spring migration from Texas. Although never abundant, whooping cranes once ranged over most of central North America. Yet destruction of wetlands for building and the killing of the birds for food and sport soon resulted in dwindling numbers. It was estimated that in 1941 there were only about 15 of the species left in North America; their numbers have now increased to about 200 as a result of successful breeding programs.*

In the southeastern section of the park, the Salt Plains extend in a dazzling landscape of salt-encrusted mud flats, salt mounds, and salt springs interspersed with grasslands. As salty water emerges from underground springs, flows across the plains, and evaporates, it leaves behind salt and other dissolved minerals. During dry years, salt mounds more than 6 feet high can form around salt springs. Rivers and ponds on the Salt Plains are ten times as salty as the sea.

For at least 9,000 years, the land that is now Wood Buffalo National Park has been inhabited by hunters, beginning with prehistoric nomads. Today, the Dene and the Metis people continue the tradition of fishing, hunting, and trapping, although certain designated wildlife species are exempt from their efforts. Like their ancestors, these people are an integral part of the complex and remarkable ecosystem of Wood Buffalo National Park.

# Gazetteer

## THE WEST AND THE ROCKIES

### REDWOOD NATIONAL PARK

*1111 Second Street*
*Crescent City, CA 95531*
*(707) 464-6101*

The park and beaches are open all year, and admission to both is free, although there is a charge for entering the state parks within the national park.

Park facilities include a visitor center, exhibits, guided and self-guided tours, picnic areas, campgrounds, hiking along 40 miles of coastline and over 150 miles of forest trails, horse riding, swimming, and fishing. Three primitive walk-in campsites are also available. Swimmers are warned to be aware of the undertow and tides. In the summer, a bus shuttles visitors between the Redwood Information Center and Tall Trees Grove.

In the vicinity of the park, Humboldt Lagoons State Park and Patricks Point State Park both lie south of Orick on US 101. Six Rivers National Forest and the Hoopa Valley Indian Reservation are due east of US 101.

### POINT LOBOS STATE RESERVE

*(408) 624-4909*

Four miles south of Carmel, this reserve is open all year from 9 a.m. to 7 p.m. spring through fall; 5 p.m. in winter. An admission charge is made per car. No pets are permitted.

Almost due east of Carmel, off US 101 near Soledad, stands Pinnacles National Monument, Paicines, CA 95043, which is open throughout the year; admission is charged. Park facilities include a visitor center, exhibits, self-guided tours, picnic areas, and campgrounds, but the region is a particular favorite of hikers and mountain climbers. Trails range from easy to extremely strenuous and from 1 mile in length to more than 7 miles.

In the Point Lobos vicinity, Andrew Molera State Park and Pfeiffer-Big Sur State Park are both south of Carmel on SR 1.

### YOSEMITE NATIONAL PARK

*P.O. Box 577*
*Yosemite National Park, CA 95389*
*(209) 372-0200*

The park is open all year as are its access roads with the exception of Tioga Pass Road (SR 120) which is only open from Memorial Day to November 1. Admission is charged. Chains may be required at any time of year.

Park facilities include a visitor center, exhibits, guided and self-guided tours, picnic areas, campgrounds, hiking, mountain climbing, horse riding, swimming, boating, fishing, bicycle trails, cross-country ski trails, cabin rental, overnight accommodation, and restaurant.

# SEQUOIA AND KINGS CANYON NATIONAL PARKS

*Three Rivers, CA 93271*
*(209) 565-3341*

These parks are open all year, but the remote areas are not accessible in winter, the high mountain passes rarely open before July 1, and Generals Highway, which connects the two parks, is regularly closed by heavy snow in winter. An admission permit is required and is valid for four days. Chains may be required in the winter months.

Park facilities include a visitor center, exhibits, guided and self-guided tours, picnic areas, campgrounds, hiking, mountain climbing, horse riding, fishing, cross-country ski trails, overnight accommodation, and restaurant.

Devils Postpile National Monument, (619) 934-2289, is administered by these parks. It is open approximately mid-June through October. Admission is free. Facilities include a visitor center, guided tours, picnic areas, campgrounds, hiking, horse riding, swimming, and fishing.

The Inyo, Sequoia, and Sierra national forests surround the area, and the California Bighorn Sheep Zoological Area adjoins the eastern border of Kings Canyon National Park.

# SAN ANDREAS FAULT

Since the entire San Andreas Fault system runs for more than 1,000 miles, passing through North America from northwest of San Francisco to the Gulf of Mexico, it is difficult to treat it as a single tourist attraction. Its importance as a natural wonder, however, is indisputable.

The Bear Valley Visitor Center at Point Reyes National Seashore contains interpretive displays of earthquake geology, and the Earthquake Trail from the center follows the path of the fault for three-quarters of a mile.

# POINT REYES NATIONAL SEASHORE

*Point Reyes, CA 94956*
*(415) 663-1092*

The park and the visitor center at Bear Valley are open all year, and admission is free. Park facilities include a visitor center, exhibits, guided and self-guided tours, picnic areas, campgrounds, hiking, horse riding, swimming, fishing, bicycle trails, and restaurant. The stream water is undrinkable, so hikers and campers should carry a canteen of water. The Earthquake Trail is of particular interest.

Muir Woods National Monument, Mill Valley, CA 94941, (415) 388-2595, lies south of the seashore on SR 1. It is open daily from 8 a.m. to sunset, and admission is free. Facilities include a visitor center, exhibits, guided and self-guided tours, hiking, and restaurant. Picnicking and camping are both prohibited.

Golden Gate National Recreation Area is due south and east of Muir Woods.

# DEATH VALLEY NATIONAL MONUMENT

*Death Valley, CA 92328*
*(196) 786-2331*

The Furnace Creek Visitor Center is open daily from 8 a.m. to 8 p.m. from November to Easter and from 8 a.m. to 5 p.m. the rest of the year, but visits to the overall area are not regulated by either admission charges or opening hours. Most visitors come here between early November and late April; Easter week, Thanksgiving, and Christmas are particularly popular times.

Because of the heat, tours of the valley are not recommended during summer. Visitors who must cross it then are advised to carry extra water and to travel at night when the temperature is lower. Any water taken from the valley springs should be boiled or purified before drinking. Storage tanks along the park roads contain radiator water for cars.

National park facilities include a visitor center, exhibits, guided and self-guided tours, picnic areas, campgrounds, hiking, horse riding, swimming, bicycle trails, overnight accommodation, and restaurant.

# CRATER LAKE NATIONAL PARK

*P.O. Box 7*
*Crater Lake, OR 97604*
*(503) 594-2211*

The park is open all year, and admission is charged for every vehicle. The north entrance road and Rim Drive are closed from mid-October to July. Of the hiking trails, only Cleetwood Trail provides access to the lake; it also leads to the sole tour boat landing.

Park facilities include a visitor center, exhibits, guided and self-guided tours, picnic areas, campgrounds, hiking, fishing, snowmobile routes, cross-country ski trails, overnight accommodation, and restaurant.

South and east of the park along US 97 lies the Klamath Basin, which includes Butte Valley Wildlife Area, Klamath Wildlife Area, Lava Beds National Monument, Modoc National Forest and Winema National Forest. The park is surrounded to the south by the Winema, Rogue River, and to the west by the Umpqua National forests, and the Rogue-Umpqua Divide Wilderness is west of SR 230.

# OLYMPIC NATIONAL PARK

*600 East Park Avenue*
*Port Angeles, WA 98362*
*(206) 452-4501*

The park is open all year, but parts of the high country are often closed by snow between early fall and June or July. Admission is free from late September to mid-May; the rest of the year, an entry permit, which is good for seven days admission, must be purchased at the Heart o' the Hills, Soleduck, Elwha, Mora, Hoh, or Staircase entrance.

Park facilities include a visitor center, exhibits, guided and self-guided tours, picnic areas, campgrounds, hiking, mountain climbing, horse riding, swimming, boating, fishing, cross-country ski trails, overnight accommodation, and restaurant.

Olympic National Forest touches the larger section of the park on all sides but the north. There, near Sequim, visitors will find the Dungeness National Wildlife Refuge and the Olympic Game Farm. The narrow section of the park that borders the Pacific also adjoins the reservations of the Quinault, Hoh, Quileute, Ozette, and Makah Indians.

## MOUNT RAINIER NATIONAL PARK

*Tahoma Woods, Star Route*
*Ashford, WA 98304*
*(206) 569-2211*

The park is open all year, as are the Nisqually entrance and the Nisqually-Paradise Road unless the road is threatened by avalanches or storms. All other roads in the park are closed in the winter. Every car must purchase an entry permit, which is valid for seven days.

Park facilities include a visitor center, exhibits, guided and self-guided tours, picnic areas, campgrounds, hiking, mountain climbing, fishing, snowmobile routes, cross-country ski trails, overnight accommodation, and restaurant.

The park is surrounded by wilderness areas—Norse Peak and William O. Douglas to the east, Tatoosh to the south, Glacier View to the west, and Clearwater to the north. Federation Forest State Park also lies north of the park, west of Greenwater on SR 410.

## YELLOWSTONE NATIONAL PARK

*P.O. Box 168*
*Yellowstone National Park, WY 82190*
*(307) 344-7381*

Most of the park and its many facilities are open from May to October. Weather permitting, park roads are open to cars from about May 1 to October 31. The road between Cooke City, Montana, and Gardiner, Wyoming, is open all year, but only accessible between November and May from the northern park entrance near Gardiner; the Cooke City entrance can only be used between about May 30 and October 15. Because of the roaming wildlife, the maximum speed limit is 45 mph.

Drivers are urged to be extremely alert for animals on the road and to pull off into roadside parking areas to observe them. In summer, early morning and late evening are the best times to spot wild animals. Animals should always be viewed from a distance, and under no circumstances should bears be approached or fed.

Snowmobiles may use the park roads from mid-December to mid-March, depending on road conditions. An admission permit for a private vehicle is valid for seven days in both Yellowstone and Grand Teton national parks; a single entry can be purchased for bicycle, foot, bus, or horseback entry.

Park facilities include a visitor center, exhibits, guided and self-guided tours, picnic areas, campgrounds, hiking, horse riding, boating, fishing, snowmobile routes, cross-country skiing, overnight accommodation, and restaurant.

Four national forests encircle the park: Targhee, Gallatin, Shoshone, and Bridger-Teton, and the Absaroka Wilderness Area adjoins it to the east.

## GRAND TETON NATIONAL PARK

*P.O. Drawer 170*
*Moose, WY 83012*
*(307) 733-2880*

The park is open all year, although most park facilities are only available from early June to mid-September. John D. Rockefeller Memorial Parkway is closed in winter by heavy snow. A seven-day entry permit is valid for both Grand Teton and Yellowstone national parks.

Park facilities include a visitor center, exhibits, guided and self-guided tours, picnic areas, campgrounds, hiking, mountain climbing, horse riding, swimming, boating, fishing, snowmobile routes, cross-country ski trails, overnight accommodation, and restaurant.

Like Yellowstone, this park is bordered by the Bridger-Teton and Targhee national forests. A National Elk Refuge and the Jackson National Fish Hatchery lie along the eastern boundary of the park, north of Jackson.

## DEVILS TOWER NATIONAL MONUMENT

*Devils Tower, WY 82714*
*(307) 467-5370*

The park is open all year, and an admission fee is charged per vehicle or per person or bus passenger. About 3 miles from the east entrance, a visitor center is open daily: 8 a.m. to 4:45 p.m. (May 1 to June 17 and day after Labor Day to September 30); 8 a.m. to 7:45 p.m. (June 18 to Labor Day).

Facilities include a visitor center, exhibits, guided and self-guided tours, picnic areas, campgrounds, hiking, mountain climbing, and fishing. Visitors are allowed to climb the monument, and there are more than 80 distinct routes to the top. But the climb is difficult and extremely tiring, and each climber must sign in with a park ranger before and after attempting the ascent.

Black Hills National Forest spreads to the east of the monument, and Keyhole State Park can be visited to the south of it, off US 14.

# THE SOUTHWEST AND MEXICO

## GREAT SALT LAKE, UTAH

Filling a large portion of the northwestern corner of the state, the lake is only crossed by the 102-mile Southern Pacific Railroad line between Ogden and Lucin.

The Sawtooth National Forest touches the state border to the northwest of this vast natural attraction; the Wasatch-Cache National Forest lies to the east and south. The Bonneville Speedway sits between the western arm of Great Salt Lake and I-80, and 32 miles west of Brigham City, off I-84 and I-15, is the Golden Spike National Historic Site, which marks the spot where the first transcontinental railroad was completed.

Southeast of Salt Lake City on SR 92, visitors can explore Timpanogos Cave National Monument—R.R. 3, Box 200, American Fork, UT 84003, (801) 756-5238. Weather permitting, the cave is open every day from 8 a.m. to 3:30 p.m., from mid-May to mid-October. Tours are restricted to 20 people, and tickets must be bought at the visitor center. The visitor center and museum are open daily, from 8 a.m. to 5:30 p.m. June through August and from 8 a.m. to 4:30 p.m. during the rest of the year. Travelers are advised to arrive early, since the tours fill up quickly.

## BRYCE CANYON NATIONAL PARK

*Bryce Canyon, UT 84717*
*(801) 834-5322*

The park is open throughout the year, and the admission fee allows entry for 14 days. Park facilities include a visitor center, exhibits, guided and self-guided tours, picnic areas, campgrounds, hiking, horse riding, cross-country ski trails, overnight accommodation, and restaurant.

West of the park, off SR 14, Cedar Breaks National Monument, P.O. Box 749, Cedar City UT 84720, (801) 586-9451, encompasses a giant natural amphitheater. Only 10 miles farther west, off I-15, stand Zion National Park and Zion Canyon, Springdale, UT 84767, (801) 772-3256, a spectacular wilderness of cliffs and canyons that are open all year; the entry permit is good for 14 days.

Park facilities include a visitor center, exhibits, guided and self-guided tours, picnic areas, campgrounds, hiking, mountain climbing, horse riding, snowmobile routes, cross-country ski trails, overnight accommodation, and restaurant. Hiking trails vary from easy to strenuous, and summer heat makes hiking more difficult.

Twenty miles west of Kanab travelers can visit Coral Pink Sand Dunes State Park.

## RAINBOW BRIDGE NATIONAL MONUMENT, UTAH

*Administered by Glen Canyon National Recreation Area*
*P.O. Box 1507,*
*Page, AZ 86040*

Once quite inaccessible, the monument can now be reached by boat from Lake Powell as well as by foot and on horseback. Admission is free. Park facilities include self-guided tours, hiking, boating, and fishing.

Since the bridge is located on the Navajo Indian Reservation, hikers cannot use the trails without a permit from the Navajo tribe, which can be obtained by writing to the Navajo Nation, Recreational Resources Department, Box 308, Window Rock, AZ 86515.

The Navajo Reservation completely surrounds the national monument. Glen Canyon National Recreation Area borders the reservation to the north. Boating on Lake Powell can be arranged here, as can full-day and half-day trips to Rainbow Bridge.

## MONUMENT VALLEY NAVAJO TRIBAL PARK

*(801) 727-3287*

The park straddles the Utah-Arizona border, not far from Four Corners Monument, where Arizona, Utah, New Mexico, and Colorado meet. The park is open daily from 7 a.m. to 8 p.m., last entrance at 6:30 p.m. Admission is charged. Park facilities include a visitor center and both guided and self-guided tours.

West of Kayenta stands the Navajo National Monument, Box 3, Tonalea, AZ 86044, (602) 672-2366, where visitors can explore the natural ruins called Keet Seel and Batatakin. South of Monument Valley and 3 miles east of Chinle, Canyon de Chelly National Monument (Box 588, Chinle, AZ 86503, (602) 674-5436) is part of the Navajo Indian Reservation. Navajo guides lead tours through the canyon, as do park rangers. Only the trail from White House Overlook to the White House Ruin can be taken without an authorized park or Navajo guide.

## GRAND CANYON NATIONAL PARK

*P.O. Box 129*
*Grand Canyon, AZ 86023*
*(602) 638-7888*

The canyon's South Rim remains open all year, but there are heavy snow falls on the North Rim so it is usually only open from mid-May to mid-November. The admission fee to the park purchases a seven-day entry permit.

Facilities include a visitor center, exhibits, guided and self-guided tours, picnic areas, campgrounds, hiking, horse riding, fishing, overnight accommodations, and food. Advance reservations are strongly recommended for all the park's attractions, including mule rides, river trips, backcountry hikes, and camping facilities.

Because the South Rim draws the largest proportion of visitors, parking is difficult here during the summer months, but a free shuttle bus follows two routes to the South Rim between Memorial Day and Labor Day. Despite accumulated snow on the South Rim in winter, trails usually remain open into the canyon. Sightseeing buses, helicopter and airplane tours of the canyon, one-hour and half-day horseback rides, and raft trips through the canyon on the Colorado River can all be arranged through the park lodges and local facilities.

The Painted Desert, part of the Navajo Indian Reservation, adjoins the park's eastern side; the Kaibab National Forest lies to the north and south, and the Havasupai Indian Reservation is also to the south. Glen Canyon Recreation Area touches the park's northeastern tip, while Lake Mead National Recreation Area touches the southwestern tip.

## METEOR CRATER

This natural wonder is not administered by any federal or state authority and can be visited at any time free of charge.

To the west, Sunset Crater National Monument, Route 3 Box 149, Flagstaff, AZ 86004, (602) 527-7042, presents an awesome sight just north of Flagstaff. Admission is charged to each car; the fee also includes entry to Wupatki National Monument, (602) 527-7042, to the north. The lava flow at Sunset Crater is crossed by both a self-guided trail and a paved road; good walking shoes are strongly recommended for exploring the site. Visitors may picnic here, and camping is allowed from mid-May to mid-September.

Between Meteor Crater and Flagstaff itself, off I-40, Walnut Canyon National Monument (Walnut Canyon Road, Flagstaff, AZ 86004, (602) 526-3367) displays the ruins of an ancient pueblo. Self-guided trails pass the cliff dwellings and trace the canyon rim; both trails may be closed by snow in winter or spring.

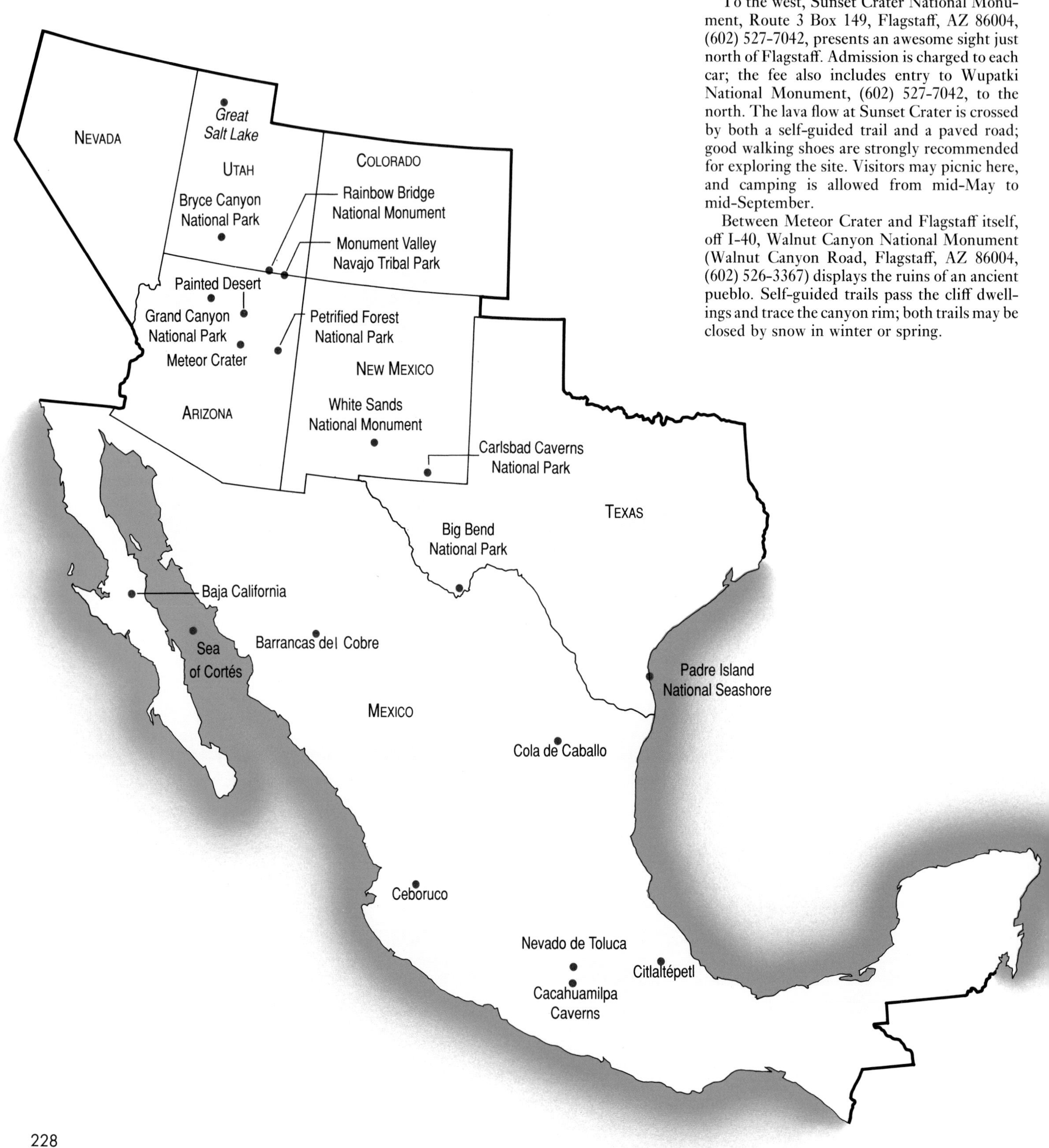

## PETRIFIED FOREST NATIONAL PARK

*Petrified Forest National Park, AZ 86028*
*(602) 524-6228*

The park is open every day and charges admission for each motorized vehicle or for each person arriving by other means. Opening hours are from 7 a.m. to 8 p.m. June through August; 8 a.m. to 6 p.m. in May and September; and 8 a.m. to 5 p.m. during the rest of the year.

Park facilities include a visitor center, exhibits, self-guided tours, picnic areas, hiking, and restaurant. No campgrounds or overnight accommodation exist in the park. Only wilderness backpack camping is permitted, for which a free permit must be obtained at a visitor center.

East of the park, across the state line into New Mexico and east of Ramah on SR 53, El Morro National Monument (Route 2 Box 43 Ramah, NM 87321, (505) 783-4226) is a striking, natural landmark of sandstone, carved with ancient petroglyphs. The monument is open every day except Christmas; the visitor center is open from 8 a.m. to 7 p.m., June 1 to Labor Day; from 8 a.m. to 5 p.m. during the rest of the year. Admission is charged to view the massive Inscription Rock and cascading waterfall. Self-guided tours are available.

## CARLSBAD CAVERNS NATIONAL PARK

*3225 National Parks Highway*
*Carlsbad, NM 88220*
*(505) 785-2232*

The park is open every day except December 25. The admission charge for entry to the caverns is based on the visitor's age, but admission to the park itself is free. Between May 28 and September 1, the visitor center is open from 8 a.m. to 7 p.m. and tours run continuously between 8:30 a.m. and 5 p.m. At all other times, the visitor center is open from 8 a.m. to 5:30 p.m. and tours run between 8:30 a.m. and 3:30 p.m.

Walking shoes with rubber soles and a sweater or light jacket are highly recommended for the cavern tours. The complete trip, or Blue Tour, covers about 3 miles and lasts about three hours. The less strenuous Big Room trip, or Red Tour, covers 1¼ miles and lasts about 90 minutes. Park facilities include exhibits, guided and self-guided tours, picnic areas, hiking, and restaurant.

Lincoln National Forest adjoins the western border of the park, and the Guadalupe Mountains National Park lies due south of the forest, across the New Mexico-Texas border. Off US 285 outside Carlsbad is the Living Desert State Park.

## WHITE SANDS NATIONAL MONUMENT

*P.O. Box 458*
*Alamogordo, NM 88310*
*(505) 479-6124*

The park is open every day except December 25 and charges admission for every private vehicle. The visitor center, which is the only source of drinking water in the park, is open from 8 a.m. to 7 p.m. from Memorial Day to Labor Day and from 8 a.m. to 4:30 p.m. the rest of the year. Park facilities include exhibits, guided and self-guided tours, picnic areas, and hiking. Tours are given from 7 a.m. to 10 p.m. from Memorial Day to Labor Day, and from 7 a.m. to half an hour after sunset during the rest of the year.

A 16-mile round-trip journey can be made along Dunes Drive daily, between 8 a.m. and 10 p.m. from Memorial Day to Labor Day and between 8:30 a.m. and half an hour after sunset the rest of the year. The San Andres National Wildlife Refuge lies due west of the park, and the Aguirre Springs National Recreation Area to the south.

## BIG BEND NATIONAL PARK

*Big Bend National Park, TX 79834*
*(915) 477-2251*

The park is open throughout the year and charges admission for every vehicle for a week's entry permit. Park facilities include a visitor center, exhibits, guided and self-guided tours, picnic areas, campgrounds, hiking, horse riding, boating, fishing, overnight accommodation, and restaurant.

Hikers are advised to carry drinking water and usually require a gallon a day. Drivers are advised to fill their gas tanks before entering the park, where distances are vast and the service stations generally close at 5 p.m. There is no public transportation to or through the park.

## PADRE ISLAND NATIONAL SEASHORE

*9405 S. Padre Island Drive*
*Corpus Christi, TX 78418-5597*
*(512) 949-8068*

The seashore is open to visitors 24 hours a day, every day of the year, for an admission fee charged for each car or each person. Park facilities include a visitor center, exhibits, self-guided tours, campgrounds, hiking, horse riding, swimming, boating, fishing, and hunting. A 5-mile stretch of the beach is reserved exclusively for pedestrians.

Immediately north of the park lie Padre Balli County Park and Mustang Island State Park; slightly farther north is the Aransas National Wildlife Refuge. Immediately south, visitors will find the Laguna Atascosa National Wildlife Refuge, Brazos Island State Park, and Port Isabel Lighthouse State Historic Site.

## MEXICO

Anyone who visits Mexico's natural wonders will be traveling in a country that covers more than 761,000 square miles of plateaus, mountains, valleys, and canyons. Its 31 states and one Federal district contain few navigable rivers, but the temperate north and tropical south are nourished by rain, most of which falls between May and October. The heat is most intense along the coasts and in the lower altitudes of the interior, where jungles and swamps are common.

Proof of citizenship and a tourist card are required to enter the country; inquire about the regulations before leaving home. U.S. car insurance is not valid in Mexico, so separate arrangements should be made by all drivers. For the most popular travel seasons—December through February and June through August—confirmed reservations for accommodation are strongly suggested. Spanish is the national language, but English is widely spoken.

## OGLALA NATIONAL GRASSLAND

*270 Pine Street*
*Chadron, NE 69337*
*(308) 432-3367*

This natural grassland covers 94,334 acres, across which local ranchers herd their livestock at certain times of the year. Toadstool Park lies just inside the southern border and contains a single small recreation area with picnic units and a reconstructed sod house.

To the south, Fort Robinson State Park and Nebraska National Forest are respectively west and south of Crawford. Still farther south, off SR 29, is Agate Fossil Beds National Monument (Box 27, Gering, NE 69341, (308) 436-4340) which is open daily throughout the year free of charge. The removal of fossils, rocks, and plants is strictly prohibited. Visitors are cautioned to look out for rattlesnakes.

# THE CENTRAL STATES

## BADLANDS NATIONAL PARK

*P.O. Box 6*
*Interior, SD 57750*
*(605) 433-5361*

The park is open all year, and admission is charged for vehicles and for hikers and bikers between late May and September. Park facilities include a visitor center, exhibits, guided and self-guided tours, picnic areas, campgrounds, hiking, and restaurant.

Climbing here can be dangerous since the slopes are steep and can give way underfoot, and the weather is unpredictable. No fires are permitted. In the Sage Creek Wilderness Area, the north unit of the park, the only trails are those cut by bison, so a topographical map is strongly recommended for hikers.

Buffalo Gap National Grassland surrounds the north unit of the park, and the south unit and Palmer Creek unit lie within the Pine Ridge Indian Reservation. Driving south along SR 27, visitors will reach the Wounded Knee Massacre National Historic Site.

## BLACK HILLS NATIONAL FOREST

Spectacular natural scenery spread over 1.2 million acres. Information about the history and management of the forest can be obtained at the Pactola Reservoir Visitor Center, which is open seven days a week between Memorial Day and Labor Day.

The forest contains Jewel Cave National Monument, Route 1 Box 60AA, Custer, SD 57730, (605) 673-2288. This site, one of the longest caves in the world, has its own visitor center, exhibits, and picnic areas. It offers a Scenic Tour (admission fee according to visitor's age) from early May to September; tour groups do not exceed 25 people. There is also a Historic Tour (admission charge according to age), led between mid-June and mid-August, which is quite strenuous—children under six are not permitted on this tour—and a Spelunking Tour between mid-June and mid-August, for which a fee is charged; this tour is limited to ten people at a time, who must be very fit and at least 16 years old. Sensible, rubber-soled shoes and a sweater or light jacket are recommended for all visitors.

In the vicinity lie Bear Butte State Park, which is north of Sturgis off SR 79, and Custer State Park and Wind Cave National Park, both of which are east of Black Hills National Forest off SR 87. A broad band of Buffalo Gap National Grassland surrounds the southern end of the forest.

## OZARK NATIONAL SCENIC RIVERWAYS

*P.O. Box 490*
*Van Buren, MO 63965*
*(314) 323-4236*

The park contains more than 134 miles of the Current and Jack Fork rivers and their streams and tributaries. It is open, free of charge, all year, and most visitors take to the waters on Saturdays in the summer—only about 2 percent visit the park in the winter.

Facilities include exhibits, guided tours, picnic areas, campgrounds, hiking, horse riding, swimming, boating, fishing, hunting, and restaurant. Concessions in 19 locations are authorized to rent canoes and provide shuttle services. Swimming is permitted, but visitors are warned not to jump or dive into the water without first testing its depth. Water cannot be consumed unless it is boiled or treated first.

The Ozark Mountains contain roughly 4,000 caves, many of which can be explored by hikers and mountain climbers. Visitors are advised to check with a park ranger before entering any cave and to carry several light sources into it.

## ISLE ROYALE NATIONAL PARK

*87 North Ripley Street*
*Houghton, MI 49931*
*(906) 482-0984*

The park is open from mid-April through October and full park services are available from mid-June through Labor Day. Admission is free. Travel to the park is only by seaplane or boat, for which reservations are required.

Park facilities include a visitor center, guided and self-guided tours, picnic areas, campgrounds, hiking, boating, fishing, overnight accommodation, and restaurant. Swimming is permitted but unpopular since Lake Superior is extremely cold and leeches appear during warmer seasons.

Across the lake to the west stands Grand Portage National Monument, Box 666, Grand Marais, MN 55604, (218) 387-2788, once a key site in the extensive web of waterways that carried the fur trade. The monument is open every day from mid-May to mid-October; admission is charged.

## MISSISSIPPI RIVER

A single river more than 2,000 miles long, running through the United States from Lake Itasca, Minnesota, to the Gulf of Mexico and connecting a network of 15,000 miles of navigable waterways, the Mississippi is one of the world's busiest commercial waterways and one of North America's best-loved natural wonders. Exploring it from source to delta will lead travelers into ten states and a number of state and national parks.

North Dakota
Isle Royale National Park
Lake Superior
Lake Huron
South Dakota
Black Hills National Forest
Badlands National Park
Minnesota
Wisconsin
Michigan
Lake Michigan
Lake Erie
Oglala National Grassland
Iowa
Nebraska
Illinois
Indiana
Ohio
Kansas
Missouri
Ozark National Scenic Riverways
Oklahoma
Arkansas
Mississippi River

# THE EAST AND SOUTHEAST

## EVERGLADES NATIONAL PARK

*P.O. Box 279*
*Homestead, FL 33030*
*(305) 247-6211*

The park is open all year and charges admission, but only to those who enter it at the main entrance, on SR 9336 southwest of Homestead. Facilities include a visitor center, exhibits, guided and self-guided tours, picnic areas, campgrounds, hiking, boating, fishing, bicycle trails, overnight accommodation, and restaurant. Some services are limited or unavailable between May 1 and mid-December.

Hiking trails vary from short and easy to long (14 miles) and quite strenuous. Five boardwalk or blacktop nature trails extend between the park headquarters at the main entrance and Flamingo. Canoe trails are marked and canoes can be rented, as can small skiffs and houseboats; sightseeing boats travel to the Ten Thousand Islands area and the mangrove swamps. Boats can also be taken into Florida Bay, but they cannot land on most bay islands; these are closed to protect nesting birds.

Wilderness tram tours are available from November to April, departing from Flamingo Lodge, and the Shark Valley Tram Tour leaves Shark Valley, off US 41, daily on the hour if weather permits; reservations for the latter must be made several weeks in advance November through May. Be prepared for mosquitoes.

To the south, on US 1 near Key Largo, John Pennekamp Coral Reef State Park is open daily from 8 a.m. to sunset, and glass-bottom boats make three trips daily to the living coral reef offshore. Separate charges are made for admission to the park and for the boat trip, for which reservations are recommended.

## MAMMOTH CAVE NATIONAL PARK

*Mammoth Cave, KY 42259*
*(502) 758-2328*

The park is open all year and admission to it is free. Facilities include a visitor center, exhibits, guided and self-guided tours, picnic areas, campgrounds, hiking, horse riding, boating, fishing, accommodation, and restaurant. Over 70 miles of self-guided nature trails are available at all times; park rangers lead surface walks from mid-June through August.

Cave tours range from $1\frac{1}{4}$ to 6 hours. All depart from the visitor center, from which schedules and prices can be obtained. Tour reservations can be made through Ticketron and are recommended, since group sizes are limited. Visitors are advised to wear good walking shoes and a sweater or jacket.

## OKEFENOKEE SWAMP PARK

*Waycross, GA 31501*
*(912) 283-0583*

South of Waycross on SR 177, the park serves as the northern entrance to the entire Okefenokee Swamp. The admission fee to the park includes a 2-mile boat trip through the swamp, and other cruise boats and canoe rentals are also available. The park contains exhibits, wildlife shows, and outdoor displays on Pioneer Island.

Okefenokee National Wildlife Refuge, Route 2, Box 338, Folkston, GA 31537, (912) 496-3331, occupies a large portion of the swamp, and can be reached through the Suwannee Canal Recreation Area on its eastern border, Stephen C. Foster State Park to the west, and Okefenokee Swamp Park to the north. The refuge provides facilities for fishing, boating, canoing, and camping, and there are self-guided canoe trails. The refuge manager must issue permits for canoe trips of two to five days; reservations can be made up to two months in advance.

The Suwannee Canal Recreation Area, with its visitor center, exhibits, and walking trails, is open every day except December 25, from 7 a.m. to 7:30 p.m. March 1 to September 30 and from 8 a.m. to 6 p.m. during the rest of the year. Admission is charged.

## GREAT SMOKY MOUNTAINS NATIONAL PARK

*Gatlinburg, TN 37738*
*(615) 436-1200*

Equally divided between Tennessee and North Carolina, the park is open all year and admission is free. Facilities include a visitor center, exhibits, guided and self-guided tours, picnic areas, campgrounds, hiking, horse riding, fishing, bicycle trails, and accommodation.

The Appalachian Trail crosses the park from southwest to northeast and is the most heavily used foot trail in the park, but there are more than 900 miles of foot and horse trails to wander. Fishermen enjoy an equally vast choice of streams, but visitors from out-of-state will need a license from Tennessee or North Carolina. Fees are charged at all ten developed campgrounds, and reservations are recommended from May 15 to October 31 at Cades Cove, Elkmont, and Smokemont.

Cherokee National Forest adjoins the northeast and southwest borders of the park, and the Cherokee Indian Reservation lies just inside the southern boundary. Due south of Townsend, off US 321, Tuckaleechee Caverns are famous for the onyx formations in the main cave.

## GEORGIA'S STONE MOUNTAIN PARK

*(404) 498-5600*

The park is due east of Atlanta off I-285. It is open every day from 6 a.m. to midnight and admission is charged to the beach complex; there is also a charge for parking. Along with Stone Mountain, the park contains recreational facilities including golf, tennis, a water park, and a roller-skating trail. A hiking trail up Stone Mountain itself leads from the western side of the mountain to the summit.

The Stone Mountain Historical Trail circles the mountain with an 8-mile hike, and steam trains make the circular journey every day except December 24 and 25, from 10 a.m. to 8 p.m. in the summer and from 10 a.m. to 5:30 p.m. for the rest of the year. During the summer, the mountain can be viewed from the water on 30-minute lake cruises that leave the marina every hour. A cable car also operates to the summit every day, from 10 a.m. to 8 p.m. in the summer and from 10 a.m. to 5:30 p.m. the rest of the year; it is closed December 24 and 25.

Also east of Atlanta, on US 78, Yellow River Game Ranch, (404) 972-6643, contains a zoo with both wild and domestic animals, some of which roam freely and can be fed. The ranch is open Monday through Friday, from 9:30 a.m. to dusk between Memorial Day and Labor Day and from 9:30 a.m. to 6 p.m. for the rest of the year. Admission is charged.

# BLUE RIDGE MOUNTAINS

From Great Smoky Mountains National Park in North Carolina and Tennessee to Shenandoah National Park in Virginia, the Blue Ridge Parkway (200 BB&T Building, 1 Pack Square, Asheville, NC 28801, (704) 259-0701) runs for nearly 500 miles along the ridge of the Appalachians; the southernmost 350 miles of the road follow the crest of the Blue Ridge Mountains.

Sites along the spectacular, uninterrupted scenic drive are designated by mileage markings that indicate their distance from the northern end of the parkway; all these points of interest are free. The road is open all year, but snow and ice may close portions of it. North and south of Asheville, high sections of the road are often closed from about mid-November to March or April. Picnic areas, hiking trails, food, and drinking water can be found all along the parkway; lodging is available from May to November (and straight through the year at Peaks of Otter Lodge); and nine campgrounds are open between May 1 and early November, depending on the weather. Fees are charged at all of them.

Points of interest along the road include the Richland Balsam Trail (near Mile 431) which wanders through woodland usually found 1,000 miles to the north; Emerald Village (Mile 331) where the North Carolina Mining Museum and the Gemstone Mine are located; and the James River Wayside (Mile 63.6), which examines the history of the James River and the Kanawha Canal. Waterrock Knob (Mile 451.2) provides a sweeping 360 degree view of the southern Appalachians.

# CAPE HATTERAS NATIONAL SEASHORE

*Route 1, Box 675*
*Manteo, NC 27954*
*(919) 473-2111*

The sandy stretches of this seashore are public property, so visitors enjoy free access to them and to the ocean at all times. Roads from the north and the west connect the seashore to the mainland. At the seashore's southern end, Ocracoke can be reached by toll ferry from Swanquarter, NC, in $2\frac{1}{2}$ hours and from Cedar Island, NC, in $2\frac{1}{4}$ hours; reservations are recommended. A free ferry connects Ocracoke Island to Hatteras Island; it runs every day and the journey lasts 40 minutes.

Park facilities include a visitor center, exhibits, guided and self-guided tours, picnic areas, hiking, swimming, boating, fishing, and hunting. Five campgrounds are open through the summer; sites can be reserved through Ticketron. Both the ocean and the sands can be treacherous; motorists are advised to keep to the roads and swimmers should only enter the water where lifeguards are on duty.

At Pea Island National Wildlife Refuge on Hatteras Island, local and migrating birds can be viewed from the observation decks.

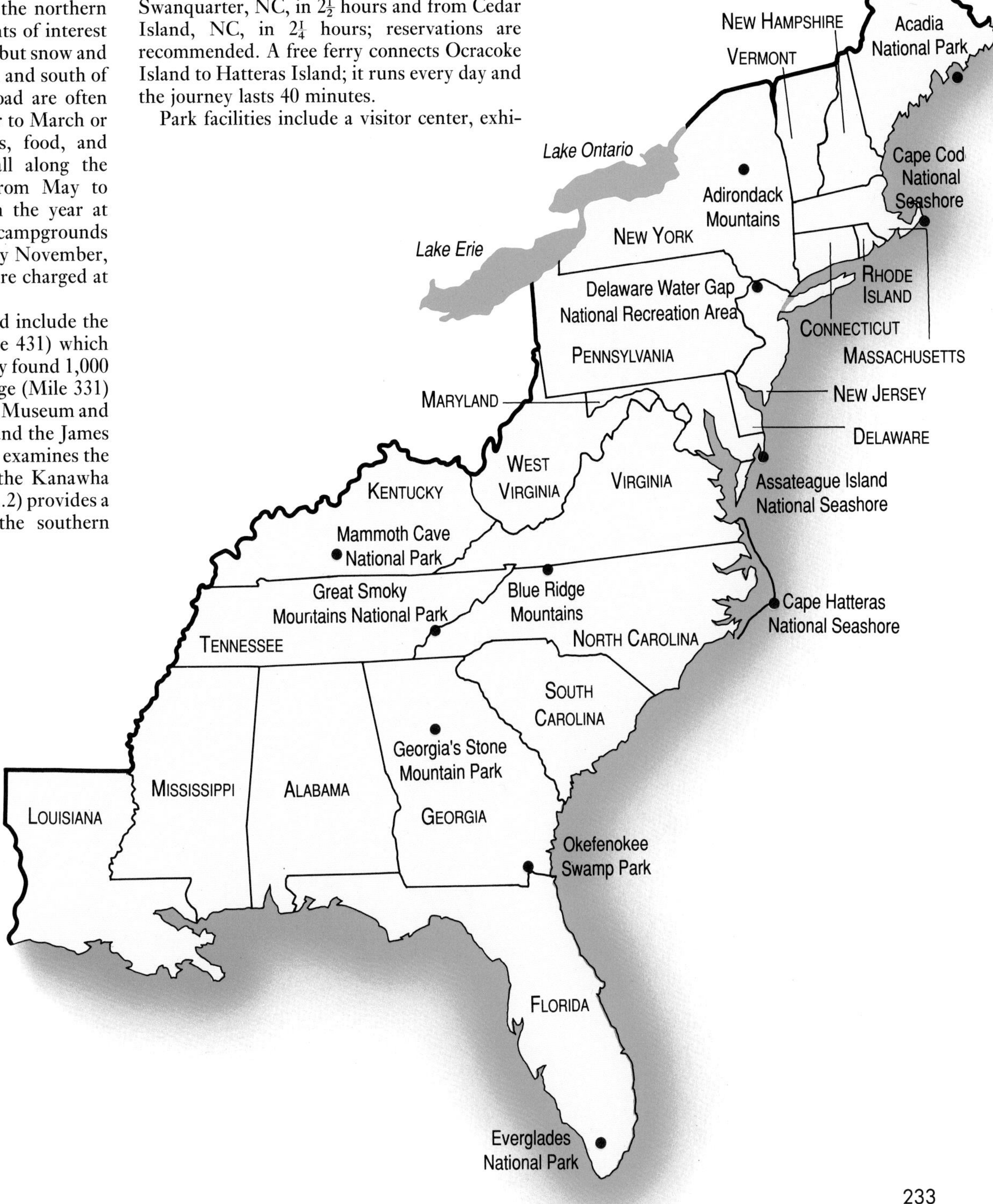

# ASSATEAGUE ISLAND NATIONAL SEASHORE

*Route 2, Box 294*
*Berlin, MD 21881*
*(301) 641-1441*

Assateague Island comprises three public areas: Assateague Island National Seashore, Chincoteague National Wildlife Refuge, and Assateague State Park. Admission is charged to the seashore, whose facilities include a visitor center, exhibits, guided and self-guided tours, hiking, swimming, boating, fishing, and hunting.

There is free access to campsites for backpackers and canoists at the Maryland end of the island. The three on the ocean side are open year-round for hikers only; the four bayside camps are open March 1 to October 31. Canoe trips, nature walks, and fishing and clamming demonstrations are available daily from July 1 to Labor Day.

Pocomoke River State Park lies half a mile west of the island, and Blackwater National Wildlife Refuge is farther west.

# DELAWARE WATER GAP NATIONAL RECREATION AREA

*Bushkill, PA 18324*
*(717) 588-2435*

Cutting through the Kittatinny Ridge of the Appalachians, the gap can be visited at any time of the year, free of charge. Park facilities include a visitor center, exhibits, guided and self-guided tours, picnic areas, hiking, campgrounds, mountain climbing, swimming, boating, fishing, hunting, snowmobile routes, and cross-country ski trails.

The Delaware River runs the length of the gap, offering many opportunities for canoing and rafting. Lifeguards oversee swimmers at Milford and Smithfield beaches from mid-June through Labor Day. Bicycles and horses can easily negotiate many of the park's roads, and hikers can enjoy 25 miles of the Appalachian Trail. During the winter months, visitors can skate on the frozen lakes and small ponds or cut their surface for ice fishing.

East of Montague at the north end of the park, High Point State Park encircles the highest point in the state of New Jersey.

# CAPE COD NATIONAL SEASHORE

*South Wellfleet, MA 02663*
*(508) 349-3785*

The national seashore, the narrow strip of dunes and beach extending along the eastern edge of the cape, is open all year. No admission is charged, but there is a charge for parking during the summer.

Park facilities include a visitor center, exhibits, guided and self-guided tours, hiking, horse riding, swimming, fishing, hunting, bicycle trails, overnight accommodation, and restaurant. Picnics are allowed on all the beaches and in the four designated picnic areas, but open fires must be authorized by permit. Visitors will need a state license for freshwater fishing and a town license for shellfishing.

Scattered around the curve of the cape are the Wellfleet Bay Wildlife Sanctuary in South Wellfleet; Sealand of Cape Cod and the Cape Cod Museum of Natural History in Brewster; Ashumet Holly Reservation and Wildlife Sanctuary in Falmouth; and the National Marine Fisheries Service Aquarium in Woods Hole.

Accessible only by car and passenger ferry, Martha's Vineyard and Nantucket Island lie across Nantucket Sound. Car reservations are required on the Hyannis Port-Nantucket and Nantucket-Martha's Vineyard ferries; the latter only operates during the summer.

On Martha's Vineyard, the Oak Bluffs State Lobster Hatchery is only open to the public in summer. Visitors will also enjoy the Felix Neck Wildlife Sanctuary off Edgartown-Vineyard Haven Road; the visitor center is open daily from 8 a.m. to 4:30 p.m. and grounds open daily between 8 a.m. and 7 p.m. and admission is charged. Attractions on Nantucket include an aquarium, the Museum of Natural Science (whose observatory is open on Wednesday evenings in July and August, weather permitting), and the Nantucket Whaling Museum.

# ADIRONDACK MOUNTAINS

The Adirondacks, their widespread foothills, and their 2,800 lakes and ponds blanket almost one-quarter of New York state. Six million acres fall within the boundaries of Adirondack Park, almost half of which is wilderness. Recreational activities in the park include the entire range of winter and summer sports; complete information is available from the Department of Environmental Conservation, 50 Wolf Road, Albany, NY 12233.

The Adirondack Museum, (518) 352-7311, in Blue Mountain Lake comprises 20 buildings that contain displays on every aspect of life in the mountains. The museum is open every day from 9:30 a.m. to 5:30 p.m. from Memorial Day weekend to October 15; admission is charged.

Lake George and Lake Placid both offer extensive facilities for camping, riding, skiing, boating of all kinds, tennis, and golf. Roughly 200 miles of hiking trails fan out from Lake Placid.

# ACADIA NATIONAL PARK

*P.O. Box 177,*
*Bar Harbor, ME 04609*
*(207) 288-3338*

The three sections of the park lie on Mount Desert Island, which is reached via SR 3; on Schoodic Peninsula, which is on SR 186; and on Isle au Haut, to which a passenger ferry runs in summer only. The park is open all year, and there is an entrance fee.

Park facilities include a visitor center, exhibits, self-guided tours, picnic areas, two campgrounds (reservations are required in summer for the one at Blackwoods), hiking, mountain climbing, horse riding, swimming, boating, fishing, bicycle trails, snowmobile routes, cross-country ski trails, overnight accommodation, and restaurant. The visitor center is open daily from 8 a.m. to 6 p.m. between June 15 and early October, and from 8 a.m. to 4:30 p.m. between May 1 and June 14 and during October.

A 2-mile stretch of road on Mount Desert Island remains open all year, but snow often closes the park's loop road in winter. Park naturalists regularly guide cruises around Baker Island, Bass Harbor, Frenchman Bay, and the Cranberry Islands to explore the region's geology, wildlife, and marine life.

# ALASKA AND HAWAII

## DENALI NATIONAL PARK AND PRESERVE

*P.O. Box 9*
*Denali Park, AK 99755*
*(907) 683-2686*

Originally established as Mount McKinley National Park in honor of its most renowned natural feature, Denali is open all year and admission is charged. Access from SR 3 is always good, but Denali Highway, SR 8, from Paxson is only open from about early June to mid-October.

The Denali Park Road, which starts at the park's eastern entrance on SR 3, is open from early June to mid-September; it runs roughly 90 miles into the park but is only paved for the first 14.8 miles. Visitors must proceed by shuttle bus after driving those first miles.

Park facilities include a visitor center, guided and self-guided tours, campgrounds, hiking, mountain climbing, fishing, overnight accommodation, and restaurant. There are float trips on the Nenana River and guided wildlife tours; reservations are recommended for the latter during July and August.

## GLACIER BAY NATIONAL PARK AND PRESERVE

*Bartlett Cove*
*Gustavus, AK 99826*
*(907) 697-2230*

A total of 3,283,168 acres of glacial peaks and inlets, the park extends from Cross Sound to the Canadian border. Access to the region is by plane or boat; daily flights connect Juneau and Gustavus, where charter vessels are available.

Every morning from mid-May to mid-September, an eight-hour guided boat tour leaves Glacier Bay Lodge, at the park headquarters at Bartlett Cove. There are also overnight tours, backpacking trips, and raft trips down the Alsek River. Private vessels cannot enter Glacier Bay without a permit.

Park facilities include guided tours, campground, hiking, mountain climbing, boating, fishing, hunting, overnight accommodation, and restaurant. Orientation for campers is given twice daily at Glacier Bay Lodge. Visitors are warned that night temperatures, even in summer, may drop to near freezing.

## HAWAII VOLCANOES NATIONAL PARK

*Hawaii National Park, HI 96718*
*(808) 967-7311*

The park is open daily throughout the year, and admission is charged. Facilities include a visitor center, exhibits, self-guided tours, picnic areas, campgrounds, hiking, mountain climbing, overnight accommodation, and restaurant.

Crater Rim Road, an 11-mile drive around the Kilauea Caldera, offers the best orientation to the park. Paved roads lead toward the summit of Mauna Loa, and marked trails attain it; before hiking to the summit, visitors must leave their names at the Kilauea Visitor Center.

The park's three drive-in campgrounds can be used without charge or advance reservations, but visits to each one cannot exceed seven days per year. Hikers who wish to stay in a shelter or cabin overnight must register at park headquarters.

## HALEAKALA NATIONAL PARK

*P.O. Box 369*
*Makawao, Maui, HI 96768*
*(808) 572-9306*

Open all day every day for an admission charge, the park is in two sections that are not directly connected by road. Haleakala Crater can be reached from Kahului on SR 37, 377, and 378. The Ohe'o section, 10 miles south of Hana at the east end of Maui, can be reached on SR 36, on the north side of the island. The road to it along the south shore, SR 31, is not fully paved and can be dangerous in stormy weather.

Park facilities include a visitor center, exhibits, self-guided tours, picnic areas, campgrounds, hiking, horse riding, and hunting. There are no roads in the park. Hikers can choose between short, easy trails and full-day treks through the crater. Camping, by permit only, is restricted to campgrounds and cabins and limited to two nights at any location and a maximum of three nights per month.

## KAUAI

The natural splendor of the island makes its resort areas, in Koloa on the south coast and Wailua on the east coast, extremely popular with visitors. Golf, tennis, swimming, camping, fishing, and hiking can all be enjoyed throughout the year. The south shore is preferred for surfing in summer and swimming in winter; the reverse applies to the north shore. Visitors should be aware of the strong undertow and changeable currents, which can make the seas treacherous. Boats can be chartered for deep-sea fishing excursions.

The scenic coast road, SR 56 and SR 50, encircles nearly the whole island, but dense vegetation on the Na Pali Coast and through the interior renders them largely inaccessible to cars. However, Na Pali Coast State Park is accessible by chartered boat, and helicoptor tours of the coast and the island can be arranged.

Recreational facilities are scattered throughout the various state parks: Haena, Wailua River, Kokee, and Waimea Canyon. Wailua River State Park also contains Fern Grotto, to which excursion boats travel daily on the longest navigable river in the islands.

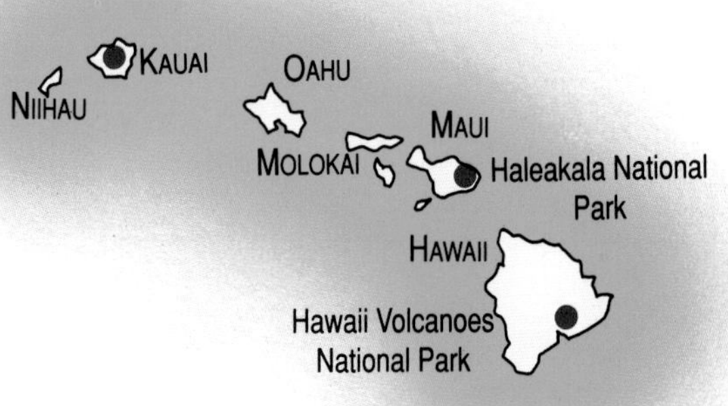

# CANADA

## NIAGARA FALLS

Both the New York and the Ontario sides of the falls have developed extensive facilities for serving and accommodating visitors. For visitor information, phone (716) 278-8010 in New York or (416) 356-6061 in Ontario. Domestic and international flights land in Buffalo, from which shuttle buses carry visitors to Niagara Falls between 8:30 a.m. and 8:30 p.m. daily. Long-distance buses and trains travel directly to Niagara Falls.

A large range of guided tours, including plane and helicoptor tours that fly over the falls, are available. Among the most popular attractions are the "Maid of the Mist" boats, which sail directly in front of the falls and into Horseshoe Basin, and the Cave of the Winds trip along wooden walkways that extend to within 25 feet of the base of the falls. The latter begins on Goat Island, which separates the American and Canadian falls, and provides paved roads and footpaths that present breathtaking views. Sightseeing trains called Niagara Viewmobiles can also be boarded on Goat Island.

The falls are illuminated nightly for up to $3\frac{1}{2}$ hours after dusk. Some of the parks and floral displays, like Wintergarden on the New York side and Queen Victoria Park on the Ontario side, are also illuminated after dark; free concerts are presented in Queen Victoria Park on Tuesday evenings from mid-June through Labor Day.

## BAY OF FUNDY

The bay is surrounded by scenic and historical wonders on all sides. On the north shore, Fundy National Park (P.O. Box 40, Alma, New Brunswick) is both a recreational park and wildlife sanctuary; it is open all year, and admission is charged. Facilities include swimming, tennis, golf, guided and self-guided tours, and trout fishing. Most activities are available between the end of May and mid-September; cross-country skiing and snowshoing are common from December through March.

In Saint John, the unusual Reversing Falls can be seen at the mouth of the Saint John River near Highway 100; the falls reverse direction with the tides. Grand Manan Bird Sanctuary on Grand Manan Island, which is the northern terminal of the Atlantic flyway, is accessible by boat from Black's Harbor, Maine. On the north shore of Chignecto Bay in Hopewell Cape, The Rocks Provincial Park emerges from the sea at low tide; visitors descend to the shore on a stairway to explore the cracks and caves in the cliff walls.

On the Nova Scotia coast, the restraining dikes that allowed marshland to be turned into farmland can still be seen along the Minas Basin shoreline near Grand Pre. Grand Pre National Historic Park, open from May 15 to October 15, between 9 a.m. and 6 p.m. every day, free of charge, contains willow trees said to be more than 300 years old.

## DINOSAUR PROVINCIAL PARK

*Brooks, Alberta, Canada*
*(403) 378-4342*

Northeast of Brooks, off Trans-Canada Highway 1, the park is open all year free of charge; donations are accepted. Visitors can take the self-guided trails, but entry to most of the park is allowed only on the guided bus tours and hikes that start from the ranger station during the summer months. Facilities include campgrounds, picnic sites, and fishing.

The Provincial Wildlife Research Center in Brooks contains a pheasant hatchery. Due south of Brooks off SR 873, Kinbrook Island stands in Lake Newell. Accessible by causeway, the island is popular with fishermen and a favorite haunt of bird watchers, since it is directly in the path of the migratory flyway.

## GLACIER NATIONAL PARK

*Glacier and Mount Revelstoke National Parks*
*P.O. Box 350*
*Revelstoke, British Columbia,*
*Canada VOE 2SO*
*(604) 837-5155*

The park is open all year, and an admission fee is charged. Since the region receives some of the heaviest snowfall in the world and is subject to avalanches, travel can be difficult in winter. The Trans-Canada Highway is protected at the most dangerous spots by concrete snow sheds, and earth dams serve as snow protection as well.

Facilities in the park include exhibits, guided and self-guided tours, campgrounds, picnic sites, fishing, hiking, mountain climbing, and skiing. Illecillewaet Valley is the most popular area for cross-country skiing, and a network of hiking trails extends from the Illecillewaet campground. Climbers and overnight hikers must register at the park's administration office before and after each trip.

East of Golden, Yoho National Park (Box 99, Field, British Columbia, Canada VOA 1GO, (604) 343-6324) spreads across the western slope of the Rocky Mountains. Its natural wonders include the Burgess Shale fossil beds, where more than 120 species of fossils have been found; visitors must obtain a permit to view the beds at Mount Burgess and Mount Stephen.

Admission is charged to the park, which is open all year, but most facilities are available during the summer only. Facilities include hiking, mountain climbing, fishing, horse riding, cross-country skiing, snowshoeing, ice climbing, and winter camping.

## COLUMBIA ICEFIELD

*Jasper National Park*
*P.O. Box 10*
*Jasper, Alberta, Canada TOE 1EO*
*(403) 852-6161*

Although access to some areas may be impossible in winter, the park is open all year, and admission is charged. The icefield, in the form of the Athabasca Glacier, is clearly visible from Icefield Parkway, Highway 93, and can be visited by snowmobile. From late May to late September, snowmobile tours of Athabasca

Glacier begin at the Icefield Center and last 1½ hours. Park facilities also include guided tours, campgrounds, picnic sites, skiing, horse riding, fishing, cross-country ski trails, mountain climbing, and hundreds of miles of hiking trails. Full-day and half-day raft tours on the Athabasca River are available from June 15 to September 15.

At Sunwapta Pass, Jasper National Park adjoins Banff National Park (Box 900, Banff, Alberta, Canada TOL OCO, (403) 762-3324), which offers a wide selection of sports and recreational facilities, similar to those in Jasper, along with miles of scenic roads and hiking trails. Campgrounds are filled on a first-come, first-served basis; reservations are not accepted. Snow tires and/or chains are required on all vehicles in winter.

## WOOD BUFFALO NATIONAL PARK

*Box 750*
*Fort Smith, Northwest Territories,*
*Canada XOE OPO*
*(403) 872-2649*

Sprawling across the border between Alberta and the Northwest Territories, the park is open all year free of charge. Its gravel roads can be used from May 1 to November 1; a winter road joins Fort Smith and Fort Chipewyan. Facilities include a visitor center, guided and self-guided tours, exhibits, campgrounds, picnic sites, canoing, fishing, boating, caving, hiking, and cross-country ski trails.

Trips to Wood Buffalo National Park leave from the park office on Portage Avenue in Port Smith throughout the summer. The annual Wood Buffalo Frolics in mid-March include log-chopping and muskrat-skinning competitions. North of the park at Hay River, the yearly Ookpik Carnival, also in March, features dog and snowmobile races and a hockey tournament.

# Index


## A

Abbott Ridge Trail 212
Acadia 132
Adirondack Mountains 126, 132
Admiralty Island 182
Alaska Range 180
Algonquin Peak *170*
Allegheny Mountains 44, 158
Alley Spring 120
Alma Beach 209
Alum Cove 123
American Falls 204–6
animals: Assateague 164; badlands 110; Baja California 98–100; Big Bend 90–1, 92–3, *94*; Blue Ridge *158*; Bryce Canyon *62*; Canada 202–3; Cape Cod 168; Delaware Water Gap *166*; Everglades 136; fossilized 110, 115, 117; Glacier National Park 214; Grand Canyon 76, 77; Great Smoky Mountains *152*, 153, 155; Isle Royale 124; mangrove forest *137*, *138*; Mississippi 130; Mount McKinley 181–2, *182*; Mount Desert *175*; Okefenokee Swamp 146, *146*; Olympic Peninsula 36; Ozarks 120; Padre Island 97; Painted Desert 83; Peace-Athabasca Delta 222, *223*; prairie 52, *53*; river bottomlands 42–3, *43*; White Sands *89*; winter coloring 182
animals, marine: Baja California 100; Bay of Fundy *109*; Canada 203; Glacier Bay 186, *186*; Padre Island 96–7
Antelope Island 58
Appalachian Mountains 132, 133, 136, 150, 158, 166; Trail 150–2
Appetite Hill, Carlsbad 86
Aspinall Water Wheel 166
Atchafalaya River 131
Athabasca Glacier 218, *219*
Athabasca River 220
aurora borealis *216–17*, 217
Avalanche Crest Trail 212
avalanches 212; paths 214
Avery Island Bird Sanctuary *129*

## B

badlands 106, *107*, 117, *117*
Badlands National Monument 107
Badwater 32
Bagnell Dam 122
Bahia de Los Angeles 100
Baja California 98–100
Bakersfield 28
Barranca de Urique 102
Barrancas del Cobre 101–2, *105*
Bartlett Cove *185*
Bay Harbor 174–6
bayous, Louisiana 131, *131*
Bear Butte 112
Bear River 56, 58
Bear Valley Visitor Center 30
Bearpaw Sea 210
Beaver River Valley/trail 214
Belle Fourche River 52, *53*
Big Cypress National Reserve 138
Big Meadow 161
Big Room, Carlsbad 86
Big Spring 120–1
Billys Island 149
Birch River 220
birds: Assateague 164; badlands 110–11; bayous *131*; Big Bend 92, *93*, *94*; Big Moose Lake *171*; Cape Cod 168, *168*; Cape Hatteras *163*; Delaware Water Gap *167*; Everglades 134, *134*, 136; Glacier Bay 186; Glacier National Park 214; Grand Canyon 76; Great Smoky Mountains 153; Hawaii 194, *198*, 198–201; Isle Royale *124*; Mount Desert *176*, *177*; Mount McKinley 183; Okefenokee Swamp *146*, 148; Ozarks 120, *122*; Padre Island *96*; Peace-Athabasca Delta 222, *222*, *223*; prairie 52, *52*, *53*; river bottomlands 42
birds: marine 12, 164; Kauai 201
birds: migratory 25, 30, *58*, 133, *164*; flyways *58*, *94*, 120, 131, 161
Black Canyon 74
Black Hills 106, 108, 110
Black Mountains 158
Blanchard Springs caverns 123
Blue Mesa *82*
Blue Spring 120, *122*
Bodegas Bay 30
Bodie Island 162
Boquillas Canyon 90
Boston Mountains 123
Bourne and Sagamore bridges 168
Brady Icefield *184*
Bridal Veil Falls 20, 204
Bridge Creek 64
Bright Angel: Canyon/Creek *73*, 74; Trail 72–4
Bristlecone Loop Trail 63
Bryce Canyon 54, 60–3, 78
Buckeye Hollow 123
Buffalo National River *120*, 123
Buttonbush Nature Trail *169*

## C

Cabo San Lucas 98, *103*
Cacahuamilpa Caverns 103–4
Cades Cove 152
Canadian Pacific Railway 212, 215
Cañon Diablo meteorite 78
Cape Alva 36
Cape Hatteras Lighthouse 162, *162*
Cape Lookout National Seashore 162
Capitan Reef 84
Carmel Bay 16
Casa Grande 91
Cascade Range 38
Cathedral, the *62*
Cathedral mountain range 20, 44
Cave City 144
Ceboruco volcano 105
Chain of Craters road 194
Chantocoatlan River 103–4
Chesser Island 149
Chignecto Bay 208
Chihuahua Desert *90*, 101, 103
Chilkat State Park/River 186
Chincoteague Bay 164
Chinle Formation 82
Chippewa National Forest 128
Chisos Mountains and Basin 91–2, *92*
Chloride Cliff 32
Citlaltépetl 104
Clark mountain range 20
Clingman's Dome 150, 152
Cloud-veil Dome 44
Coast Ranges, structure *14*
Colorado River/rapids 64, *70*, 70–6, *74*, 78
Columbia Mountains 212
Columbia River 56
Copper Canyon 101–2, *105*
Corpus Christi Pass 96
Cougar Brook Valley 214
Crystal Mountain 156
Current River 120–1, *122*
Custer State Park *114*
Cypress Point *17*

## D

Dark Hollow Falls 161
Delaware River 166, *167*
Denali/Fault/Parks/Preserve 180, 183
Desert Island 174
Devils Golf Course 32
Diamond Shoals *162*
Dillon Pass *111*
Dingman's Falls *166*
Dinosaur Trail 210
dinosaurs 82, 210, *211*
Drakes Bay/Beach/Estero 30, *30*

## E

Earthquake Trail 30
earthquakes: 1906 San Francisco *28*, 30; Yellowstone 46
Echo River, Mammoth Cave 144
El Capitan 18
Elkhorn Ranch 111
Emmons Glacier 40
Emory Peak 91
Estero de Limantour 30
Everglades 133

## F

Fall River 112–15
Falling Water Creek 123
fish: Assateague 164, *164*; Big Bend 90–1, *94*; Blue Ridge 161; Delaware Water Gap 166; Everglades *137*; Glacier Bay 186; Great Smoky Mountains 153–5; Mammoth Cave 144, *145*; Mount Desert 176–7; Okefenokee Swamp 149; Ozarks 122; Wisconsin swamps *128*
fish, marine: Cape Cod 168, *169*; Cape Hatteras 162; Gulf of California 101, *103*; Padre Island 96
Flint Ridge cave system 142
floodplains 131; subtropical 110
Forbidden Canyon 64
forests: fires 50; Olympic types 36, *36*; subalpine 214
forests: rain forest *185*, 185–6; temperate 36, *36*, *37*; tropical *195*
Fort Raleigh 162
Fort Robinson 116
Fort Ross 12, 14
Frary Peak 58
Fraser River 38
Frenchman Bay 174–5
Front Royal 160
Furnace Creek 32

## G

Garcia Caverns 103
geysers 46; Firehole River *51*; *see also individual names*
Giant's Staircase *23*
Glacier Crest Trail 212
Glacier House 215
Glacier Point 18
glaciers/glacial activity 20, *23*, *26*, 27, *27*, 36, 38, 40, *40*, 44, *44*, 56, 171, 172, *173*, 174, *184*, 184–6, *187*, 204, *212*, 212–15, 218, *218*, *219*
Glen Canyon and Dam 64, 74
Goat Island 204
Gold Bluffs Beach 12
Golden Canyon 32
Grand Canyon 54, 60, 78
Grand Falls *81*
Grand Geyser *50–1*
Grandfather Mountain 158
Granite Gorge 72
Grapevine Hills *93*
Great Basin 29
Great Glacier Trail 212
Great Plains 106, 116–17, 130
Great Salt Lake 54
Great Smoky National Park 132
Greater Yellowstone Ecosystem 50
Green River 74, 145
Ground Afire 32, *32*
Guadaloupe Mountains/Ridge 84
Gulf Intercoastal Waterway 96
Gulf of California 98, 100–1
Gulf of Mexico 98

## H

Half Dome 18, *21*
Hanalei Bay *200*
Harper's Ferry 160
Havasu Canyon and Creek 72, 76
Hetch Hetchy reservoir 24
Hillman Peak 34
Hindu Temples *62*
Hoh: rain forest *37*; River 36
Holloch System, Switzerland 142
Hood Canal 36
Hoover Dam *74*
Horseshoe Falls 103, 204, *206*
hot springs 46, *46*, *48*, 112–15
House of Many Hands *68*
Hualalai volcano *195*
Hualapai River 70–2
Huasteca Canyon 103
Hurricane Creek 123
hurricanes 136, *140–1*, 141
hyenaedons 110

## I

Icefield Parkway 218
Illecillewaet Glacier 212, *215*
Indians: Algonquin *65*, 126, 170; and Mammoth Cave 142, 144, *145*; Arikara 108; Athabasca 180; Basket-maker 86; Cherokee 155; Cheyenne 112; Creek 156; Dene 223; Havasupai 72, 74; Iroquois 170; Karankawa 96; Metis 223; Miwok 20–3, 30; Navajo/Navajo reservation 64, *64*, 68, *68*, *83*; Neutral 204; Oglala Sioux 115; Paiute 20–3, 63, 64, *83*;

pictographs *67*; Pueblo *68*, 72, *73*; Seminole 136; Shoshone 32; Sioux 108, 112; Tarahumara 102–3; Teton Sioux 112
insects: Great Smoky Mountains *152*; Mammoth Cave *145*; Great Salt Lake 58
Inverness Ridge mountains 30
*Isla Blanca* 96
Isla Partida *100*
Isle au Haut 175
Isthmus of Tehuantepec 98

J

Jacks Fork River 120–1
Jackson Hole 42, 43, *44*
James River 161
Jesse James Cave 144
John Muir Trail/Wilderness 23–4
Jordan River 56
jungle 80

K

Kaibab Plateau and Trail 70–6, 78
Kaibito Plateau 78
Kalalau Valley *196*, 201
Kentucky Diamond caverns 144
Kilauea Point 201
Kilauea Volcano *189*, 190; *192*, 193, *195*
Kill Devil Hills 162
Kings Canyon 23
Kittatinny Mountain 166
Kitty Hawk 162
Klamath River 12

L

Labrador Current 174
Laguna Madre 96
Laguna Meadows 92
Laguna Ojo de Liebre 100
Lakes: Athabasca 220; Big Moose *171*; Bonneville 56, 58; Cass 128; Champlain 170; Erie 204; Fausse Pointe 131; George 173; Heart *173*; Itasca 128; Jackson's 42; Leech 128; Mead *74*; Mono 25, *25*; Okeechobee 136, 138; Ontario 204; of the Ozarks 122; Pepin 130; Peyto 218; Powell 64, 74; Quake 46; Reflection *40*; of the Sun and Moon *105*; Superior 124; Winnibigoshish 128; Yellowstone 48; Yosemite 20
Las Tres Virgenes *100*
Lassen Peak 38
Lechuguilla Cave 86–7
Lee monument *156–7*
Legend People 63
lignite fires 111
Limantour Beach/Spit 30
Limberlost 161
Little Colorado River 80, *81*
Little Missouri River 111
Long Point Light 168
Loop Brook Trail 214
"Lost John" 142
Lost Mine Peak 91
Luna Island 204

M

Magazine Mountain 123
Magdalena Bay *103*
Main Corridor, Carlsbad 86
Mammoth Cave 132–3
Mammoth Site 115
mammoths 10, 117
mangroves 133, 136, *137*
Manicouagan Crater *78*
Mansfield Channel 96
Marble Gorge *74*
Mariposa Big Tree Grove 18
Mariscal Canyon 90, *90*
Mark Twain National Forest 120
mastodons 10
Mauna Kea 194, *195*
Mauna Loa *189*, 190 *192*, 193, *195*
meadows: alpine 24, *38*, *40*, 92–3, 180; subalpine *215*
Meigs Overlook *154*
Merced Grove 18; River 20, *21*, *23*
Mesquite Flats *32*
Mexican Plateau 98, 101
Minas Basin 208
Mississippi Flyway 120, 131
Mississippi River 106, 107, 118, 126, 131
Missouri River 106, 108, 129, 130–1
Monterey Peninsula 14, 103
Monticello 160
Mounts: Bonney *212*; Cadillac 174, *174*, 175; Dawson 214; Haleakala 193, 194; Hood 193; McKinley 178, 184; Marcy 170; Mazama 34; Mitchell 158; Moran 42, 44; Olympus 36; Orizaba *98*; Owen 44; Pisgah *160*; Rainier 38; Rushmore *114*, 115; St. Helens eruption 189, 193; Waialeale 196, 198; Whitney 23
Muldrow Glacier *27*
Mustang Island 96

N

Na Pali Coast 196, 201
Nags Head 162
Nakimu Caves 214
National Elk Refuge 43
Natural Bridge 161
Nauset Beach 168
Navajo Bridge 74
Needles Highway *112*
Nevada Falls 18, 20, *23*
Nevado de Toluca 104–5, *105*
Nez Perce mountain 44
Nisqually Glacier/River/icefall 40

O

Ocean City 164
Oglala National Grassland 107
Ohio River 131
Okefenokee Swamp 133
Old Faithful geyser 46, *50–1*
Olmsted Point 18
Olympic Mountains 36
oreodonts *111*
Osage River 122
O'Shaughnessy Dam 24
Outer Banks 162
Oxbow Bend 44
Ozarks 123; plateau structure 120

P

Pamlico Sound 162
Paradise Park *38*
Paria River 60
Paunsaugunt Plateau 60
Pea Island 162
Peace River 220; dam *221*
Peace-Athabasca Delta *220*, 220–2, *221*
Pedestal Log *82*
Piedmont River 160
Pikes Peak State Park *126*
Pink Cliffs 60, 63
Pinnacle Rock *17*
Pinnacles Volcano 28
Pisgah National Forest *160*
plains, boreal 220, *220*
plants/trees: Adirondacks 173, *173*; alpine 40, *40*; Assateague 164, badlands 108, 111; Big Bend *90*, 92, *93*, *94*, 95; Blue Ridge *158*, 160, *160*, 161; Bryce Canyon *62*, 63; Cape Cod 168, *169*; Cape Hatteras *162*; eastern region 133; Everglades 136–7, *137*, 138, *139*; fossilized 152; glacial valley *44*; Glacier National Park 214; Grand Canyon 76; Great Smoky Mountains 152–3, *154*, 155; Hawaii *193*, 194, 198, *199*, *200*, 201, *201*; Isle Royale 125; Monument Valley 68; Mount Desert 177; Mount McKinley *183*; Okefenokee Swamp *146*, 148–9, *149*; Olympic Peninsula 36; Ozarks 120, 122; petrified *50*, 55, 80–3, 111, 117; prairie 52, 117; Rainbow Bridge *65*; redwood 10–12, *10*, *12*; river bottomlands *42*, 42–3; Great Salt Lake 58; single-celled 58; Stone Mountain 157
plants, aquatic: bayous *131*; intertidal 12; marine 16
plate tectonics 20, 28–9, 30, 104; and meteoritic craters 78
Point Imperial *77*
Point Reyes 16, 28; Lighthouse 30
Popocatépetl 104
Potomac River 160, 161
Prairie Creek campground 12
prairies: fires 111; preserved *116*, 116–17; salt *137*
Puerco River and Ruins *83*
Puget Sound 36
Purcell Range 212

Q

Quatre Fourche River *221*

R

Rainbow Point 63
rainfall: badlands 110; Big Bend 95; Death Valley 32; effect in Painted Desert 82–3; Everglades *137*; Great Salt Lake *59*; Kauai 196–8; Monument Valley 68; Mount Rainier 38–40; Okefenokee Swamp 148; Olympic Mountains 36; Pine Ridge 116
Red Deer River Valley 210, *210*
Red Mill watermill 120
Red River 131
Red Rock Pass 56
Redwood Creek 10
Reid Glacier *184*
Reno, 28, 29
Reversing Falls Rapids 208–9
Rio Amacuzac 104
Rio Grande 90, *90*, 91, *94*
River of Grass *137*
Riverside Geyser *51*
Roanoke: Island 162; River 161
Rogers Pass 212–15

S

Sacramento Mountains 88
Saint John River 208–9
salamanders 152, 153, *153*
salt flats 56–8, *59*
Salt Lake City 28, *57*
Salt Plains 223
San Andreas Fault 100
San Andres Mountains 88
San Benito islands 100
San Gabriel Mountains *29*
San Geronimo River 103–4
San Juan Mountains 90
Santa Elena Canyon 90
Santee-Cooper Reservoir *123*
Schoodic Point 175
Schoolroom Glacier 44
Scotty's Castle 32
Sea Lion Point 16
Sea of Cortés 55, 98, 100, *103*
Selkirk Range 212, *212*, 215
Shackleford Banks 162
Shenandoah: National Park 158, 160–1; River 160
Shiva Temple 72
Sierra de Juarez park 100
Sierra de San Pedro Martir 100
Sierra del Carmine 93
Sierra Madre ranges 93, 98, 101, 102
Sierra Nevada 10, 18; structure 20
Signal Mountain 43
Sigri, Greece 83
Skyline Drive 158, 160
Slave River 222
Smith River 12
Snake River 42, 56
Sonora Desert 100
Stevens Canyon 40
Strait of Juan de Fuca 36
St. Anthony's Falls 126
St. Lawrence River 170, 171
St. Marys River 148
Susquehanna River 166
Suwannee River 148
swamps, hardwood *128*

T

Table Rock Scenic Tunnels 206
taiga/tundra 214; preserved 180, *180*
Taioga Road 18
Teewinot Mountain 44
Tehachapi Mountains 28, 30
Telescope Peak 32
temperatures: Big Bend 92; Death Valley 32; Everglades 134; geyser field 46; Grand Canyon 76; Pine Ridge 116
Temple of Osiris *62*
Tenaya Creek 20

Teton Range 42, *42*, 44
Theodore Roosevelt National Park 111
Thousand Islands 171
Tioga Pass 18, 24, 25
Toadstool Geologic Park 117, *117*
Tobin Harbor *124*
Tomales Bay and Point 30
tornadoes 118, *119*
Toroweap Overlook *74*
Tower Junction *50*
Trans-Canada Highway 212, 214, 215, *215*
Treaty of Laramie 112
Tularosa Basin 88
Tule Elk Range 30
Tuolumne: Grove 18; Meadows and River 24–5

U

Urique Canyon 102, *105*

V

Valley of the Dinosaurs 210
Vernal Falls 18, *23*
volcanoes, volcanic activity 34, *34*, 38, 46, *48*, 52, 55, 104–5, 112, 179, *188*, 189, *189*, 190–4, *190–5*, 196; *pahoehoe/'a'a 189*, 193, *195*; underwater 190; *see also individual names*

W

Wailua Falls/River 196, *199*
Waimea Canyon 201, *201*
Wall of Windows *62*
Wall Street (Bryce Canyon) *62*
Wasatch Mountains 58
Weber River 56
Welch Spring 120
Whirlpool Rapids 206
White River 107, 108, 110, 123
Wichita Falls *119*
Willow Flats 44
Wind Cave National Park 115
Wisconsin Glacier 171
Wizard Island *34*

Y

Yosemite Falls 18, *18*, 20, *21*
Yovimpa Point 63
Yucatán Peninsula 98, 136

Z

Zabriskie Point 32
Zion Canyon 60, 78

# Acknowledgments

*r = right; l = left; t = top; c = center; b = bottom*

1 James Green/Robert Harding Picture Library; 3 S. Meyers/Ardea; 4 Steve Terrill; 5*tl* Dean Lee/Oxford Scientific Films; 5*tr* Wendy Shattil & Bob Rozinski/Oxford Scientific Films; 5*b* David Muench; 6 David Muench; 10/11 David Muench; 12/13 Tony Stone Associates; 13/17 David Muench; 17 Heather Angel/Biofotos; 18/19 David Muench; 20*l* M. Bedmai/Photo Network; 20*r* Muir-Hanna Trust, Holt Atherton Center for Western Studies, University of Pacific; 21 David Muench; 22/23 William M. Smithy Jr./Planet Earth Pictures; 24/25 David Muench; 25 Heather Angel/Biofotos; 26 Stephen Morley/Susan Griggs Agency; 26/27 Thomas Kitchin/Tom Stack & Associates; 27 Gerald Corsi/Tom Stack & Associates; 28/29 David Parker/Science Photo Library; 29 Eli Reed/Magnum Photos; 30/33 David Muench; 34/35 David Muench; 35 Steve Terrill; 36/37 Steve Terrill; 37 David Muench; 38/39 David Muench; 40 Jeff Foot/Bruce Coleman; 40/41 Steve Terrill; 42/43 David Muench; 43 Franz J. Camenzind/Planet Earth Pictures; 44/45 François Gohier/Ardea; 46/47 Guido Alberto Rossi/The Image Bank; 48/49 Bard Martin/The Image Bank; 49 Gary Brettnacher/Tony Stone Associates; 50 U. Bagel/Zefa Picture Library; 50/51 François Gohier/Ardea; 51 Ian Beames/Ardea; 52/53 David Muench; 56/57 David Muench; 57 Popperfoto; 59*t* David Muench; 59*b* Pete Gasson/Planet Earth Pictures; 60/62 David Muench; 63 John Mason/Ardea; 64/65 Marc Muench/David Muench; 65 David Muench; 66/67 Ernst Haas/Magnum Photos; 67*t* Dave Lyons/Planet Earth Pictures; 67*c* Ernst Haas/Magnum Photos; 67*b* John Mason/Ardea; 68/69 David Muench; 69 Lanks/Shostal Associates/Superstock; 70/71 Pictor International; 72/73 Zefa Picture Library; 73 David Muench; 74 B. Bodin/Colorific!; 75/76 David Muench; 78/79 François Gohier/Ardea; 80/81 David Muench; 81 Heather Angel/Biofotos; 82 Heather Angel/Biofotos; 82/83 David Muench; 84/85 MPL Fogden/Bruce Coleman; 86 Chris Howes; 87 John Cancalosi/Bruce Coleman; 88/89 David Muench; 89*t* David Muench; 89*b* Bob McKeever/Tom Stack & Associates; 90/91 David Muench; 92 Tom Till/International Stock/Bob Firth Photos; 93*t* David Muench; 93*b* Steven C. Kaufman/Bruce Coleman; 94*tl* Gunter Ziesler/Bruce Coleman; 94*tr* B & C Calhoun/Bruce Coleman; 94 Leonard Lee Rue III/Bruce Coleman; 94/95 George Ancona/International Stock/Bob Firth Photos; 96/97 Tom Stack & Associates/The Image Bank; 98/99 J.P. Courau/Explorer; 100 Jack Swenson/Tom Stack & Associates; 100/101 Karl Switak/NHPA; 102 Norbert Wu/Click/Tony Stone Associates; 102/103 Richard Coomber/Planet Earth Pictures; 103 Karl Switak/NHPA; 104/105 Jadwiga Lopez/Click/Tony Stone Associates; 105 Tony Morrison/South American Pictures; 108/109 Rod Planck/Tom Stack & Associates; 110/111 Terry Donnelly/Tom Stack & Associates; 111 Badlands National Park Service; 112/113 Stephen Morley/Susan Griggs Agency; 114 R. Rowan/Susan Griggs Agency; 115 Jeff Foot/Bruce Coleman; 116/117 David Muench; 117 James P. Rowan/Tony Stone Associates; 118 Shelly Katz/Black Star/Colorific!; 118/119 A & J Verkaik/Zefa Picture Library; 120/121 David Muench; 122 John Swedberg/Ardea; 122/123 David Muench; 124/125 Bob Firth Photos; 125 Rolf Bender/FLPA; 126 David Muench; 127 Fred Mayer/Magnum Photos; 128 Fred Mayer/Magnum Photos; 128/129 David Muench; 129 Richard Kalvar/Magnum Photos; 130 Dan McCoy/Rainbow; 130/131 Eve Arnold/Magnum Photos; 131 Dan McCoy/Rainbow; 134/135 François Gohier/Ardea; 136/137 Mike Coltman/Planet Earth Pictures; 137 Dan McCoy/Rainbow; 138 Dan McCoy/Rainbow; 138/139 Brian Alker/Planet Earth Pictures; 139 Brian Rogers/Biofotos; 140/141 Weiner-Jomes-Amberg/Gamma Liaison/Frank Spooner Pictures; 141 Toby Ranklin/The Image Bank; 142/145 Chip Clarke; 146/147 David Noble; 148/149 David Muench; 149/151 John Shaw/NHPA; 152 Judd Cooney/Oxford Scientific Films; 152/153 Eric Horan; 154/155 John Shaw/NHPA; 156/157 Ken Hawkins/Stock South; 157 Rolf Richardson/Robert Harding Picture Library; 158/161 David Muench; 162/163 David Muench; 163 Eric Horan; 164/165 David Muench; 165 Brian Parke/Tom Stack & Associates; 166/167 David Muench; 167 Kenneth W. Fink/Ardea; 168/169 Stephen J. Krasemann/NHPA; 169 Eunice Harris/Aspect Picture Library; 170/171 David Muench; 171 Anna E. Zuckerman/Tom Stack & Associates; 172/173 David Muench; 174/175 Steve Terrill; 175 Frank Lane Picture Library; 176/177 Chris Howes; 180/181 Martin Grosnick/Ardea; 182 David Rowley/Planet Earth Pictures; 182/183 Duncan Murrell/Planet Earth Pictures; 184/185 Stephen J. Krasemann/NHPA; 186/187 Leo Tonchet/Susan Griggs Agency; 187 Paul Dix/Susan Griggs Agency; 189*t* Zefa Picture Library; 189*b* Krafft/Explorer; 190/191 Eric Horan; 192/194 Krafft/Explorer; 195*t* Krafft/Explorer; 195*b* François Gohier/Explorer; 196/197 David Muench; 198 Robert Harding Picture Library; 198/199 David Muench; 199 LLT Rhodes/Click/Tony Stone Associates; 200 Sheryl McNee/Click/Tony Stone Associates; 200/201 Bobbi/Click/Tony Stone Associates; 204/205 George Hunter/Click/Tony Stone Associates; 206 Thomas Kitchin/Tom Stack & Associates; 206/207 Ralph Reinhold/Oxford Scientific Films; 208/209 Gene Ahrens/Bruce Coleman; 209 Sig Brandshaw/Mach 2 Stock Exchange; 210/211 Peter Holton/Mach 2 Stock Exchange; 212/213 Ed Cooper; 214 Ed Cooper; 214/215 S. Meyers/Ardea; 215 Ed Cooper; 216 John W. Warden/Superstock; 216/217 Bryan & Cherry Alexander; 218/219 Anthony J. Lambert; 219 Don Reid/The Mach 2 Stock Exchange; 220/221 Anthony J. Lambert; 222*t* Erwin & Pegg Bauer; 222*b* Bob & Clara Calhoun/Bruce Coleman; 222/223 Anthony J. Lambert; 223 Jeff Foot/Bruce Coleman.